The Inner Island

AN EXHIBITION CURATED BY
JEAN-MARIE GALLAIS

FONDATION CARMIGNAC, PORQUEROLLES

ÉDITIONS DILECTA
PARIS, 2023

An island.
An island where we lose our bearings.
An island that makes us forget the age of civilisation.
A piece of Gondwana emerging in the Mediterranean.
An island at once powerful and fragile. A realm.
A real island, a fictive island.

Artworks.
Artworks detached from reality.
Artworks escaping geography and time.
An imaginary archipelago, secret conversations.
An ancient, vital energy. Worlds.
Islands of thought, invented islands.

Inner islands.

CHARLES CARMIGNAC

ISLAND WITHIN

ISLAND

An island is the summit of a hill that emerges above water. However, upon its approach by boat, sometimes it gives us the impression that it is floating. Once on it, that it is drifting. It is almost as if it were taking us even further away from the continent.

A shifting territory of metamorphosis, islands attract through their promise of the new or even the unknown. Because once on the other shore, on the other side, who knows what we will discover about the world and about ourselves? If the island is internal, then where are we? On an island within the island, an interiorised island akin to a remote and intimate shelter? We are undoubtedly on a thrilling drift devised by the exhibition curator, Jean-Marie Gallais, during which the mind can wander among the shadows of the real. *The Inner Island* has been the subtitle of our museum in Porquerolles from the outset. It comes from a drawing by Stephan Zimmerli (p. 180), my acolyte from the band Moriarty, who set the visit to images like a journey of the mind, oscillating around a surface line. On this circuit, the interior dimension of the island is intensified by the presence of the forest, the underground space of the Villa, and the choice of certain works whose contemplation gives rise to introspection. The option is therefore given to visitors of becoming these "researchers of the interior from the exterior", in Kandinsky's words. This theme already permeated our previous exhibitions: *The Imaginary Sea* led us into the depths of the sea and the subconscious; *Ulysses' Dream* was an odyssey of a return to the self, in the mental space of a labyrinth. This time, the exhibition fully acknowledges the rift from reality and invites us to give in to the vertigo of the faraway. It is hard to give in without the assurance of being in good hands. Jean-Marie Gallais has the energy of the great explorers, those who discover lands where no one has yet set foot. His zone of action is reality once removed, a territory richly endowed with unknown spaces, into which the multitude of extraordinary artists that he convokes throw themselves. While the journey is a gentle one, it is no less profound for that fact. His exhibition

Paint the Night, at Pompidou-Metz in 2019, modified my relationship to the nighttime. In it, there was already this attraction for the other side: the night as the other shore of the day. In *The Inner Island*, ambiguity sets in from the first steps: are we in Porquerolles or on an island that resembles it? The diurnal sky is pierced with shooting stars; the body of the island merges with our own. We traverse creature-landscapes and encounter some bizarre figures. In contact with these magnetic artworks, our little boat wends its way irresistibly through the inner worlds of the artists.

How could we have suspected that a multitude of inner worlds could be so well entangled that they could form a geography? With Jean-Marie Gallais' subtle weaving, the artists' inner islands form at least an archipelago, if not a lone and unique inner island, in which the public travels and loses itself, to the point of possibly at least finding their own. Freed of the shared notions of space, time, and habitual laws, we must adopt a different logic or become a new version of ourselves to inhabit this floating world. From one artwork to the next, from one plane of reality to the other, a powerfully uncanny atmosphere marks us and lingers on well after we have left the island. Infinite thanks go to Jean-Marie Gallais for this liberating journey to the border of dreams and to its magnificent constellation of artists, some of whose charming members crisscrossed their way about the island both day and night.

The village square will remember, among other things, games of *pétanque* with Darren Almond, before he set off to hunt the Moon, or Ryōko Sekiguchi, who suggested drinking it up on an esplanade near the church, as an inspiration for the poetic text that she signs in this catalogue. Thanks to Yann Chateigné Tytelman, whose voice freely intertwined with that of the curator throughout these pages, and to the Dilecta team for this beautiful book. Thanks to the many lenders who enabled us to present this journey, to the teams of the Fondation and of Villa Carmignac, and to all of the partners and providers who accompany us.

9

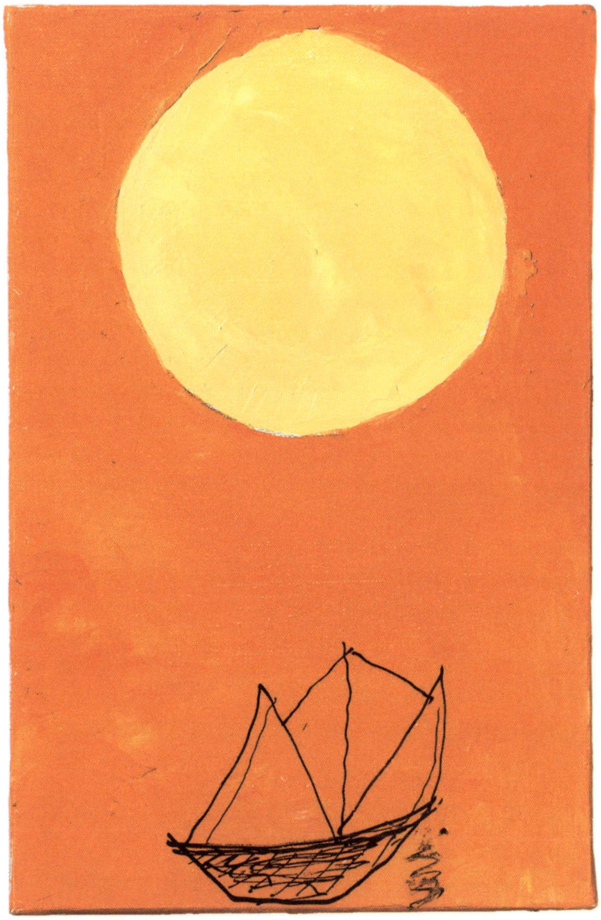

ETEL ADNAN
Planète 7, 2019,
oil on canvas, 33 × 22 cm

RYŌKO SEKIGUCHI

THE METAMORPHOSIS

OF AN ISLAND

Water determines everything.

On an island, there can be hills, mountains, plains, or valleys. Forests or cliffs. Or none of all that. But there has never been an island without water.

Water stops.

Everyone associates water with fluidity, movement, and the ephemeral. But water can be an insurmountable wall, more than a rock can, even more than a mass of metal.

Not because it stagnates.

Water, in its movement, can separate two lands. It is precisely because it is changeable that it is difficult to pin it down and affix it like a butterfly in a frame.

What is possible with a butterfly is not the case with water.

The island transforms its land into a house. Following the departure of the last boat, once the gate to the bridge that connects it to the continent has been closed, everything, on this plot of land, finds itself enclosed on the island.

Everything, except for those that are also able to live in the water.

Everything, except for swimmers, such as boar.

The island can sometimes become a cage, a prison.

Once, islands were often used as military bases, as a factory-island in the case of Inujima Island, a mining-island for Gunkan Island, sometimes even as penal colonies. Or sanatoriums to which patients suffering from contagious diseases were confined. Kings stripped of their titles were sent in exile to islands. In Japanese, this act was known as *shimanagashi*, meaning "evacuating someone as far as an island". A person was banished to this piece of land, and most often, they were condemned to remain there forever.

To withdraw themselves on a dot of land. When only the islands that we perceive off the coast appear as inhabitable lands. One more step and we would find ourselves on the island for eternity. In *The Tale of Genji*,[1] the hero decides to withdraw to Suma, to a mansion by the sea from which the island Awaji can be seen, for long enough to provide proof of his harmlessness to the court following a scandal. Melancholy seizes him when he contemplates the sea, no doubt owing to the fact of reaching the "end of the earth". The ghost of his father, the former emperor Kiritsubo, manifests himself before the people of the court and proclaims his innocence, which brings him back from these confines of land-sea-island.

The island creates an open closure towards the sea.

Might the island be, in some sense, a reverse fish tank: fussed over, conserved, enclosed by the water surrounding it?

The living organisms of an island – humans and animals alike – would they be the fish in this reverse fish tank?

Over the course of history, in the twentieth century as well, and still today, despite the size of the boats, their structures, and navigation techniques that have evolved beyond compare, many shipwrecks and boating accidents continue to occur – proving that the sea will never be a place like land.

Water can block us, but it can also propel us towards an elsewhere.

1
Work of Japanese literature from the eleventh century, attributed to Murasaki Shikibu.

People regularly venture into this liquid zone with random movements. Because an island is a limited space, like a house, the living things on an island that has become too small have often had to leave in search of a new space.

Sometimes, the sea has carried away those who dared to advance within its arms, sweeping them along, leading them into its depths; sometimes it has caused them to land on an unknown island. Shipwrecks are often the event that opens a story, such as in Daniel Defoe's *Robinson Crusoe* or Jules Verne's *Two Years' Vacation*, because they are about the ultimate encounter with the Other.

Discussions and encounters of great chance.

It is the water that decides.

The island is a condensed existence.

Everything is condensed on this very specific land.

In *The Island of the Colorblind*, Oliver Sacks, British neurologist and writer, talks about an island in the Pacific, where a surprising number of achromats live, who see absolutely no colour.

On the island of Martha's Vineyard, where a large part of the population was suffering from hereditary deafness, a sign language was developed known as MVSL *(Martha's Vineyard Sign Language)*. From the second half of the nineteenth century up until the early twentieth century, almost all of the inhabitants of the island practised this language like a maternal language.

There was also a sign language inherent to the Amami Islands, where the number of people suffering from hearing problems was high in certain hamlets.

They adapted to the phenomenon of condensation, and they developed a language so that those who had the faculty of hearing and those who did not could communicate.

They developed another way of life.

This closure by water, a crystalline safeguard, can paradoxically assist with the creation of a place in which treasures are hidden: a primitive fauna, an intact flora.

Flora, nature, everything is kept, preserved.

While the continent is a land where nothing escapes change, on an island, that which disappeared from the continent can endure, live an astonishing life.

Sign language, ancient words, languages of the past are preserved on an island.

And develop there in unique ways.

In Japan, several small islands around Okinawa Island maintain their musical traditions and their own scales.

If you believe in the definition of music as the means of entering into a relationship with the universe, you might say that each island has been able to preserve its morse code to communicate with the cosmos.

A scale, a language, a resonance, and waves inherent to each island.

A way of enunciating, of emitting a sound.

Might the island itself be a melody?

The island escapes.

Once upon a time, there lived a king who feared the dangers of the sea for his four daughters and warned them not to go swimming too far away. Which they inevitably did one day. They set out swimming off the coast, far enough to be noticed by the god of the sea. To escape the clutches of the god, three of them transformed themselves into an island and the fourth, with outstretched arms, was turned into a peninsula.

This is the genesis of the islands of Hyères and the peninsula of Giens.

Girls are often transforming themselves into
islands. Perimele, the daughter of Hippodamas,
was thrown into the sea by her father when he
discovered she was impregnated by Achelous,
the god-river who had seduced her. The latter
implored Poseidon, who turned her into
an island located at the mouth of this river.

Stories of metamorphosis are often
described as unwanted. So many nymphs
metamorphosised to escape Zeus's arms,
when it was not the god himself who
transformed (the mortal) Io into a heifer
to protect her from Hera's jealousy.

Except when it is a question of
metamorphosis of certain fish species
and a great deal of insects.

Which evolve in order to adapt.

Changing bodies, colour,
numbers of legs, or lifestyles.

Would a metamorphosis be imaginable that
was neither to adapt nor a form of mimesis,
but occurred out of pure pleasure?

Is it possible, for any girl, to transform herself into an island?

Into a torch aloe?

And for a tree to turn itself into a bird?

Is it possible for a colour to transform itself
into an island?

If something can transform itself into
an island, could an island also transform
itself into something?

Metamorphosis does not happen solely within
the imagination; some phenomena, even
the most improbable, can truly take place.

Some things transform themselves
without realising it themselves.

A legend from the islands of Yaeyama has it
that a flame-stone is found there.

A stone that turns itself a flamboyant,
incandescent red.

There, as everywhere else,
humans are attracted to the stones,
which shimmer like stars.

The dramas that then ensue,
we shall attribute to humans, but
let's leave the stones in their place.

Let's leave the stones that transform
themselves into flames as well.

All metamorphoses are admirable.

Out of flames, an island is sometimes born.

Even today, new islands
make their appearance
after volcanic eruptions.

They can also crop up through the indirect action of heat.

With the melting of polar ice,
new lands are starting to emerge.

Just as they can disappear after
an eruption, or due to erosion
caused by waves.

Zalzala Koh Island ("seismic mountain"
in Urdu) appeared after an earthquake
off the coast of Pakistan and disappeared
three years later.

The undulations of the earth,
the fiery earth, gives birth to islands
and makes them disappear.

It is occasionally possible to witness
the birth of an island.

On 23 September 1952, off the coast of Izu archipelago, sinkholes the size of real islands emerged in the sea after the eruption of an underwater volcano. The Japanese coastguard sent a ship to investigate, the *Daigo kaiyomaru*, from the bay of Tokyo to observe the phenomena reported, but the crew gave no more signs of life twelve hours after its departure. The next day and the days after that, other boats left to help them, but could find only some of the debris from the ship. Research undertaken by the US Army concluded that it must have been just above the crater of an underwater volcano at the time of an eruption.

The island is a sealed-off existence
that is in perpetual flux.

Today, the island of Martha's Vineyard
is no longer racked with problems of
deafness. The development of means
of transport enabled the island to open
up to the continent and its mixture of DNA,
which saw the individuals afflicted by
deafness disappear, and the "seeing voices",
to borrow Oliver Sacks's expression.

What seems to be condensed can be effaced
over several hundreds of years.

The life of an island can be shorter than that of a human being.

But it can have several lives:
it can appear, disappear,
and reappear.

It is another life that adapts itself,
that opens up while remaining closed,
condensed while being open.

Ah yes. There has also been one metamorphosis that was desired.

That of Philemon and Baucis, who were
transformed into two intertwined trees.
To thank this couple of poor and elderly
Phrygians for their hospitality, Zeus,
accompanied by his son Hermes, granted
them their wish to not be separated by death.

Philemon became an oak and Baucis,
a limewood tree.

One tree that grows within another,
or at the foot of another, as though in an
embrace – a scene that can be encountered
from time to time, on an island.

We also sometimes observe there
the lightning-fast evolution of a species
– whether plant, animal, or microbe
– at a pace incredibly more rapid than
on the continent.

Might the metamorphosis of these
living organisms be a desire for accelerated
evolution?

The desire to be even closer to the island?

Can a perfume transform itself into an island?

Two scents, swept up by the wind – or that lovingly combine in the air after the rain, just as two trees can come to form just one – could they be embodied in the form of an island?

It is possible for eucalyptus leaves to metamorphosise into red wine. Eucalyptus trees that grow around vines diffuse their olfactive molecules into the air, which are then deposited onto the skin of the fruit. The grape is gathered along with these olfactive visitors and its skin transmits the camphorous air into the nectar during its fermentation.

Underground water rises into the stalks of eucalyptus trees and transforms into mentholated oil, finding a home in its foliage.

The same underground water rises into other stalks and transforms into a juice in the form of grape bunches.

The islanders drink this wine that the eucalyptus loved, by sniffing the scent of its leaves at the foot of the tree.

Eucalyptus, fruit, and human become one.

Water circulates between these three living things.

On Okinawa Island, where alcohol is distilled from sugar cane, the smell of the island, similar to that of Martinique, wafts through the air.

While the water flow is circular, a scent can link up two very distant islands in an instant.

Scent is oblivious to the notion of distance.

A scent can exist not only as olfactive particles, but also by thought alone, borne by the memory of it.

All you have to do is remember it.

In the world of odours, there are no ghosts. Because a ghost has the same presence as an odour.

As present as it is ephemeral.

An odour can therefore travel through time, in a fraction of a second.

A memory of peach leaves from one
hundred years ago, just by thinking
about them, can cause their true scent
to re-emerge, here and now.

And the island itself, what can it become?

Separated from its solitary fate?

Odour is to humans what water is to fish.

The thing that can traverse the human body.

Humans are traversed by odours.

Without causing life to disappear.

Eating is the act of inevitably cutting an
organism's life short, whether plant or animal.

Odour visits us without the need
to snuff anyone out.

We can sniff an odour without harming it.
It is these odours that come to meet us.

We always live within two parallel worlds,
a visual space and a space of odours.

Odours do not map onto the visual landscape.
If we describe the space around us through
odours, it will be completely different to
the one that we see with our eyes.

If each odour had a colour, the air of the
islands would be very colourful. Made up
of colours constantly swept by the wind
and replaced by others.

Two distinct landscapes, within which
people usually live uneventfully.

In which we swim as we breathe.

Can the island be portable, be kept with you?

Can it be placed between our hands?
Or in the form of an odour?

Can the island keep us on its soil,
in the form of odours?

Could a part of ourselves remain on
the island and continue to live there?

Could water liberate the island?

Eventually, could it carry it off somewhere,
like a boat?

An island setting sail.

Carried by the wind, taking flight by beating its leaves?

With all of the trees becoming wings for the island?

Even if the water stops you,
the scent might transport you.

If an odour can metamorphosise
into an island, can an island transform
itself into a scent?

What might an island like
to metamorphosise into?

What is possible with a butterfly
is not the case with water.

But perhaps what is possible with a butterfly
might also be with an island.

Like flying, for instance.

Does a butterfly have an odour?

What might a butterfly's odour be?

In many civilisations, the butterfly
was the symbol of the breath.

Like an island?

One day, we will see a butterfly
that was once an island.

One day, we will smell an odour,
and we will think that
this scent was once an island,
an island that we once knew.

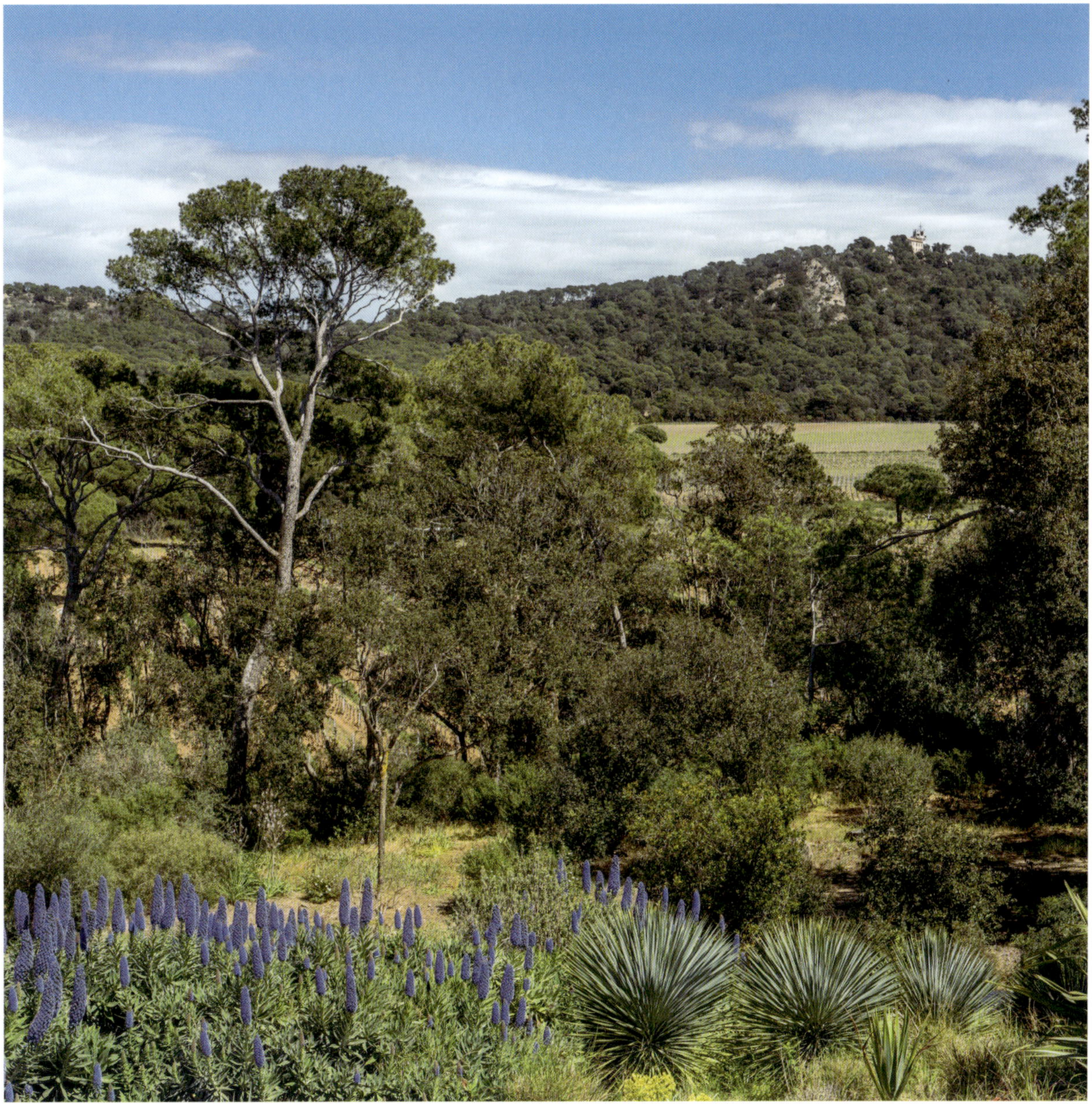

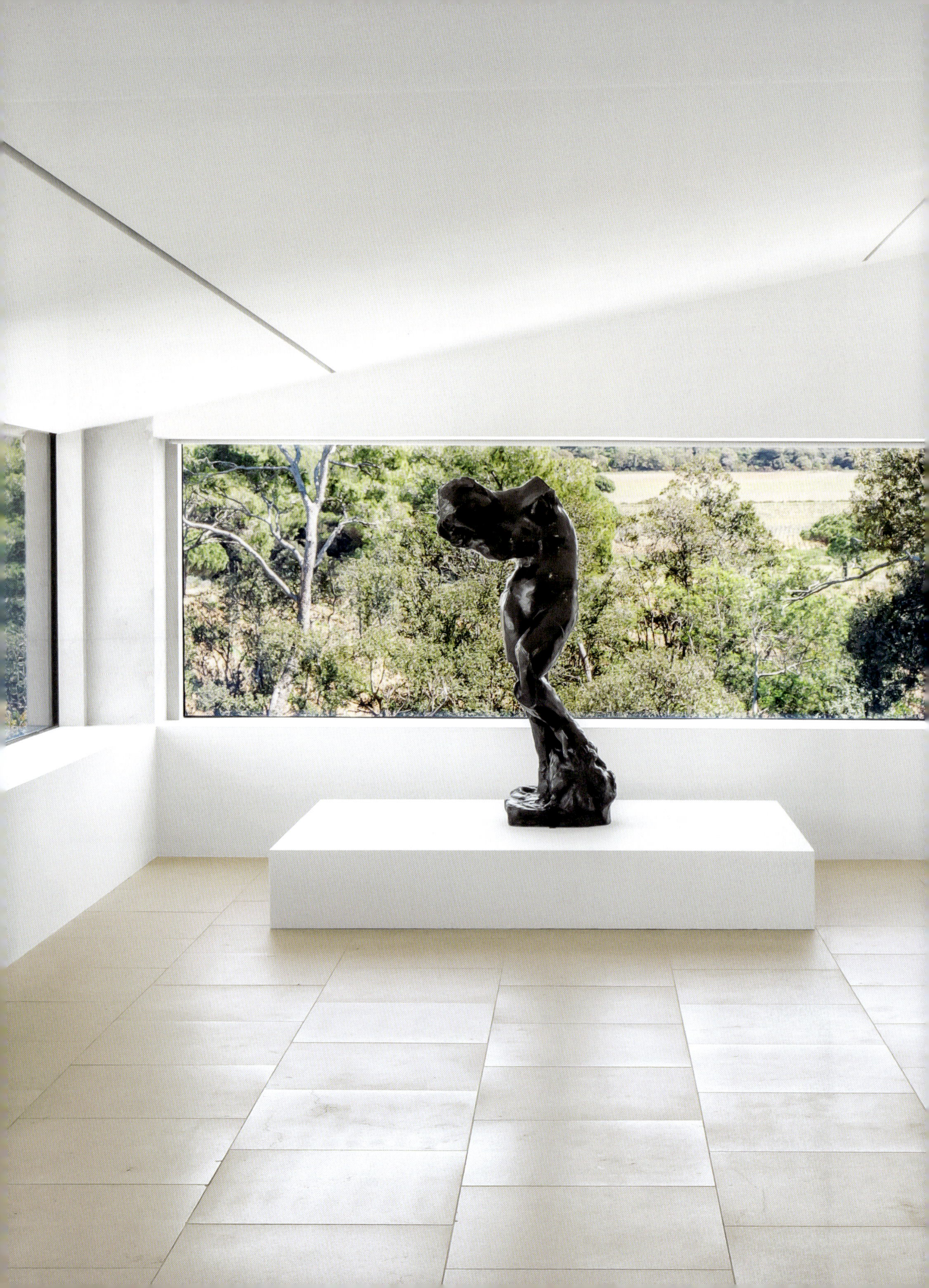

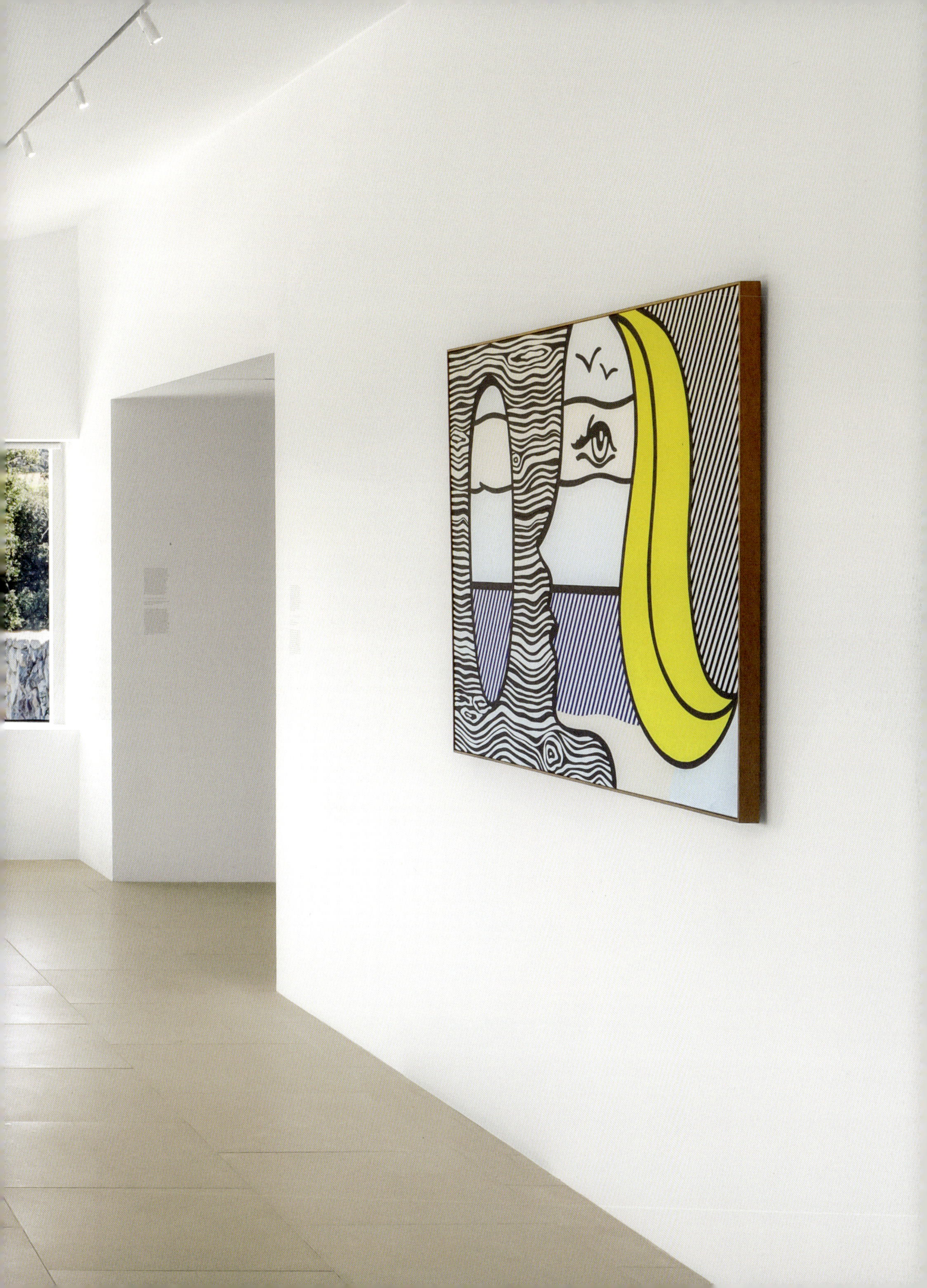

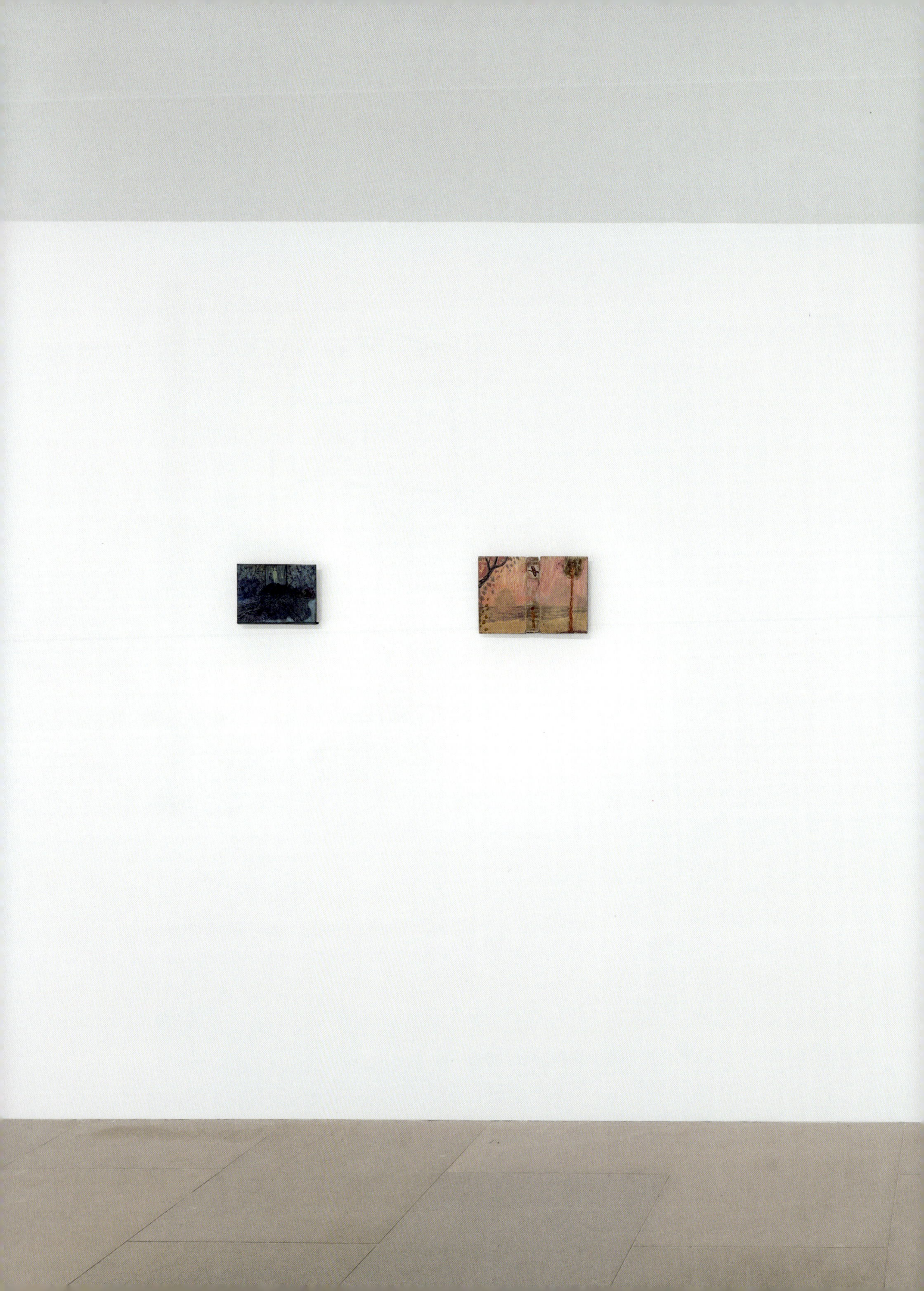

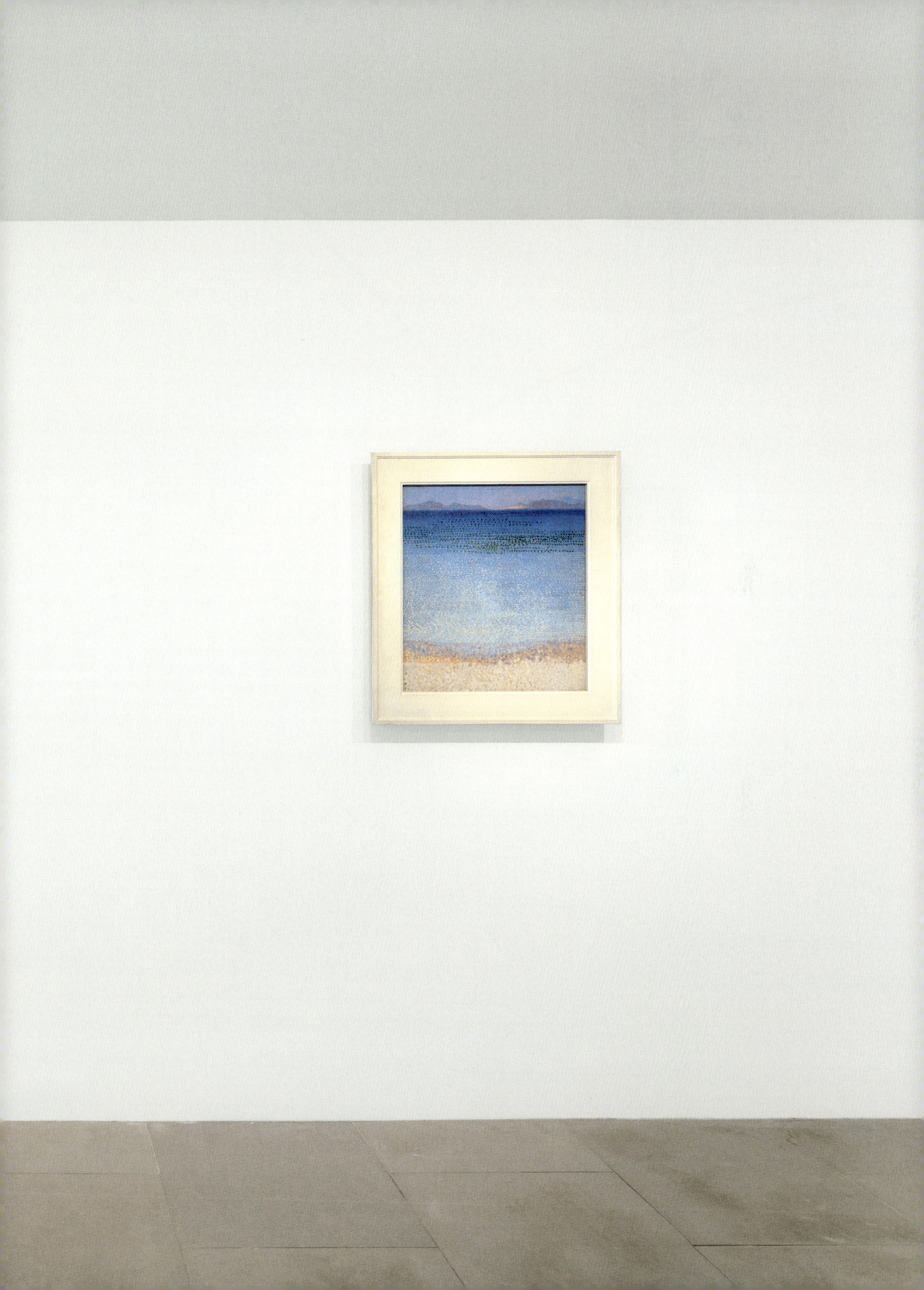

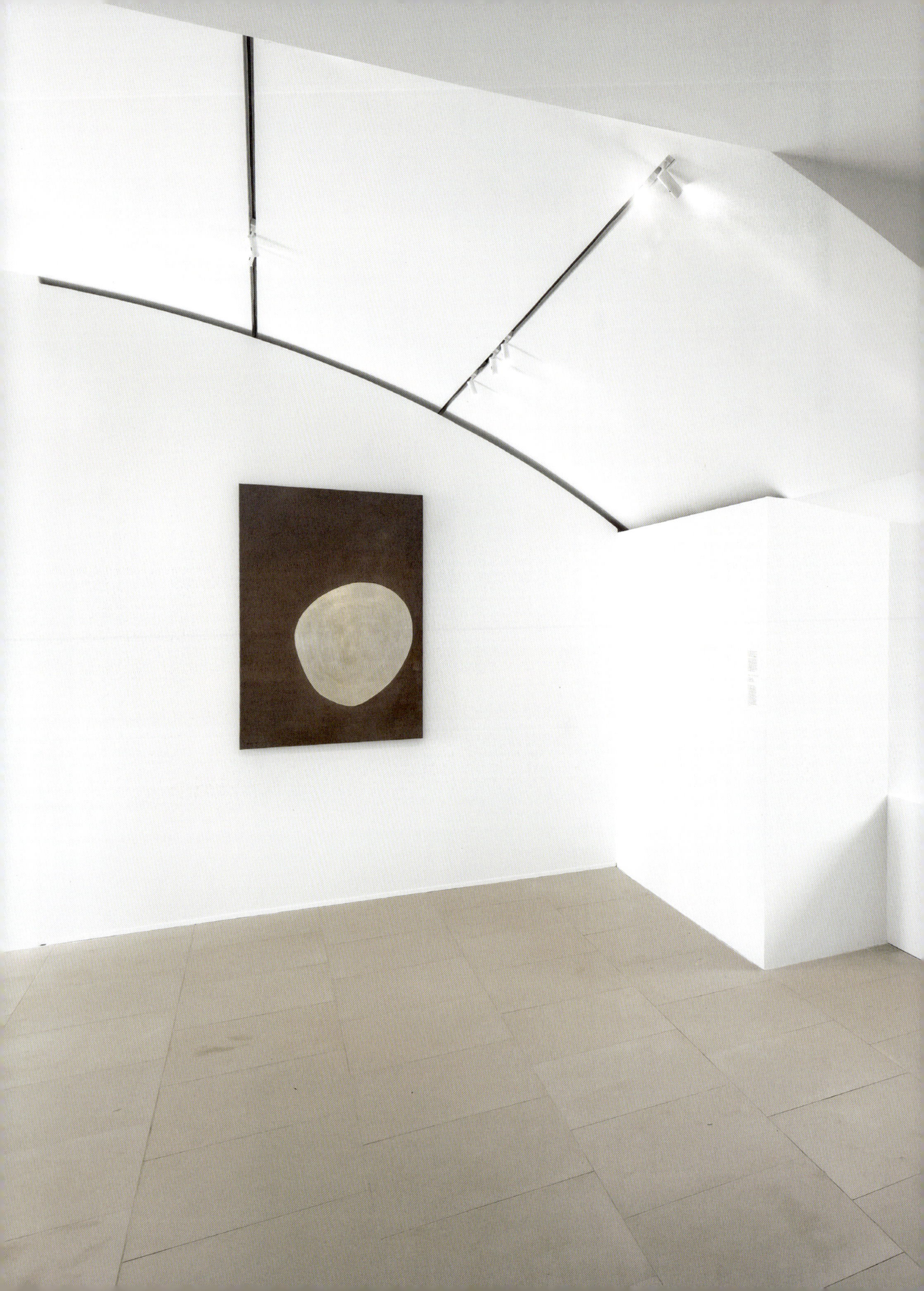

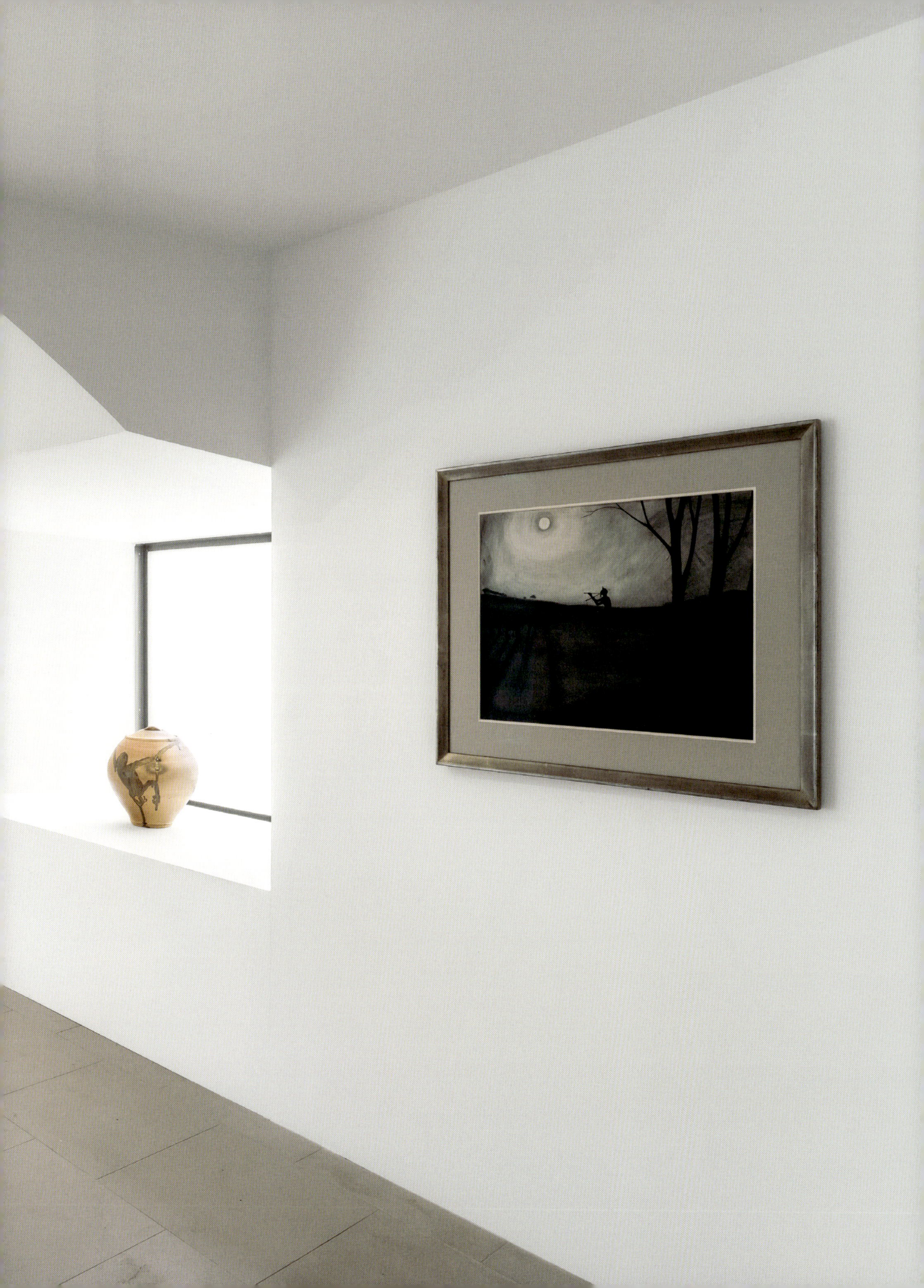

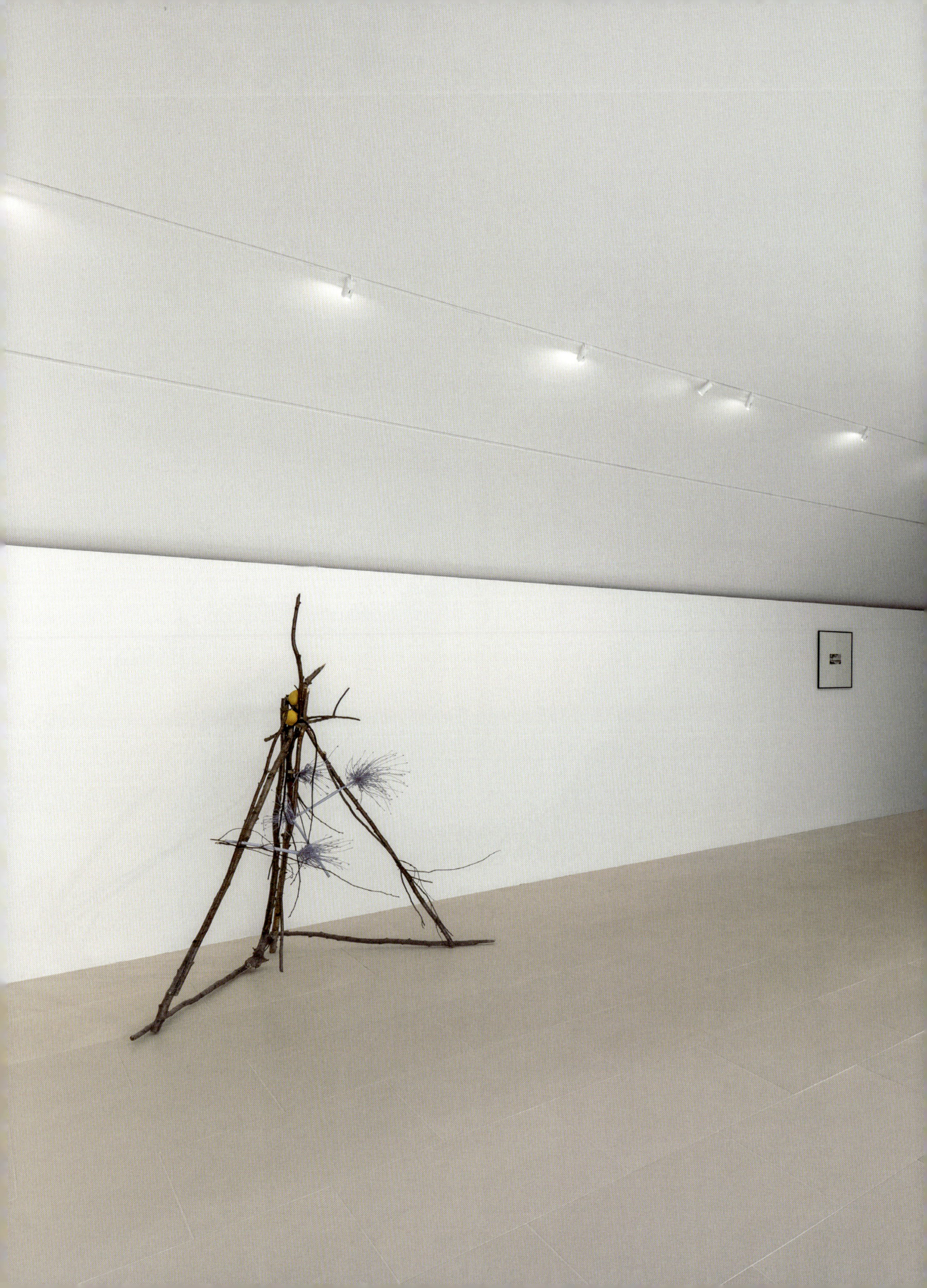

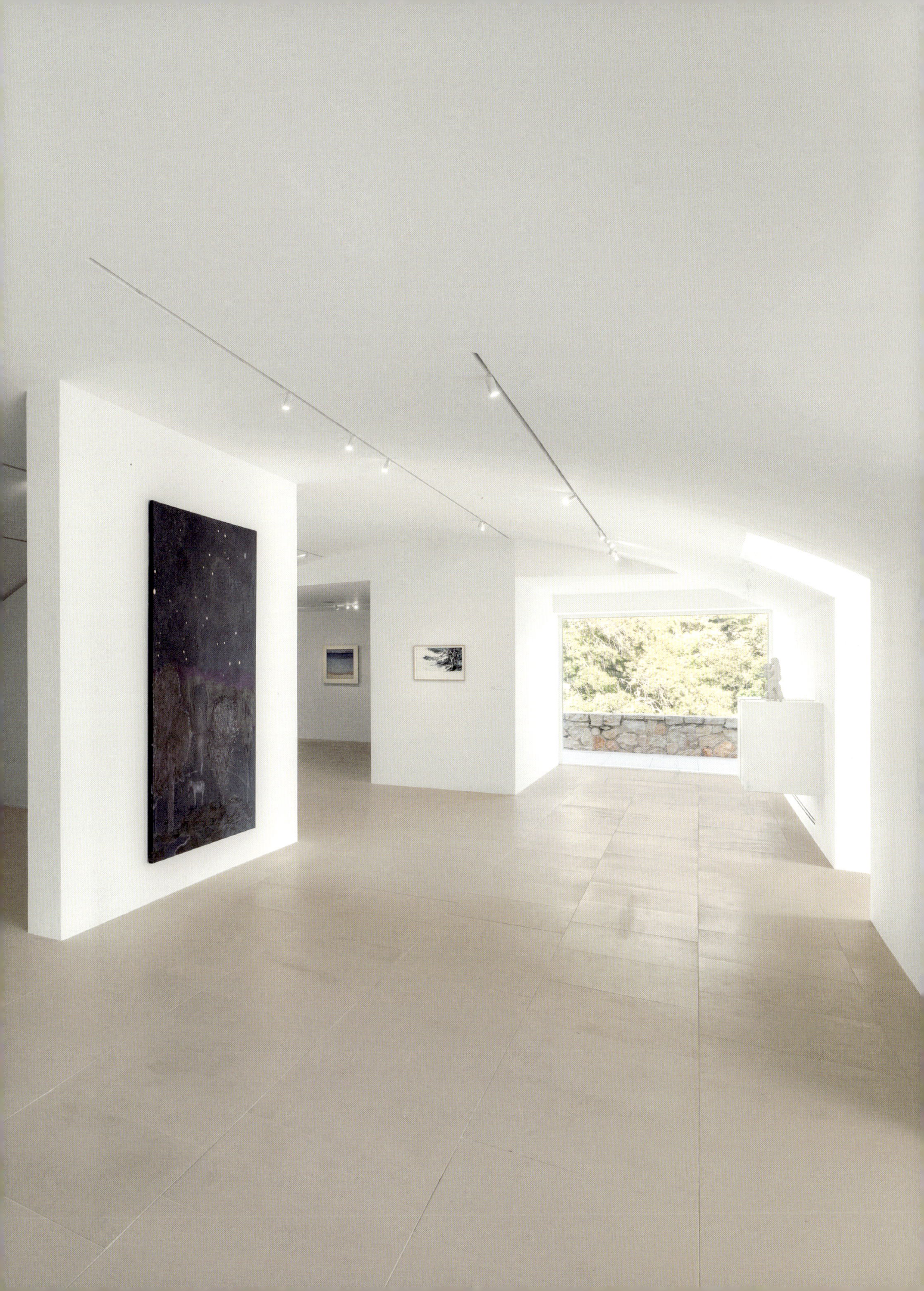

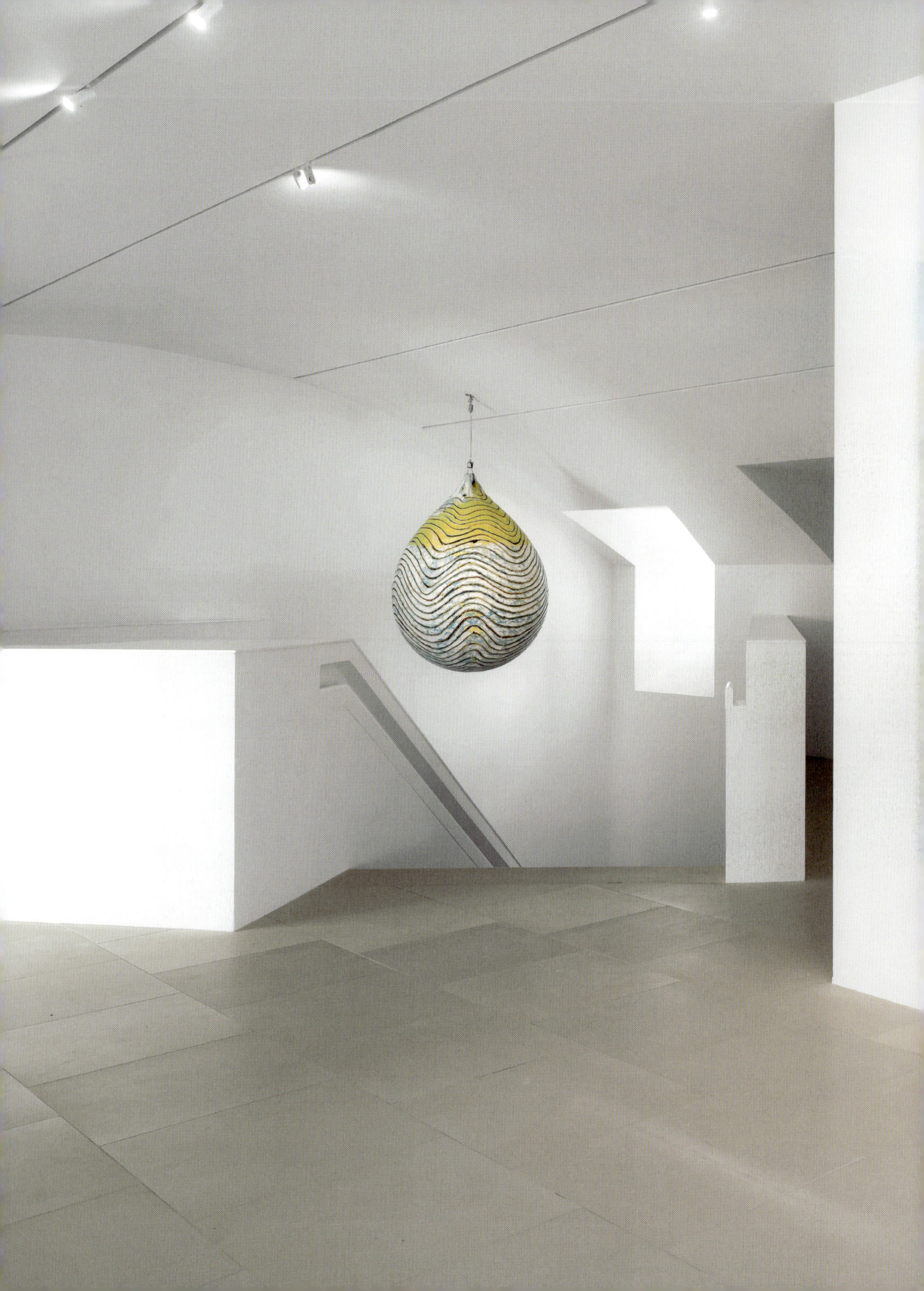

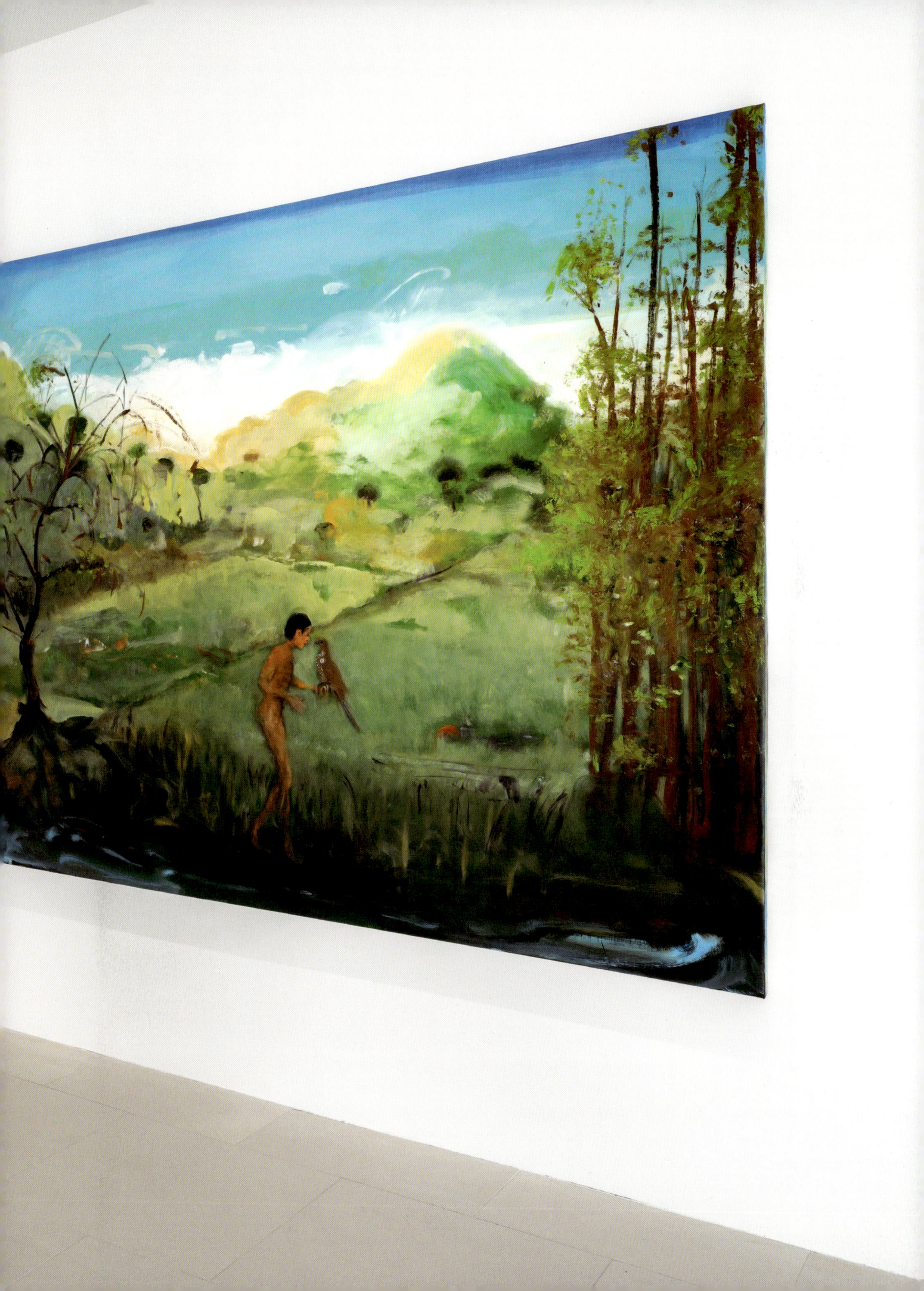

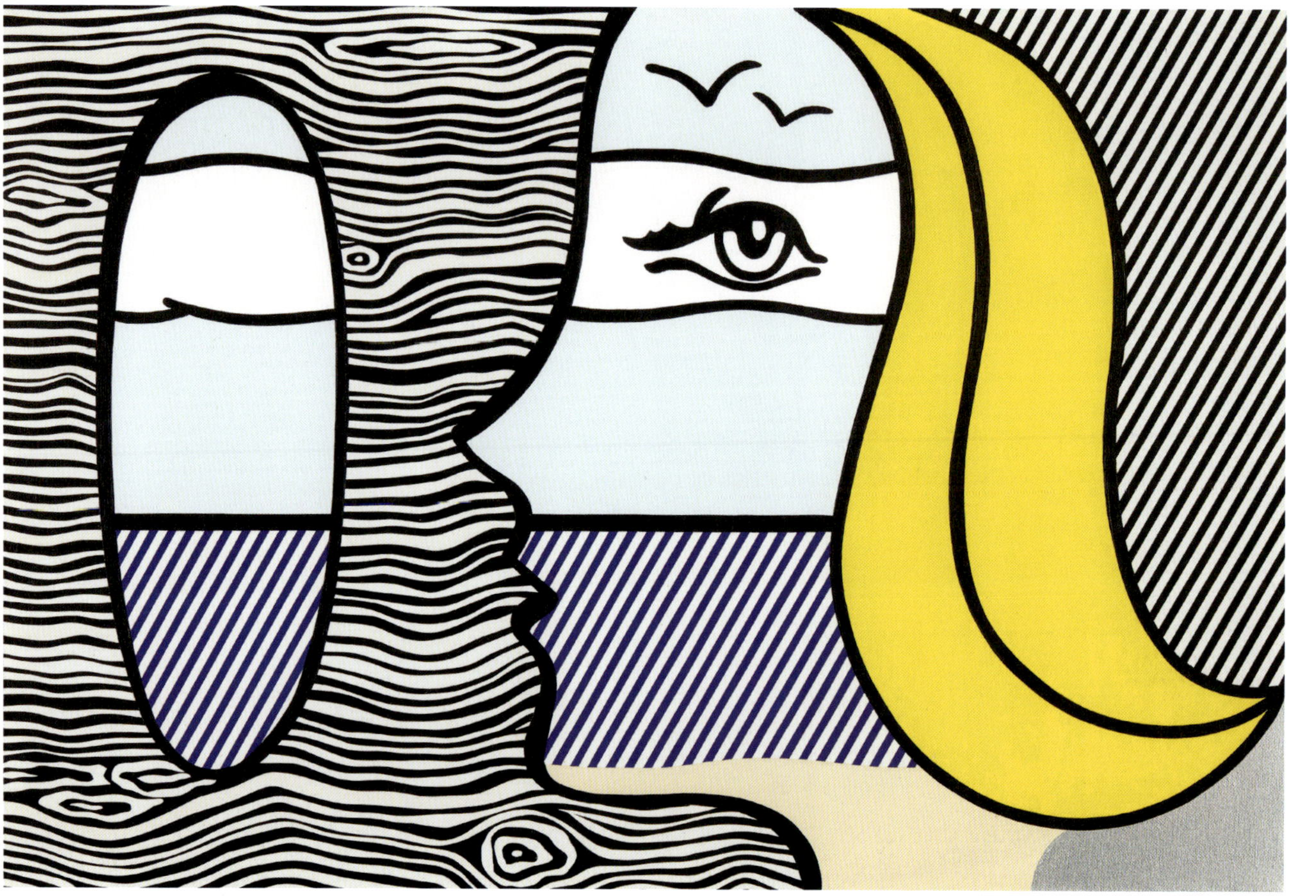

Roy Lichtenstein, *Landscape*, 1977 — oil and Magna on canvas — 101.6 × 152.4 cm

DID IT REALLY HAPPEN,

OR DID I DREAM TOO INTENSELY?

Today I did nothing.
But many things were done inside me.

ROBERTO JUARROZ
Poesia vertical decimotercero [Thirteenth Vertical Poetry], stanza 52, (our translation), 1993

LANDSCAPES WITHIN BODIES

JEAN-MARIE GALLAIS Someone told me once, and I never checked if it was true, that great scientists have often been seasoned mountaineers, with a predilection for conquering glaciers. I like to think that great artists might often have been fond of roaming around islands, with a predilection for the volcanic ones. Unlike continents, *which weigh us down*, in Édouard Glissant's words, the island presents a certain agility and malleability that is at once conceptual and physical.[1] Like glaciers, islands are mounds of shifting and threatened matter. Don't all of the concerns of an island reside in its scale? Such is the misadventure of the hero of D. H. Lawrence's *The Man Who Loved Islands* (1927), who wanders from island to island in search of one that will be neither too big nor too small and that will have a high point from which one can hope to see the sea from all sides and thus shuck off the feeling of insularity. Does this feeling even exist though? It is a mainlander speaking, so obviously an islander's account would be very different. Do we remember the first time we set foot on one of them with full awareness? Do we remember having had the sense of being on an island one day?

YANN CHATEIGNÉ TYTELMAN Embarking on an island and climbing up to a peak, isolating oneself – could we say, "insulating oneself"? – and feeling the exhilaration of heights surely represents one of the two sides of the same quest for silence, the unknown, or even ecstasy. I know when I visited an island for the first time. It was in Polynesia. I was twenty-five years old. But besides that, I've forgotten everything. A radical break with the continent or with the continuum of my life, the light of the Antipodes, the amount of humidity in the air: I saw everything through a magnifying

1
Édouard Glissant and Hans Ulrich Obrist, *The Archipelago Conversations* (New York: Isolarii, 2021)

glass. Emotions assailed me! To the point of saturation. Walter Benjamin, in exile on Ibiza Island in 1933, also described the way in which "its perfection situated it at the limits of the visible".[2] The island affected him. Islands are worlds in which perception is adjusted to scale. They are laboratories, workshops – and that might also be what interests artists. There, they experiment with vision (externally) and the visualisation of emotions (inwardly).

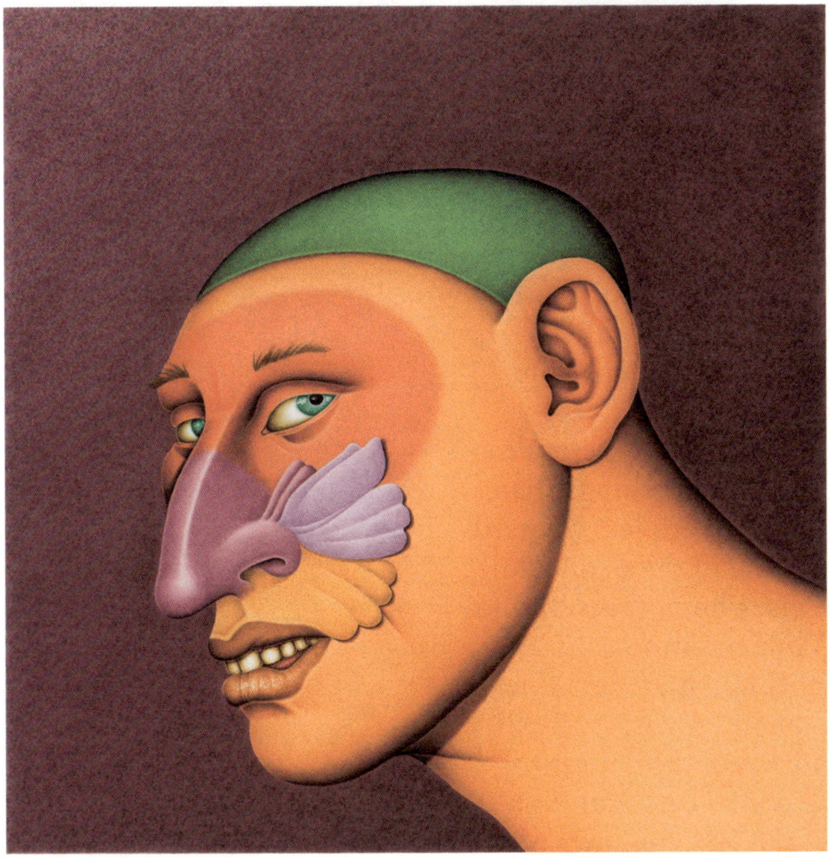

ROBERT LOSTUTTER
Garden of Opiates 9, 2012,
watercolour on paper, 45.72 × 45.72 cm

JMG This story begins in the Mediterranean, where landscapes and bodies merge, as in dreams. Porquerolles? "Many have spent time there, no one has captured it", I'm told. Who? Hannah Arendt, Charlie Chaplin, André Gide, Jean-Luc Godard, Paul Klee, Georges Simenon... I discover the story of Jean-Francis Auburtin, a painter admirative of Monet who regularly visited in the late nineteenth century to paint the island in an impressionistic style. In some of the paintings, his symbolist penchant is stronger and the atmosphere of the coves, pine trees, and rocks become conducive

2
Walter Benjamin, *The Storyteller Essays* (New York: New York Review of Books, 2019). [Translator's note: includes stories written in Ibiza in 1932-1933.]

ALBERTO SAVINIO
L'isola portatile, circa 1931,
oil painting on canvas,
32 × 41 cm

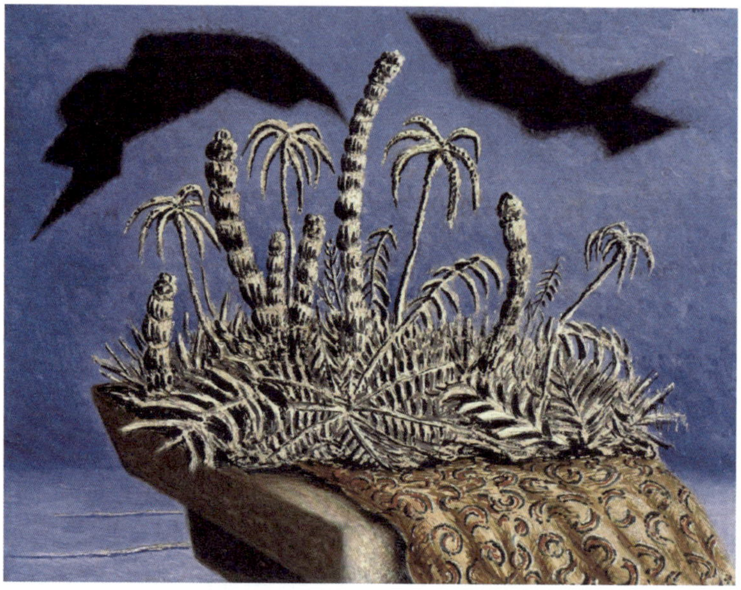

to the apparition of antique nymphs and centaurs. Auburtin stopped coming to the island when it was privatised in 1912. Its new owner, François-Joseph Fournier, decided to develop viticulture and orchards there and the artist did not find it wild enough for his taste – less picturesque, in the original sense of the word: *that which deserves to be painted*. However, there are many things that can only be encountered on Porquerolles. Bernard Plossu was able to capture some of them, all while having us believe we were elsewhere. Outside and inside at the same time. While painting eclipses, the Mediterranean represents transparency. Even the beams from the full moon illuminate beneath the surface of the water and reveal the colours of rocks and beds, depending on the configuration of the landscape. Opposite the bay windows of the Villa, a painting by Roy Lichtenstein ignores this distinction between interior and exterior, body and landscape, reality and dream. *Landscape* is comprised exclusively of textures without depth: a face and a porthole over the sea are equated. The landscape is inside and the birds are in the young woman's head, while the world around her is as smooth and opaque as veneer. Salvation comes from within. The starting point of any exploration of inner islands is *a body wrapped up in itself*, like that of *La Voix intérieure* (*The Inner Voice*, or *Meditation without Arms*), Rodin's masterpiece.

A manifesto of the autonomy of the work of art, *La Voix intérieure*, or *Méditation sans bras* is one of the sculptures that Rodin held in highest esteem among his creations. Rainer Maria Rilke said of it: "We are surprised to see that the arms are missing. Rodin experienced them, in this case [...] as something that did not fit with the body, which wanted to wrap itself up in itself."

Auguste Rodin, *La Voix intérieure* ou *Méditation sans bras* [*The Inner Voice*, or *Meditation without Arms*], 1896 — bronze — 146 × 75.5 × 55 cm

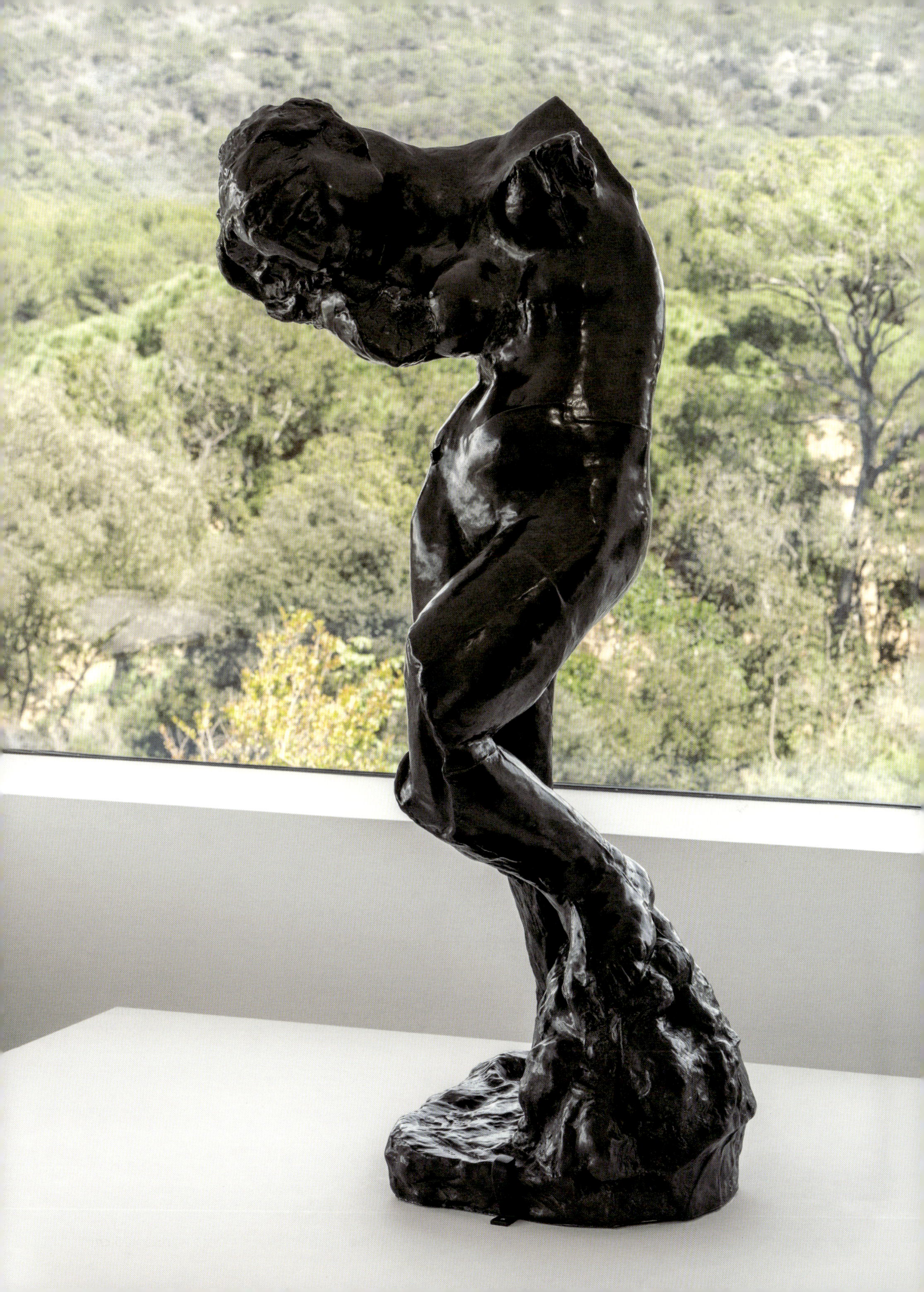

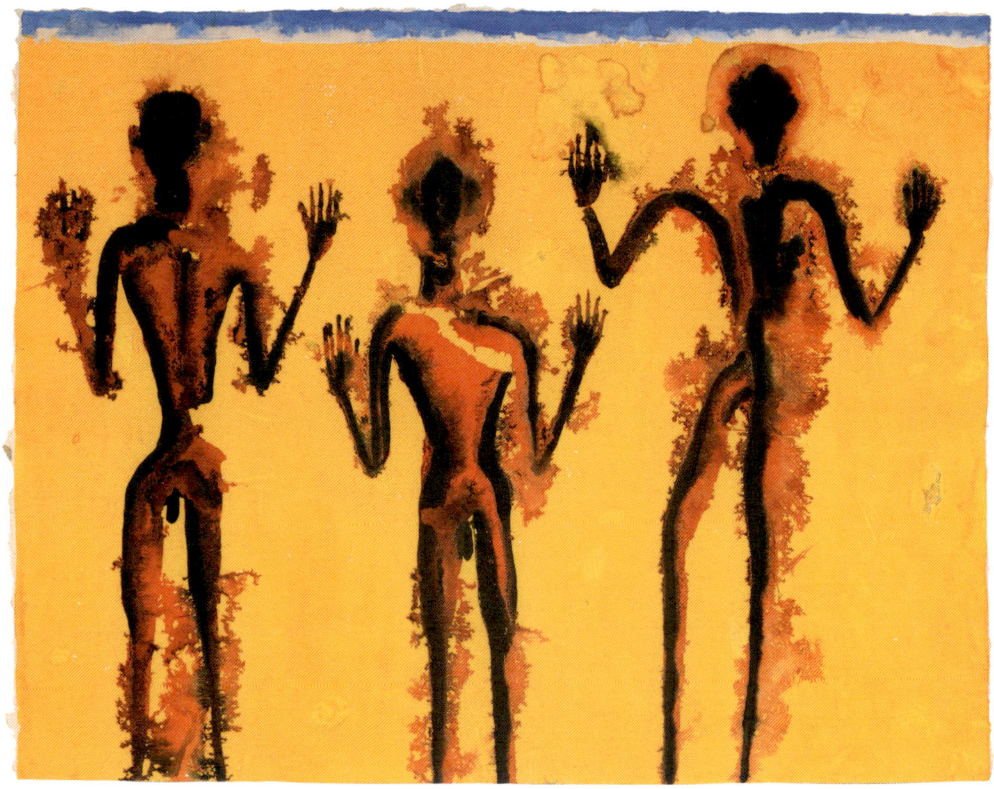

Francesco Clemente, *Fifty One Days on Mount Abu XLIV Silence*, 1995 — watercolour on paper — 53.7 × 70.8 cm

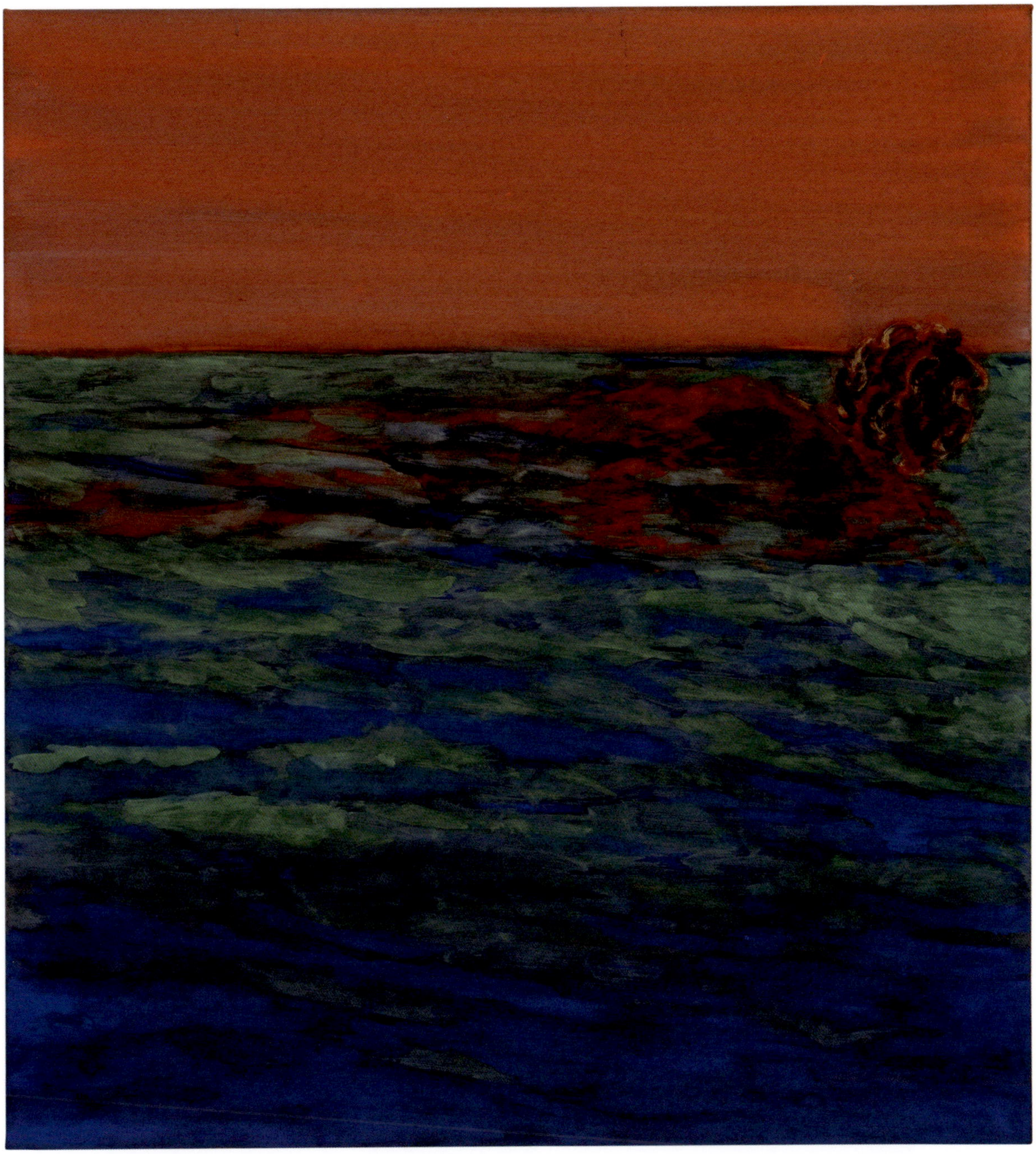

Christine Safa, *La mer, par-delà ton épaule III*, 2023 — oil on linen canvas — 146 × 135 cm

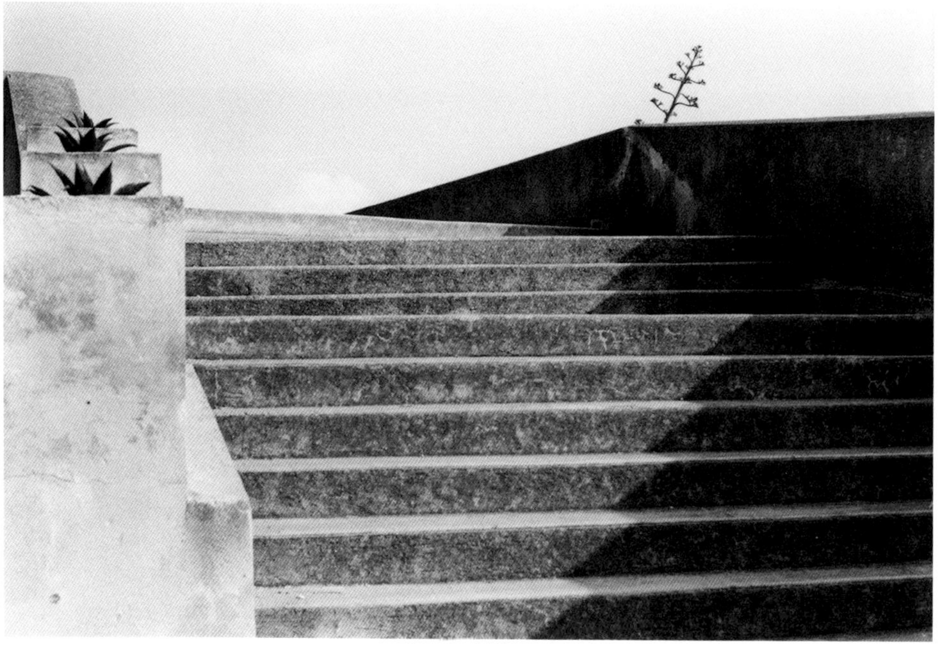

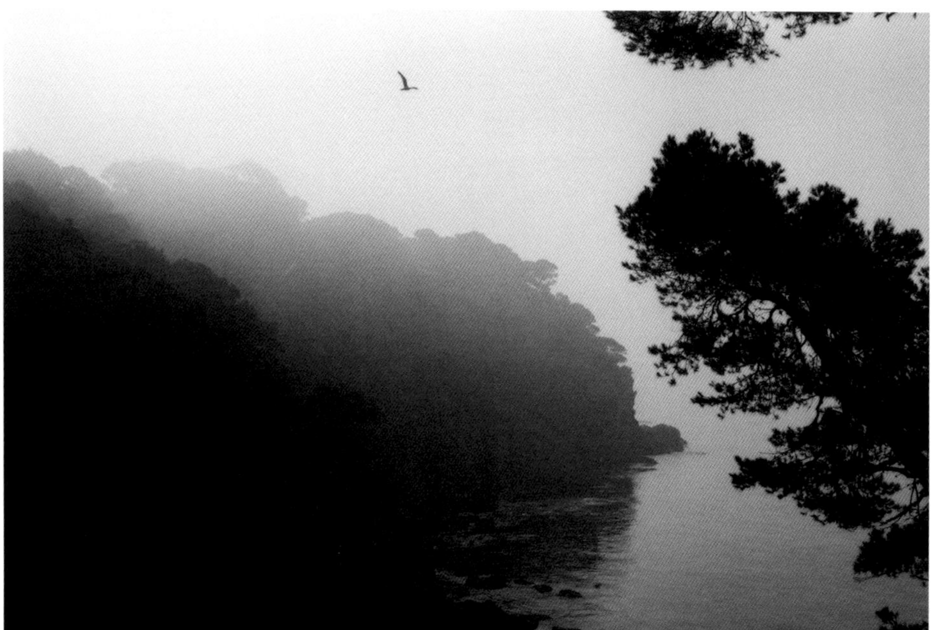

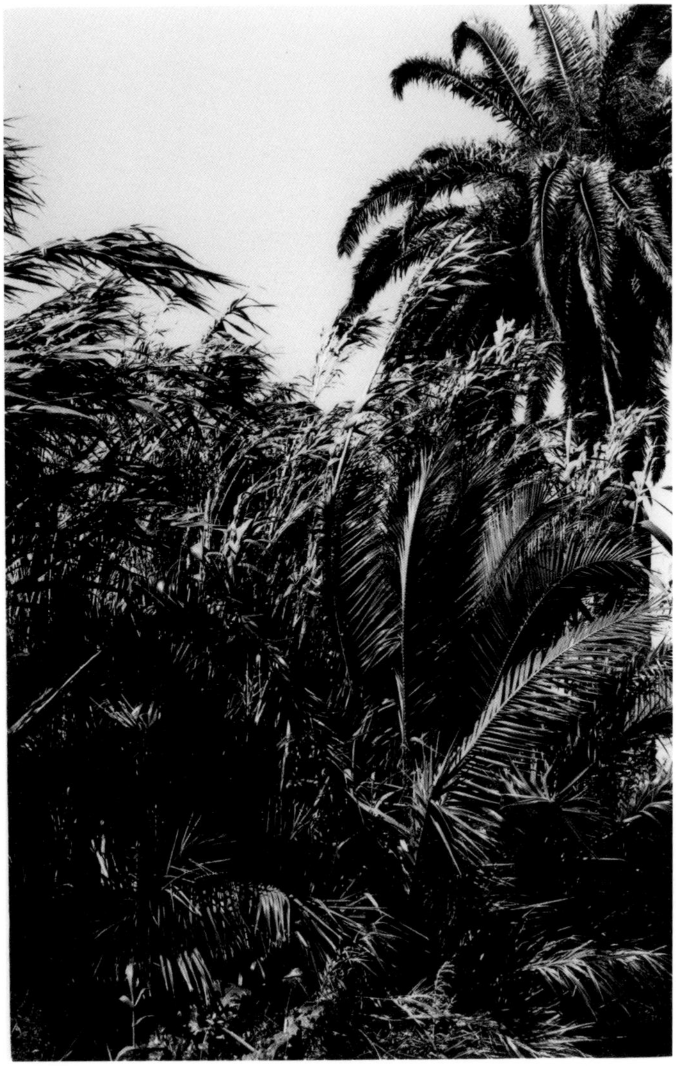

Bernard Plossu, *Île de Porquerolles,* 1976 — modern silver prints on baryta paper — 9 × 13.8 cm and 13.8 × 9 cm

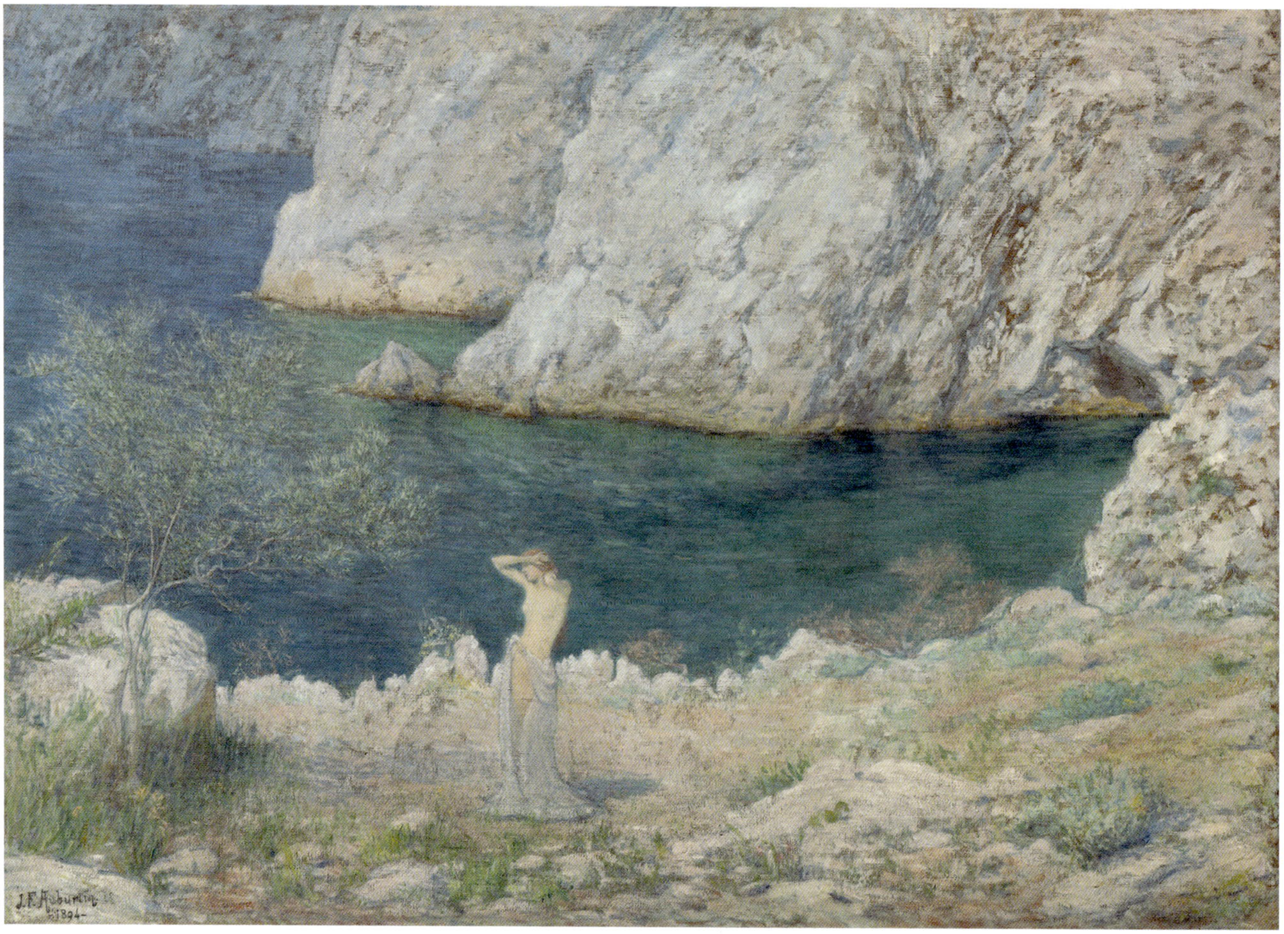

Jean-Francis Auburtin, *Le Matin (Calanque de Porquerolles)*, 1894 — oil on canvas — 113 × 162 cm

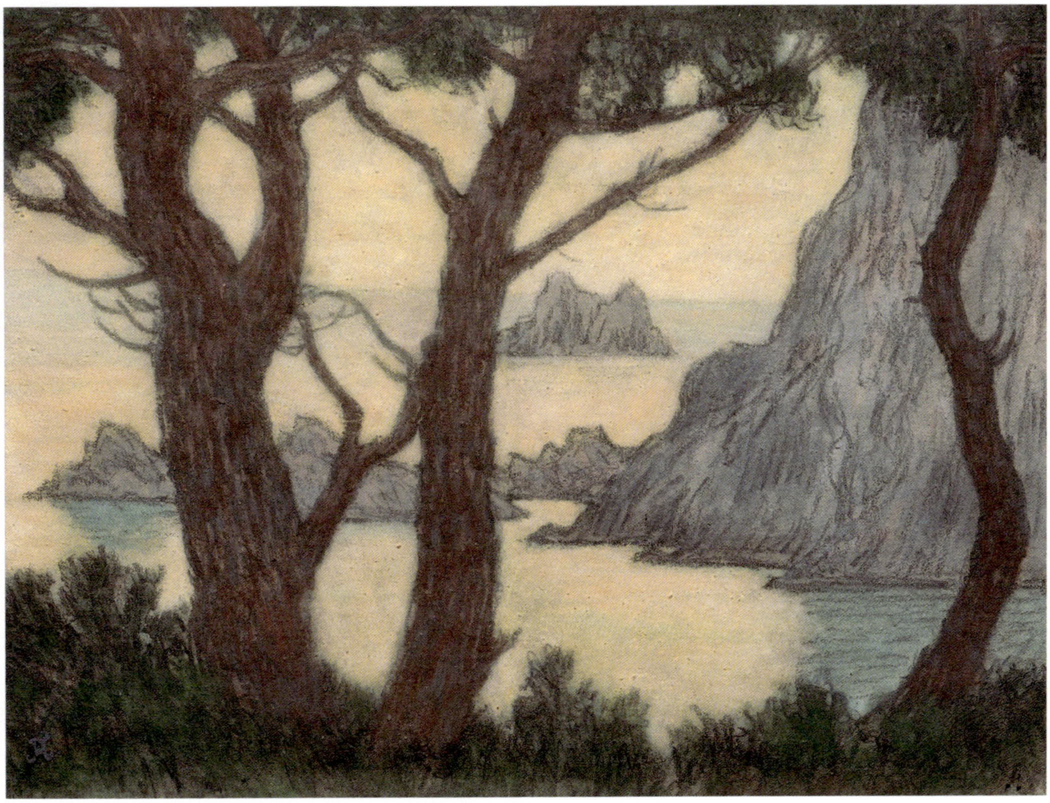

Jean-Francis Auburtin, *La Grand-Cale à Porquerolles*, 1902 — gouache on grey paper — 55.5 × 73 cm

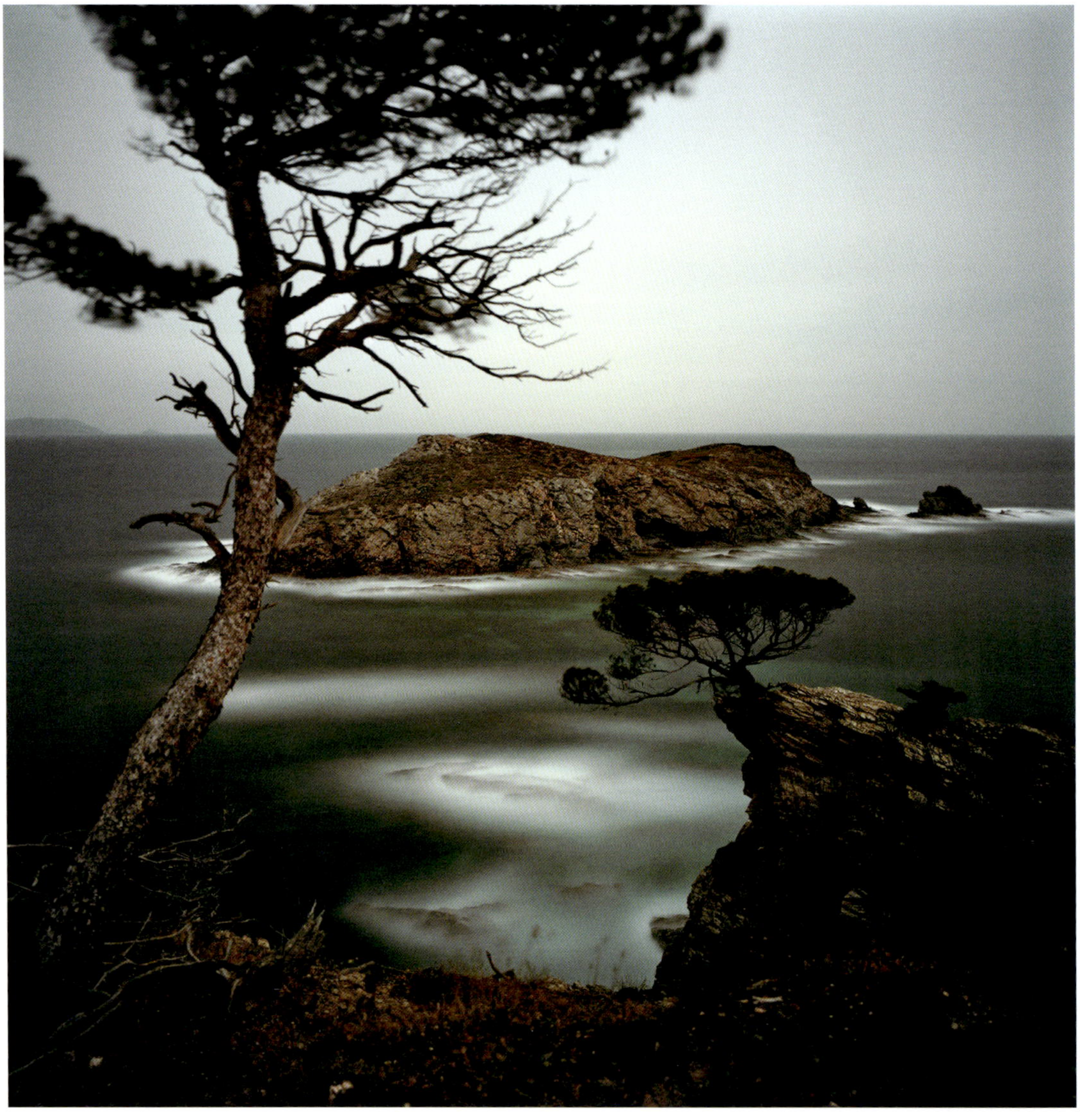

Darren Almond, *Fullmoon@Porquerolles*, 2022 — C-print — 180 × 180 cm

DAY AND NIGHT

For *The Inner Island*, Darren Almond resumed his *Fullmoon* series: images taken on nights with a full moon, all over the world. The first of these images was taken in Provence in the late 1990s. The artist had set out in search of cosmic nights of art history. He also followed in the footsteps of some of the great Romantics or went to natural sites under threat. Some of the photographs taken by night on Porquerolles with long exposure times reveal the Earth's rotation. The stars appear to be shooting, while the soft colours and lunar shadows show the landscapes – even familiar ones – in new and almost disturbing ways. The sea covers the shoreline in mist, and the island, with this new lunar appearance, becomes the terrain of a different imaginary by day.

JMG Rodin's figure is juxtaposed by the one in Jean-Francis Auburtin's painting *Le Matin* (Morning), lost in the depths of a Porquerolles landscape, and its pastel counterpoint depicting an evening light, whose figures are absent this time. Between dawn and dusk, and above all between dusk and the following dawn, a multitude of events sketch the storyboard of inner journeys. The blinding sun on the sea in Henri-Edmond Cross's work or the radiance of Anna-Eva Bergman's moons are two gateways onto these imaginary worlds that flourish in our dreams by relying on our memories. The work of art is a threshold. A space for trial and error. The night is another one. I've always wondered at what point, for each of us, fiction and reality are interdependent in our lives. Andrew Cranston recently painted what he thinks was his first childhood memory: a stag emerging from the forest before a blazing sun. Once over the shock, the child ran to the adults and told them what he saw, but his tale was met with incredulity: they thought he'd made it up. So then this awful and insoluble doubt remained: did it really happen, or did I dream too intensely?

YCT We could say that in Auburtin's, Cross's, Bergman's, and some of Cranston's paintings, the subject, or even the protagonist, is the shore. It is what defines the island: a separate geological formation, surrounded by water. It is also a thoroughfare, traversed by the waves that animate it (cosmic connection), traversed by things that return, brought back to the edge (of awareness), as memory does with recollections. For Michel de Certeau, the shore is the historian's workplace, it is a non-place, constantly changing, where one enters into conversation with the absent. It is there, he writes, that its enterprise is combined with that of dreams. I also see the shore as the place where the artist seeks to capture invisible things. Forces, presences, which are no less real. I have also had dreams on Porquerolles. Several people paid me a visit in my dreams, who had never come before. I had to make this journey, to pass this limit, to realise the extent to which this shore that haunts our imagination – as the border between the known and the unknown, dream and reality, here and beyond – is also a locus of communication.

Children are like that; they command the world, through the energy of a desperate plea, and sometimes the world obeys them.

MAURICE BLANCHOT
L'Arrêt de mort, 1948

ANDREW CRANSTON
I no what I saw, 2022,
pigment and gum Arabic and varnish on hardback book cover,
27.3 × 21.3 cm

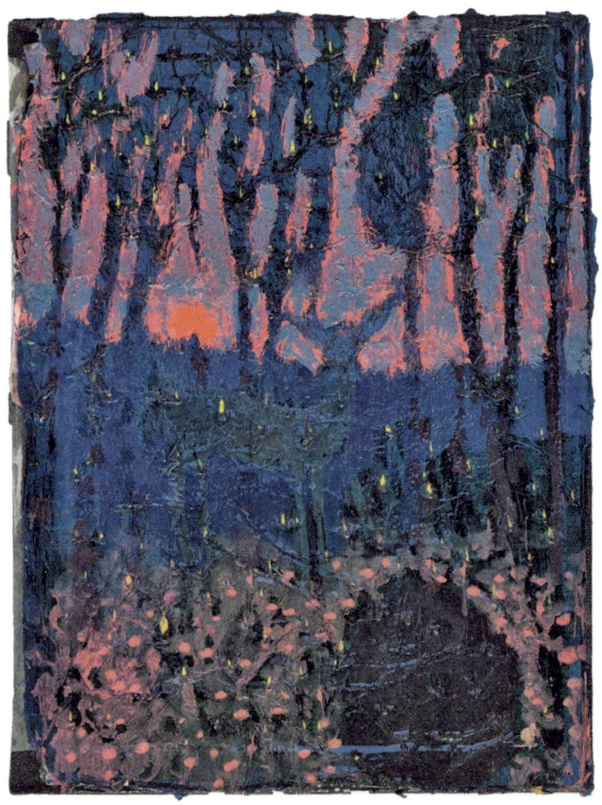

JMG As a teenager, my favourite thing was to get on a bike after dark, headphones on, and tirelessly repeat the same circuits in the courtyard and garden, in the countryside, with no light, having memorised the route. This is how all of the most extraordinary – though imprecise – stories are created. Later, I attempted to run in the middle of the night in poorly lit parks that I barely knew. Attenuated vision, the whole body absorbing the slightest bumps in the ground while taking in the night, in music, cut through with external sounds or, on the contrary, listening acutely. These deliberate alterations of perception, these intoxicating sensations, I have sometimes found again by delving into artworks, which are none other than altered realities themselves. The exhibition tries to broach this, to reconstitute the conditions of these teenage reveries.

YCT It is likely that over the next few years the experience of nighttime will only be possible in a few isolated locations: alpine areas, forests, or islands protected from light pollution and 24/7 activity. Star parks already exist: reserves of night skies where people can go to observe and, almost in a nostalgic way, *bid farewell* to the Milky Way. Because in the future, if everything continues to operate as it does today, we will only be able to connect to the heavenly bodies in what will become *islands of the night*, across the surface of the globe. The night is an essential period within an ancestral cycle. In the images that Darren Almond produces, invisible to the naked eye, we discover the night for what it really is: luminous, shifting, populated, and alive. It took a technological invention (the camera) to imagine how animals perceive their environment: for them, the dark night does not exist, it is a colourful and noisy environment. It took an island to understand this depth – fragile and essential – that the night possesses.

LEARNING TO SEE

> Seeing means opening oneself to the experience of light [...]. Perceiving things, is therefore simultaneously being perceived by them; seeing is being seen, hearing is being heard, and so on. This reversibility [is] clear in the exemplary case of two hands touching.
>
> TIM INGOLD
> *Lines: A Brief History*, 2007

JMG It is a platitude that's so lovely and accurate that we are happy to divulge it: the genius of artists resides in the depth obtained out of nothing, from a "flat surface covered with colours assembled in a certain order", according to Maurice Denis' famous phrase about painters; to fragments captured by the lens for videographers and photographers; to manipulation of materials for sculptors, etc. The question of scale is essential here too, as it is for the feeling of insularity. For Brazilian artist Lucas Arruda, the slightest brushstroke, even if it is tiny, can cause a cataclysm within a precarious landscape. For Caribbean painter and poet Frank Walter, a few daubs of raw colour on the miniature scale of a Polaroid film cartridge box is enough to evoke the whole landscape of Antigua – like an ordinary topographical and meteorological report with exacerbated hues. Landscapes as moods, as implicit portraits.

If looking at a painting makes reality look different, it is an incredibly poetic event.

LEE UFAN
Painting Saint-Victoire, 1986

Thanks to her camera, Jennifer Douzenel transfigures microevents that happen before her eyes, turning them into living tableaus. She uses it in still shots like a painter out of doors placing an easel in front of a scene. Artists are constantly teaching us how to see. To see better (major project of the nineteenth century in the West, the century of transparent architecture and the most prodigious of scientific inventions) or to see differently (major project of the twentieth and twenty-first centuries, which were no more than a series of rewritings and reinventions of our ways of seeing, framing, reframing, or looking beyond the frame). Our limited human perception is honed as soon as it is confronted with art.

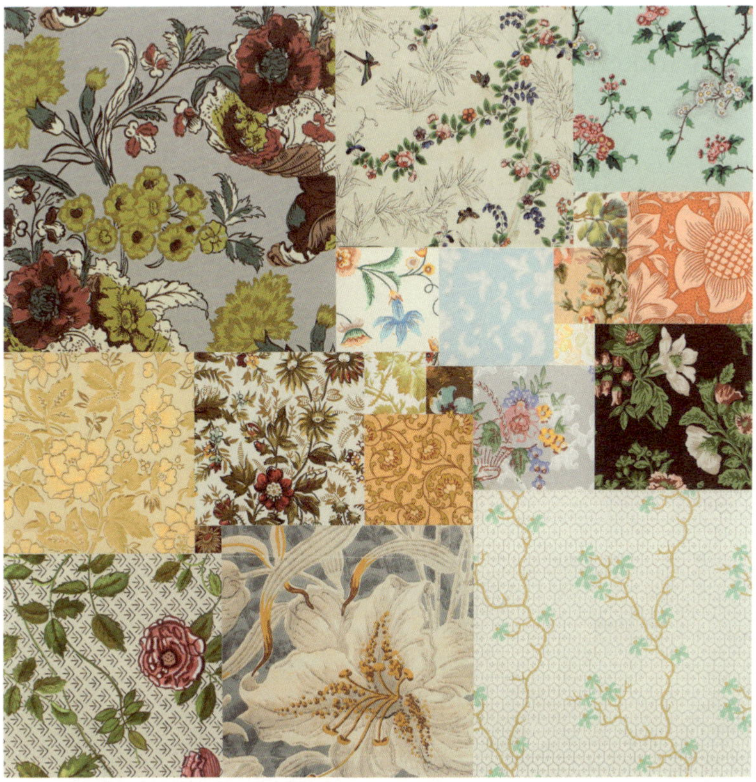

SPENCER FINCH
The Brain – is wider than the Sky (squared square of order 21 for Emily Dickinson), 2018
Collage on board, 72.4 × 72.4 cm

YCT Seeing a painting by Auburtin today means being exposed to the light, colour, and air of the island that fills the canvas and continues to permeate the exhibition space. That is how painting touches us, literally. Arruda's and Walter's artworks are not landscape paintings. They are climate paintings. Lichtenstein's *Landscape* was already an almost technical representation of the way in which we experience time and elements. We connect to the landscape not just with our eyes, but with all of our other senses as well. The character at the window, looking out to sea, is marked by what they see, what they sense and feel: they are entirely coloured by it. Arruda's paintings are like imprints, hypersensitive captures of evanescent, atmospheric evolutions. Walter's paintings can be seen as a way of taking stock of time, both its passing – repetition and difference – and the weather. The relationship that we maintain with the environment surpasses pure visuality. It is akin to immersion. In addition, this relationship occurs in both directions. Our inner climate is linked to the external climate. Lichtenstein's painting also showed this back-and-forth, this symbiosis, this way of inhaling the landscape. Our mode of perception is intrinsically linked to life. It is not a metaphor: it is actually breathing in and out.

Les Îles d'or [The Golden Isles]: Porquerolles, Port-Cros, and Le Levant were observed by Henri-Edmond Cross, who delivered in the late nineteenth century one of the most radical landscapes paintings in the history of art, focusing only on the effects of the light and pushing the horizon very high upwards. The scene is probably seen from La Courtade beach in Porquerolles. This artwork, verging on abstraction, paved the way for a whole host of modern artists.

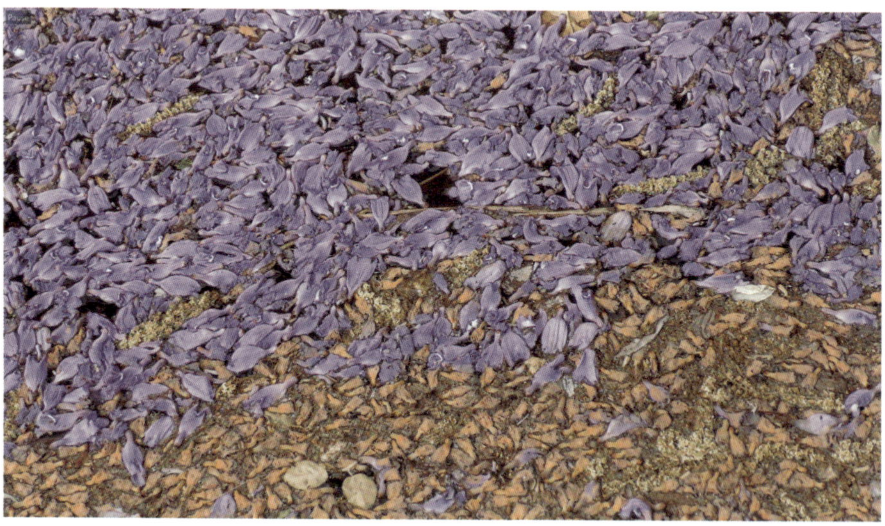

JENNIFER DOUZENEL
Petals, 2020, video, 5'20"

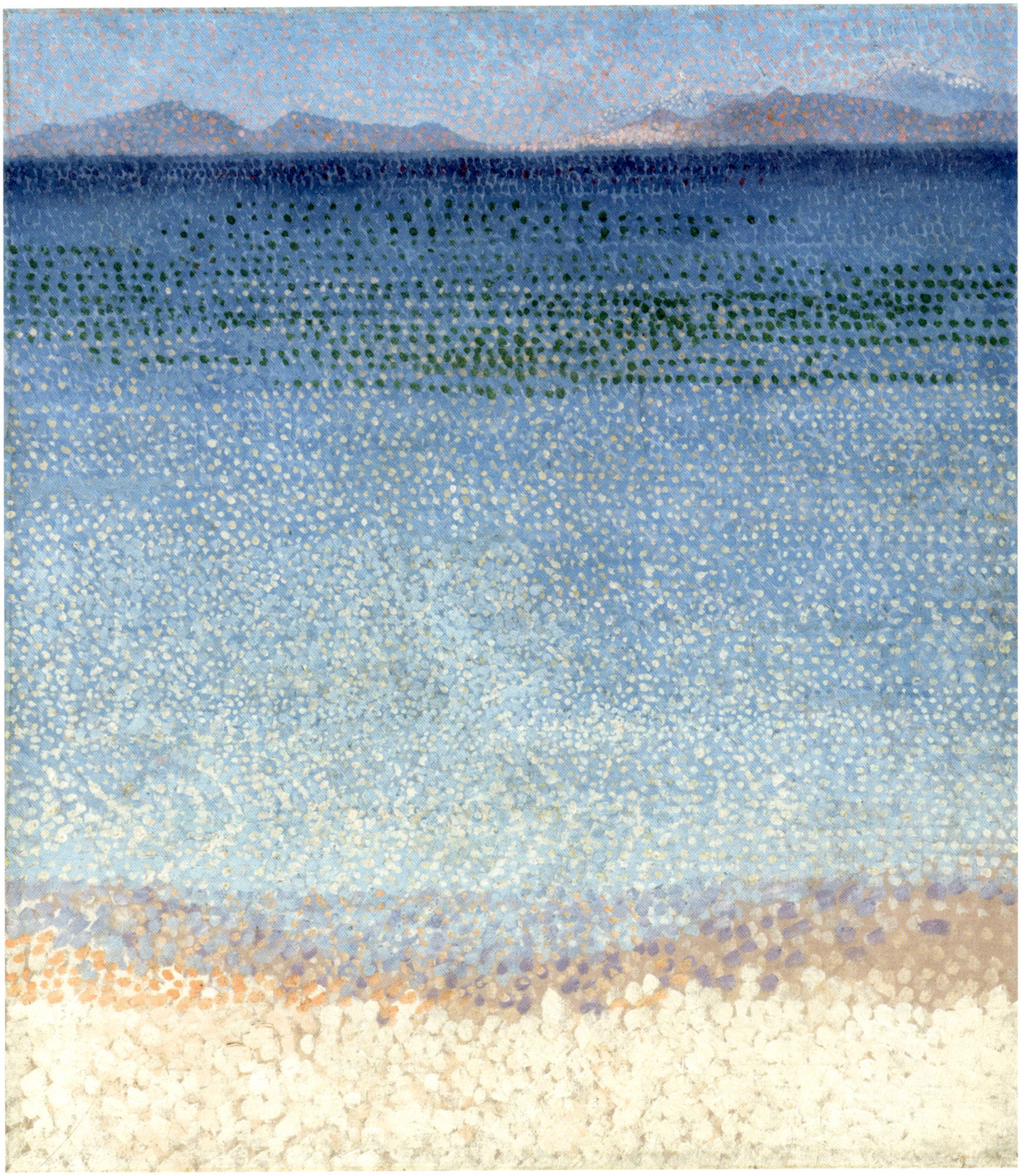

Henri-Edmond Cross, *Les Îles d'or*, 1891–1892 — oil on canvas — 59.5 × 54 cm

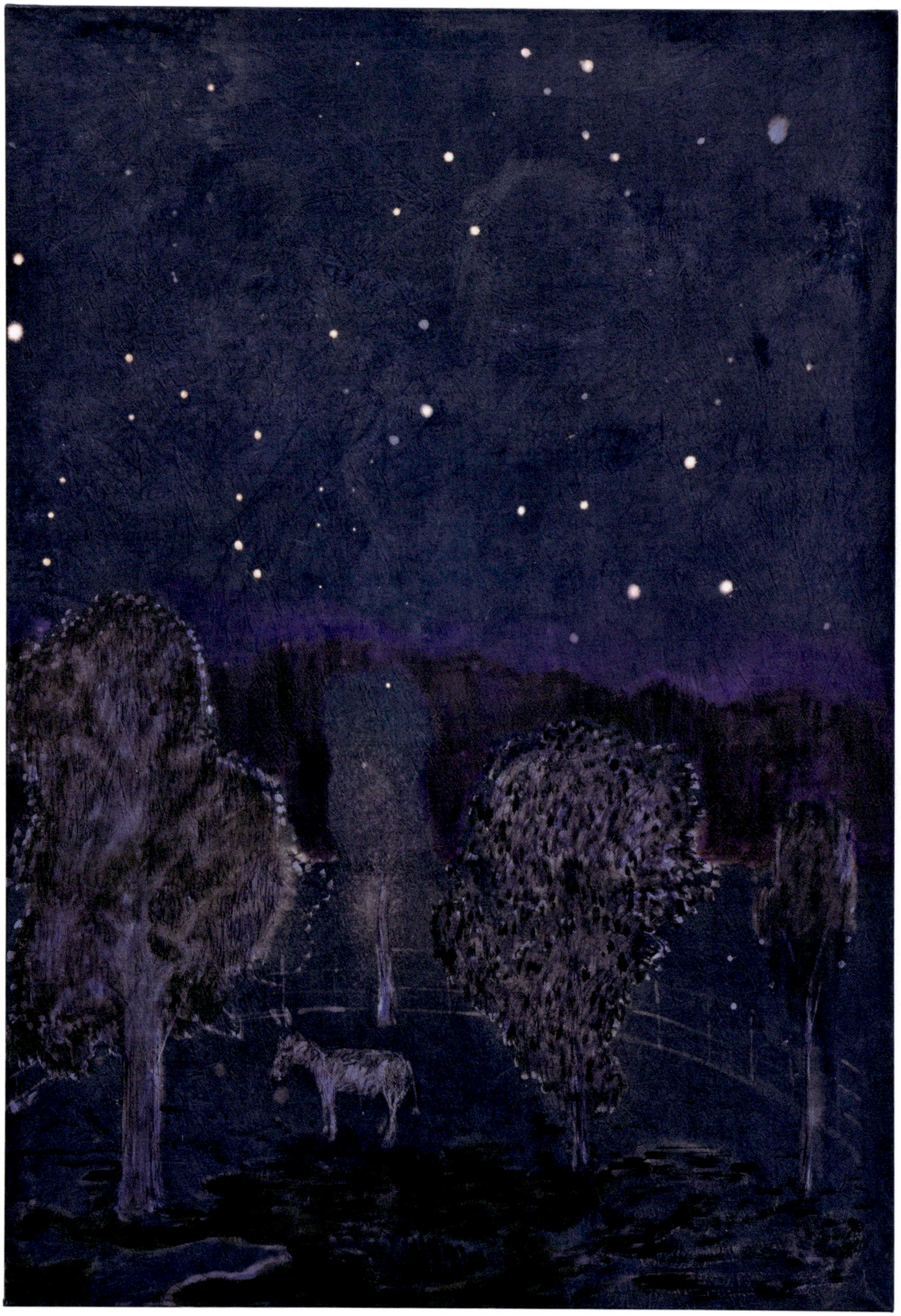

Andrew Cranston, *Starry Night with Donkey (August 1974)*, 2020 — oil on canvas — 225.1 × 160 cm

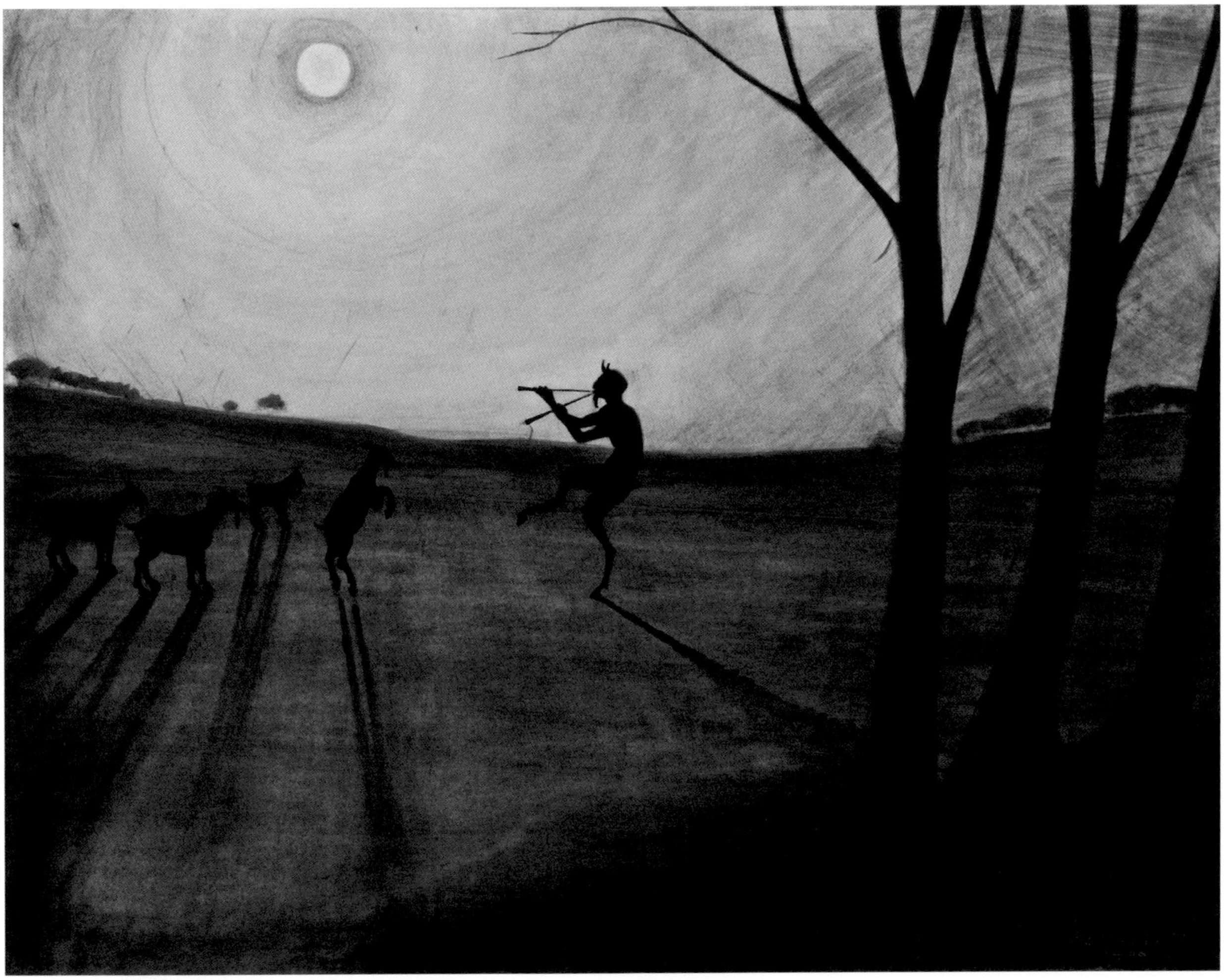

Léon Spilliaert, *Faune au clair de lune*, 1900 — Indian ink wash, paintbrush, black chalk, coloured pencil on paper — 48.9 × 63.6 cm

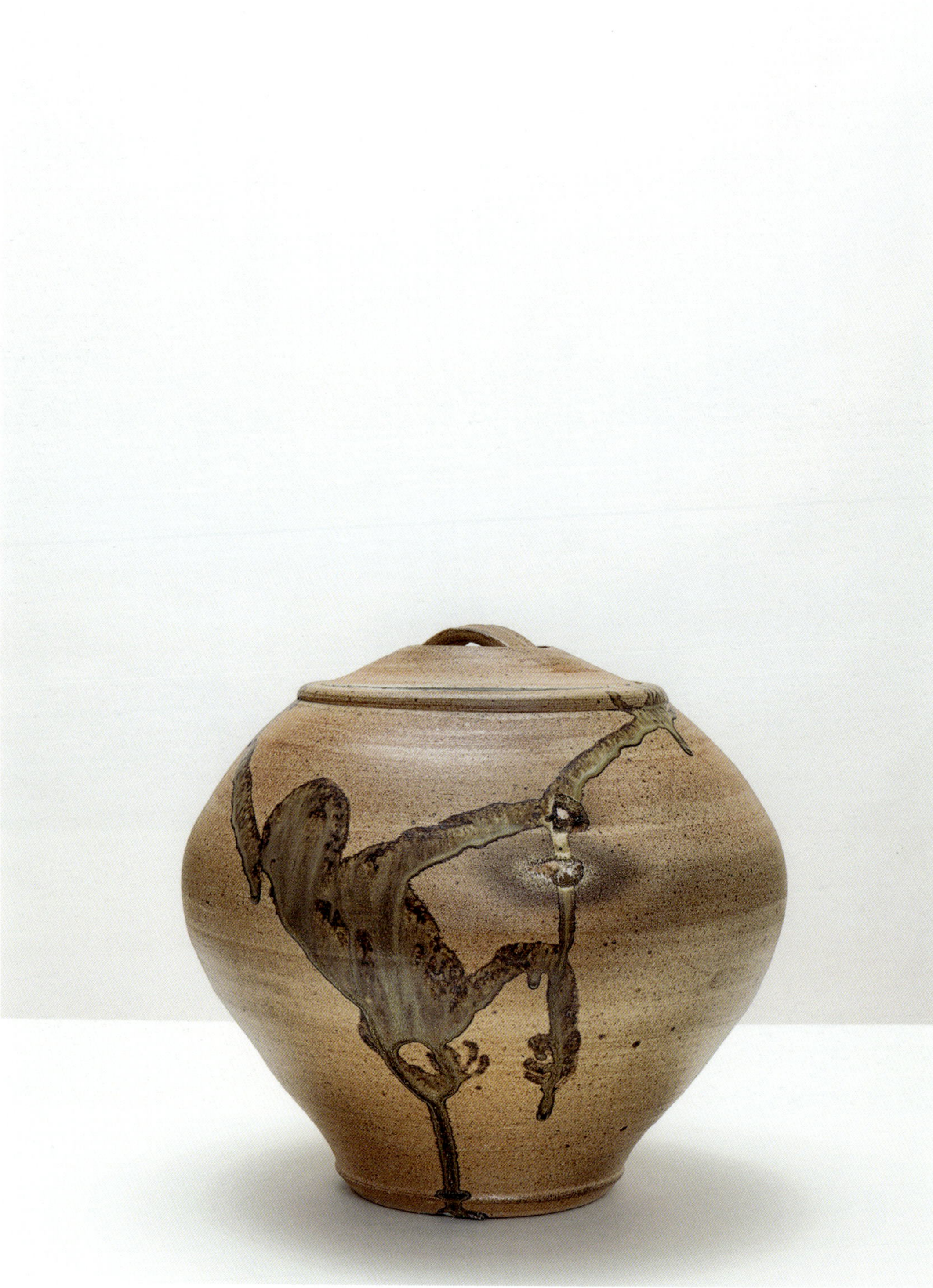

Francis Upritchard, *Moon Monkey and Dancing Monkey Urn*, 2016 — ceramic — 39 × 42.5 × 42.5 cm

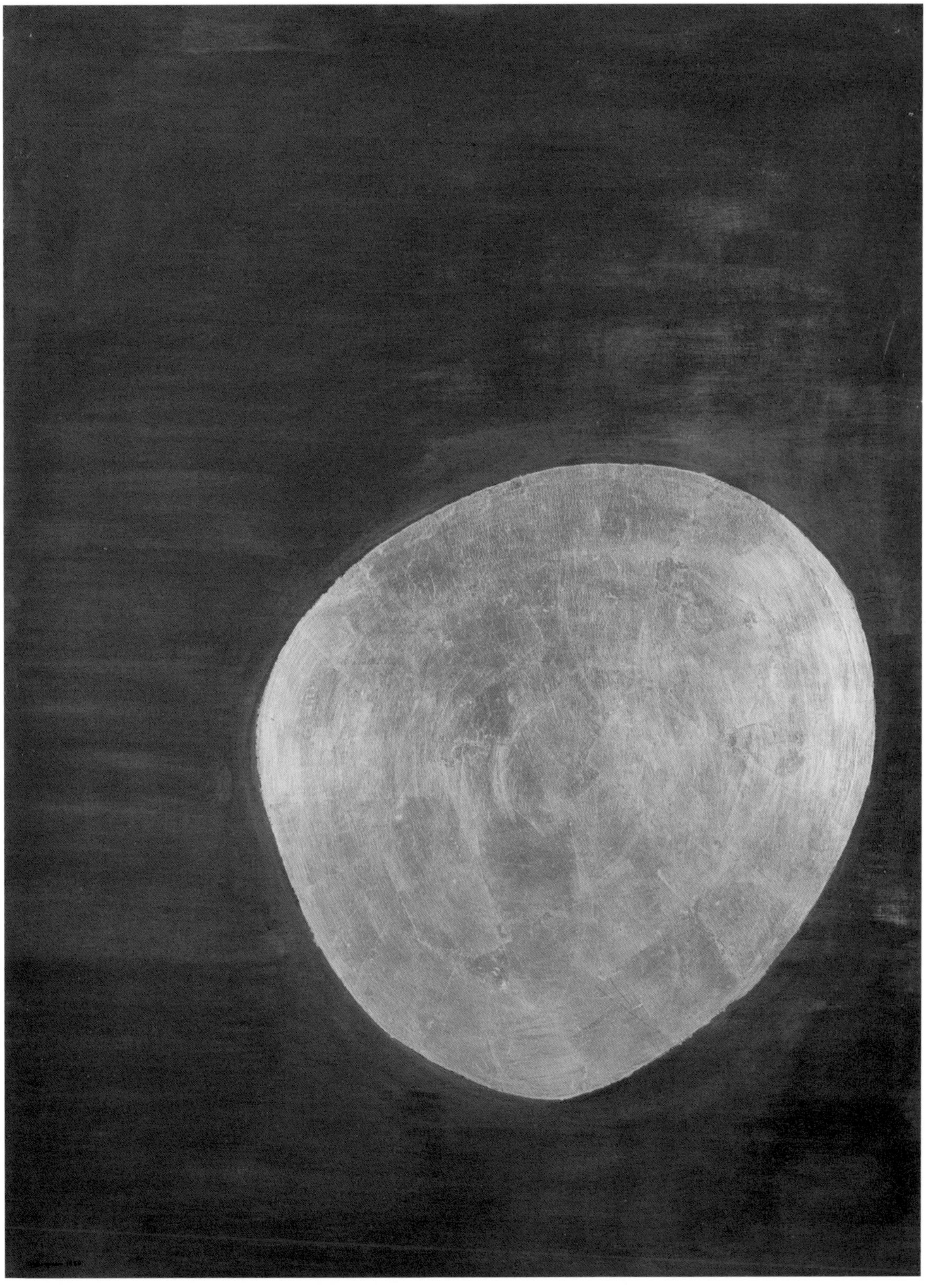

Anna-Eva Bergman, *N° 11 - 1955 Lune d'argent,* 1955 — oil and metal sheet on canvas — 130 × 97 cm

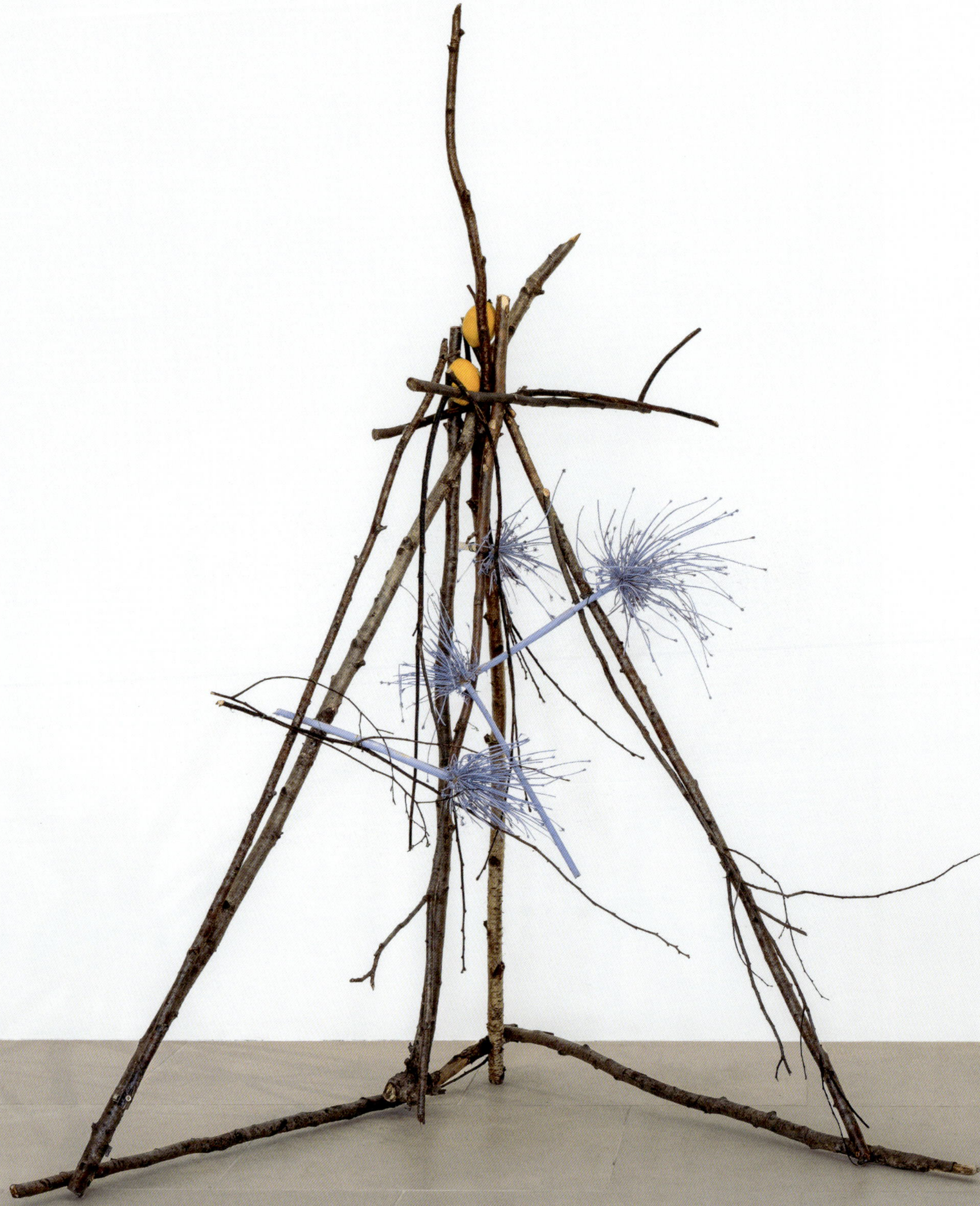

Camille Henrot, *"L'heure de s'enivrer. L'univers a-t-il un sens ?" Hubert Reeves*, 2012 — ikebana: dyed ornamental garlic (*Allium schubertii*), four-season lemons (*Citrus limon eureka*), and Holly Oak (*Quercus ilex*) — H: 181 cm

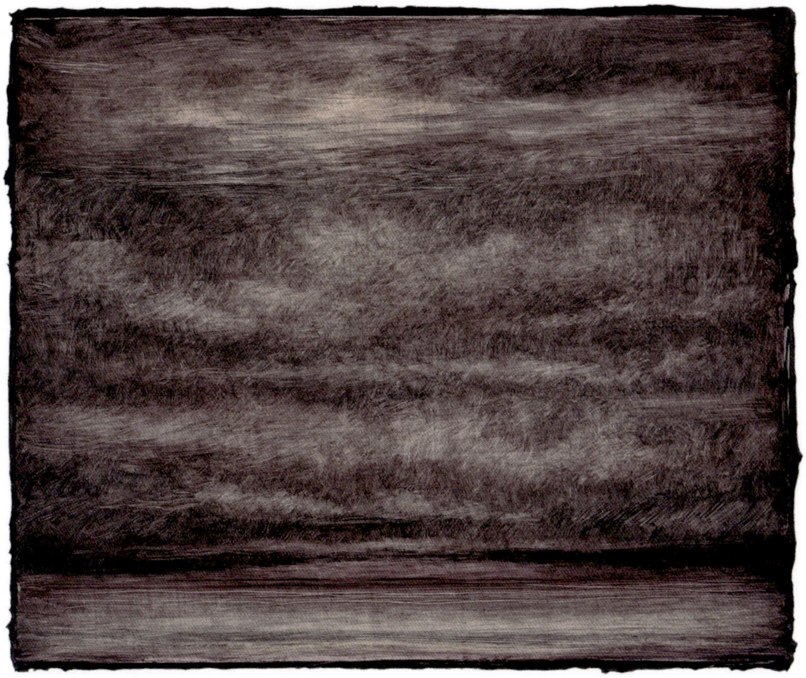

Lucas Arruda, *Untitled (from the Deserto-Modelo series)*, 2021 — oil on canvas — 18 × 22 cm

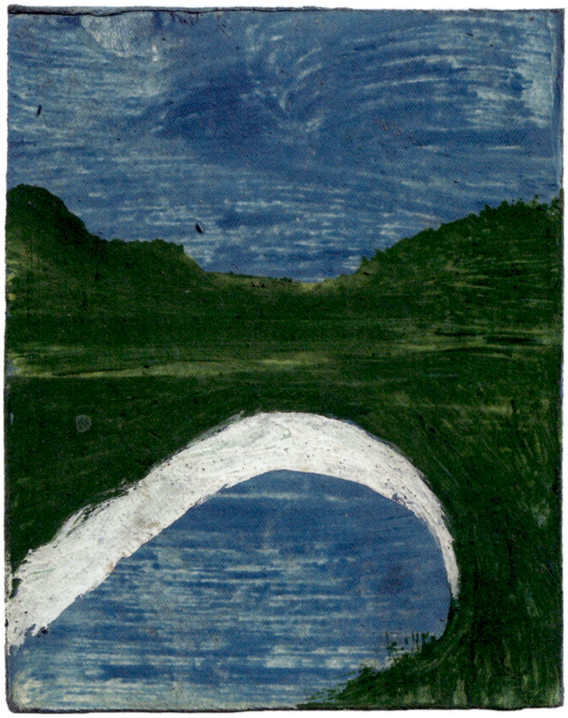

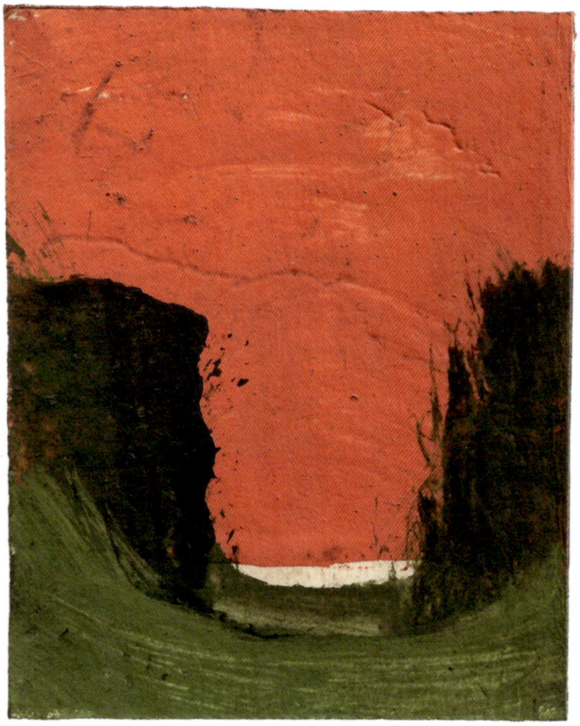

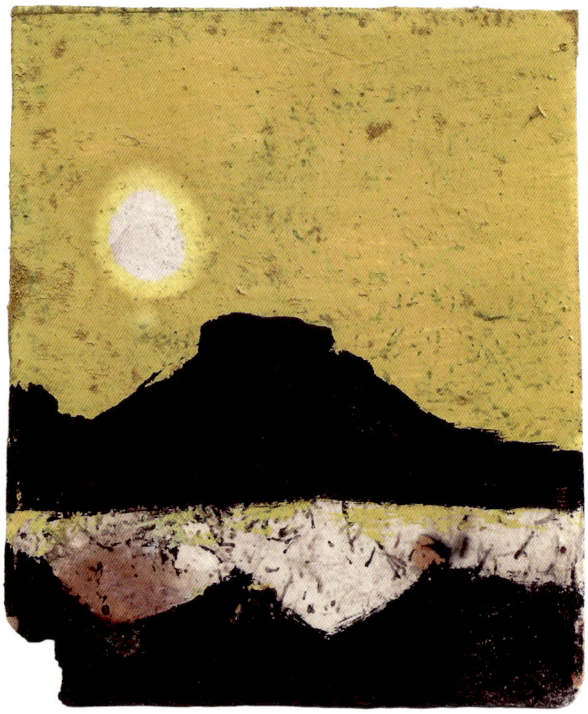

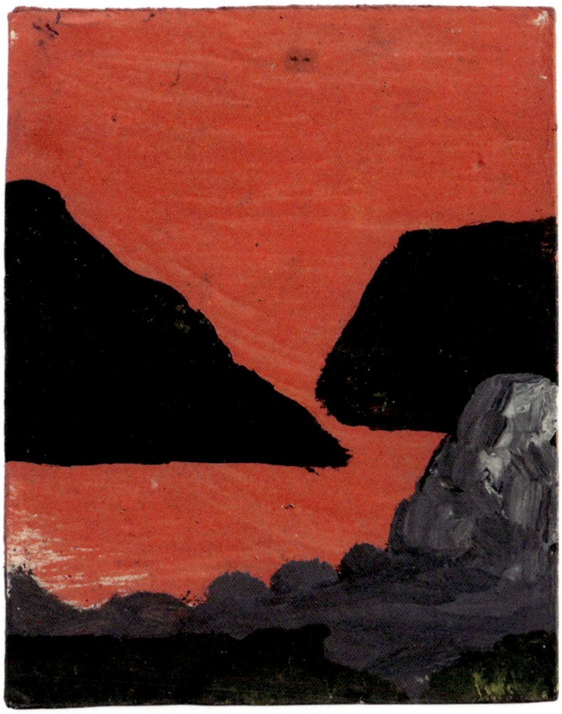

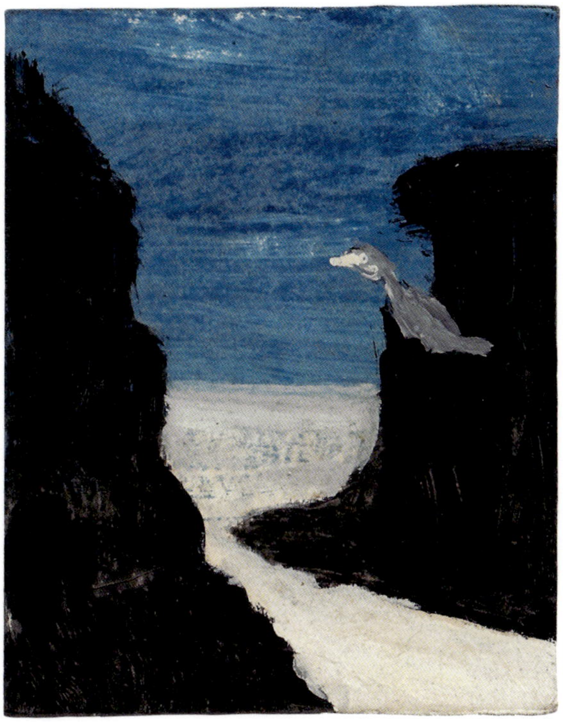

Frank Walter
Untitled (White-Edged Harbor, Green Hills), c. 1970 — oil on Polaroid film cartridge box — 10.1 × 8.1 cm
Untitled (Steep Cliffs, Red Sky, White Sea), c. 1970 — oil on Polaroid film cartridge box — 9.8 × 8 cm
Untitled (Yellow Sky, Black Bute, White Sun), c. 1970 — oil on Polaroid film cartridge box — 9.8 × 8 cm
Untitled (Hurricane Headlands), c. 1970 — oil on Polaroid film cartridge box — 10 × 8.2 cm
Untitled (Grey Bird on Black Cliff), c. 1970 — oil on Polaroid film cartridge box — 10,1 × 8.1 cm

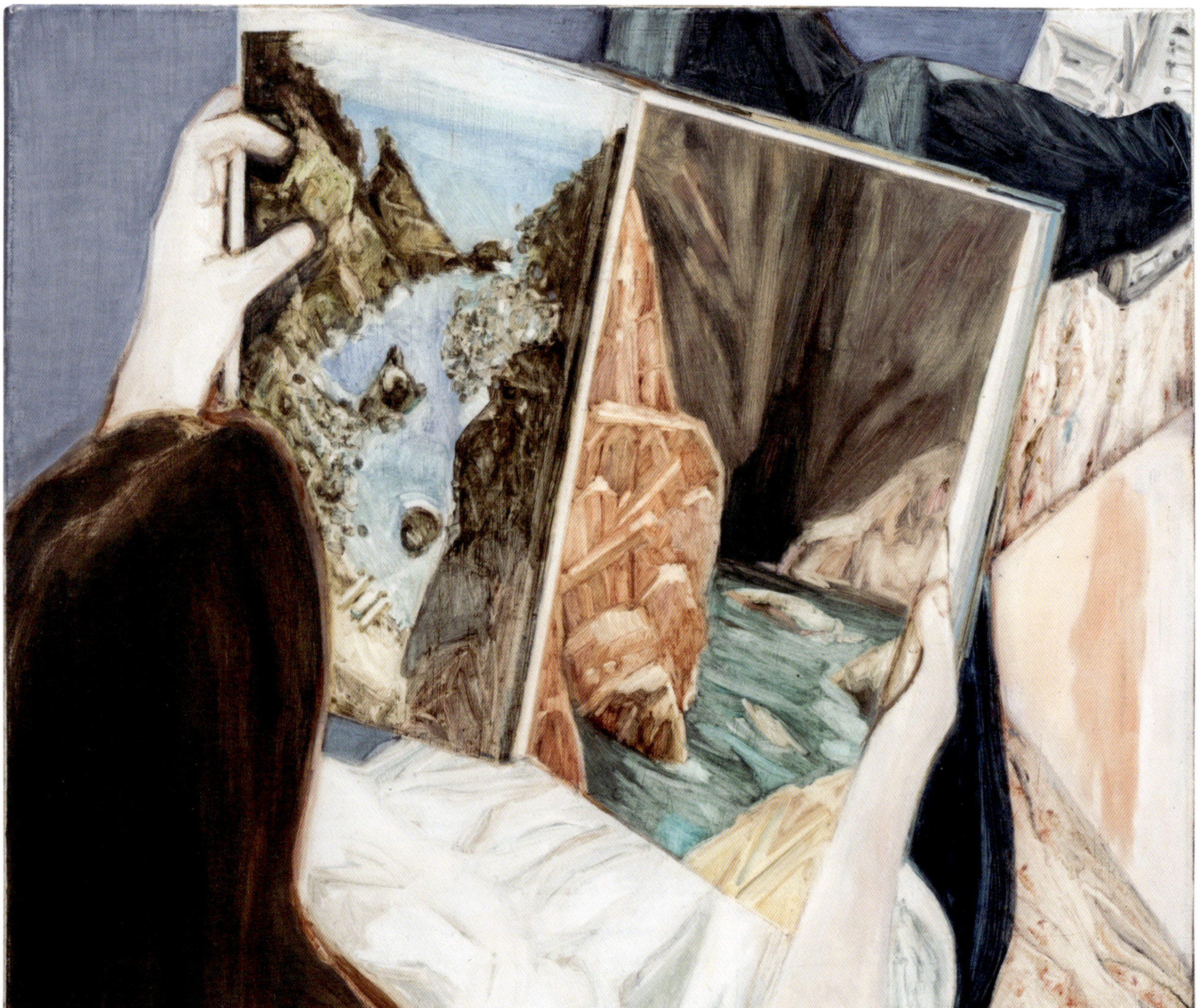

Jill Mulleady, *Badlands*, 2010 — oil on linen canvas — 46 × 55 cm

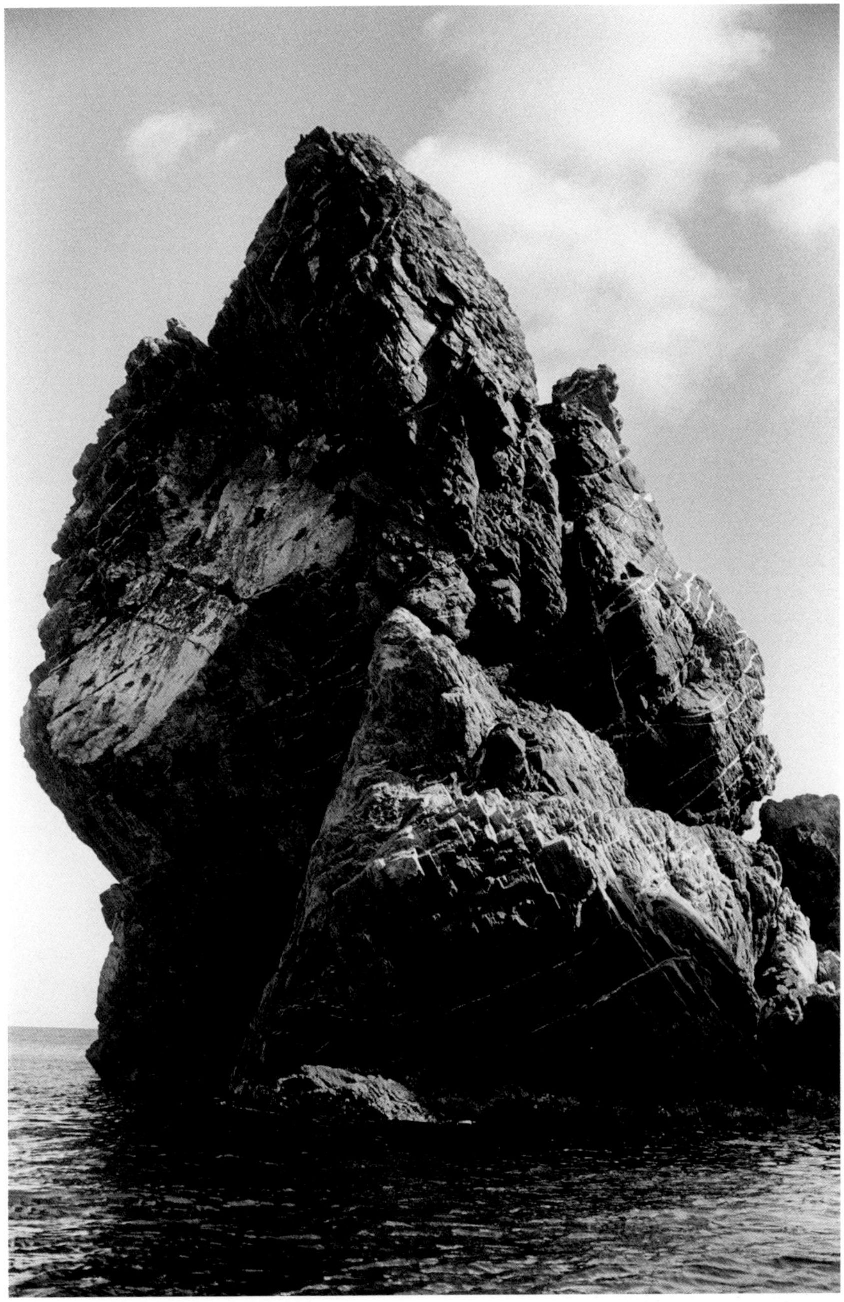

Bernard Pesce, *Les Mèdes*, 1980 — modern silver print on baryta paper — 60 × 40 cm

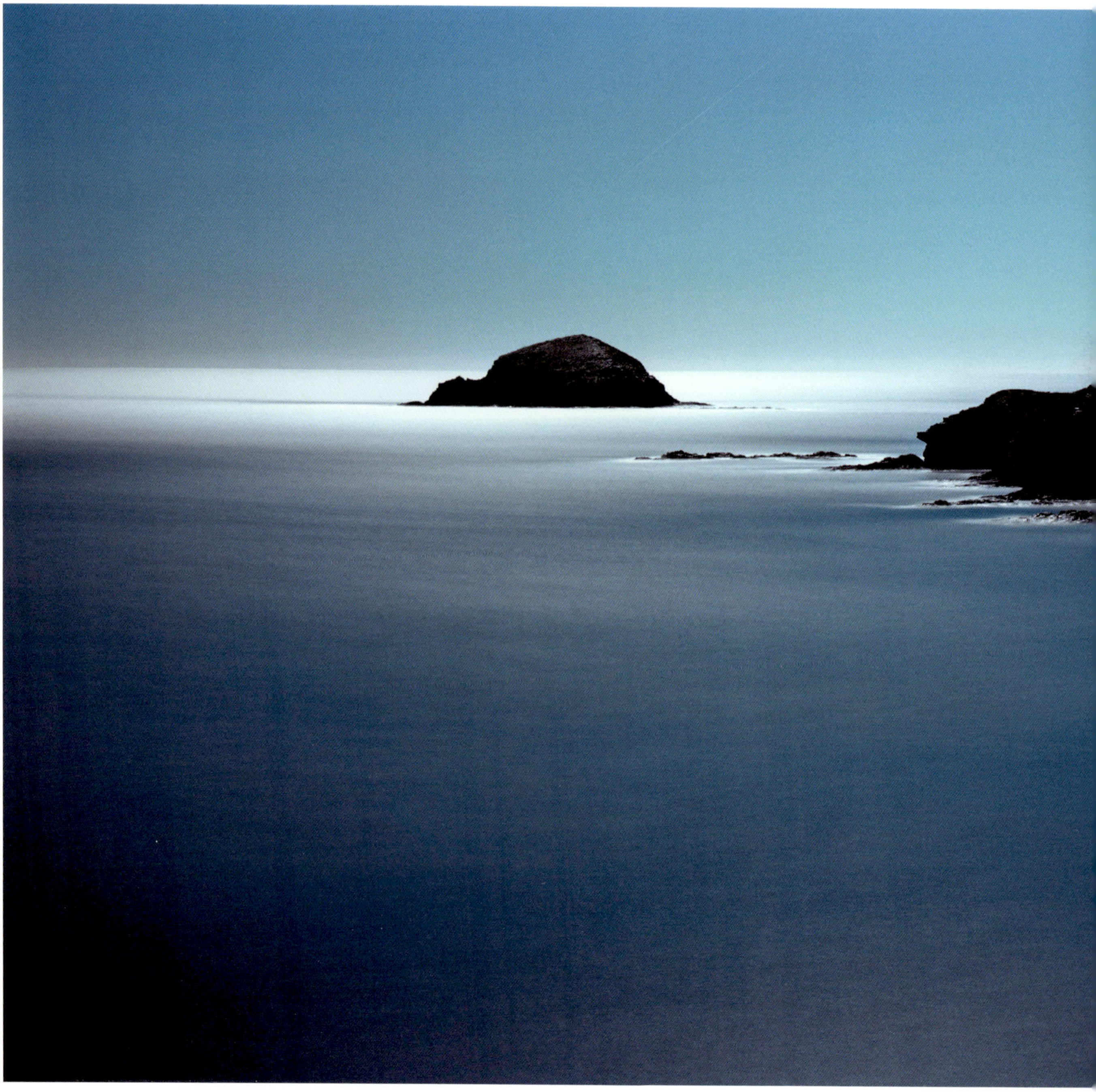

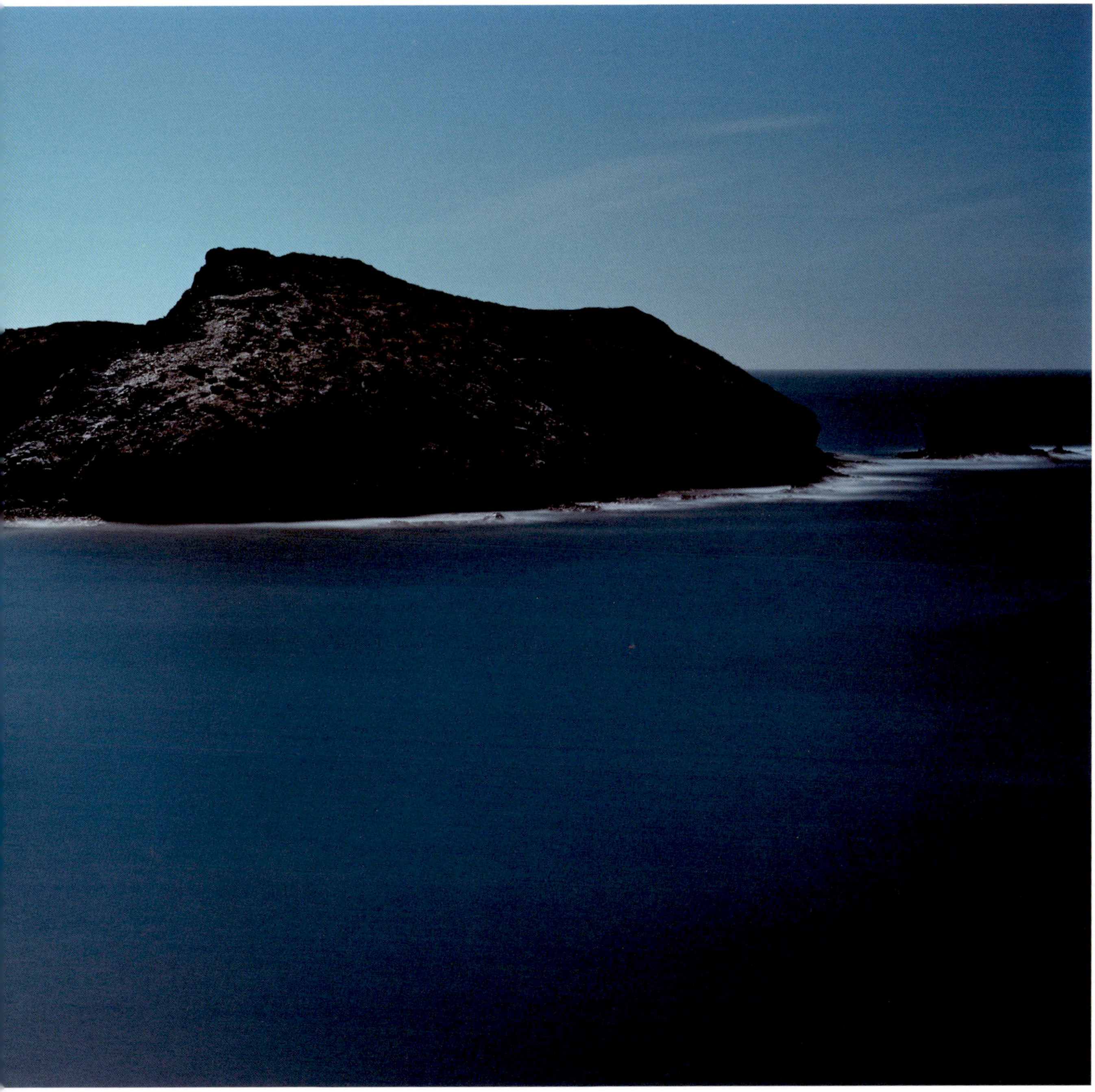

Darren Almond, *Fullmoon@Sarranier*, 2022 — C-print — 121.2 × 263.7 cm

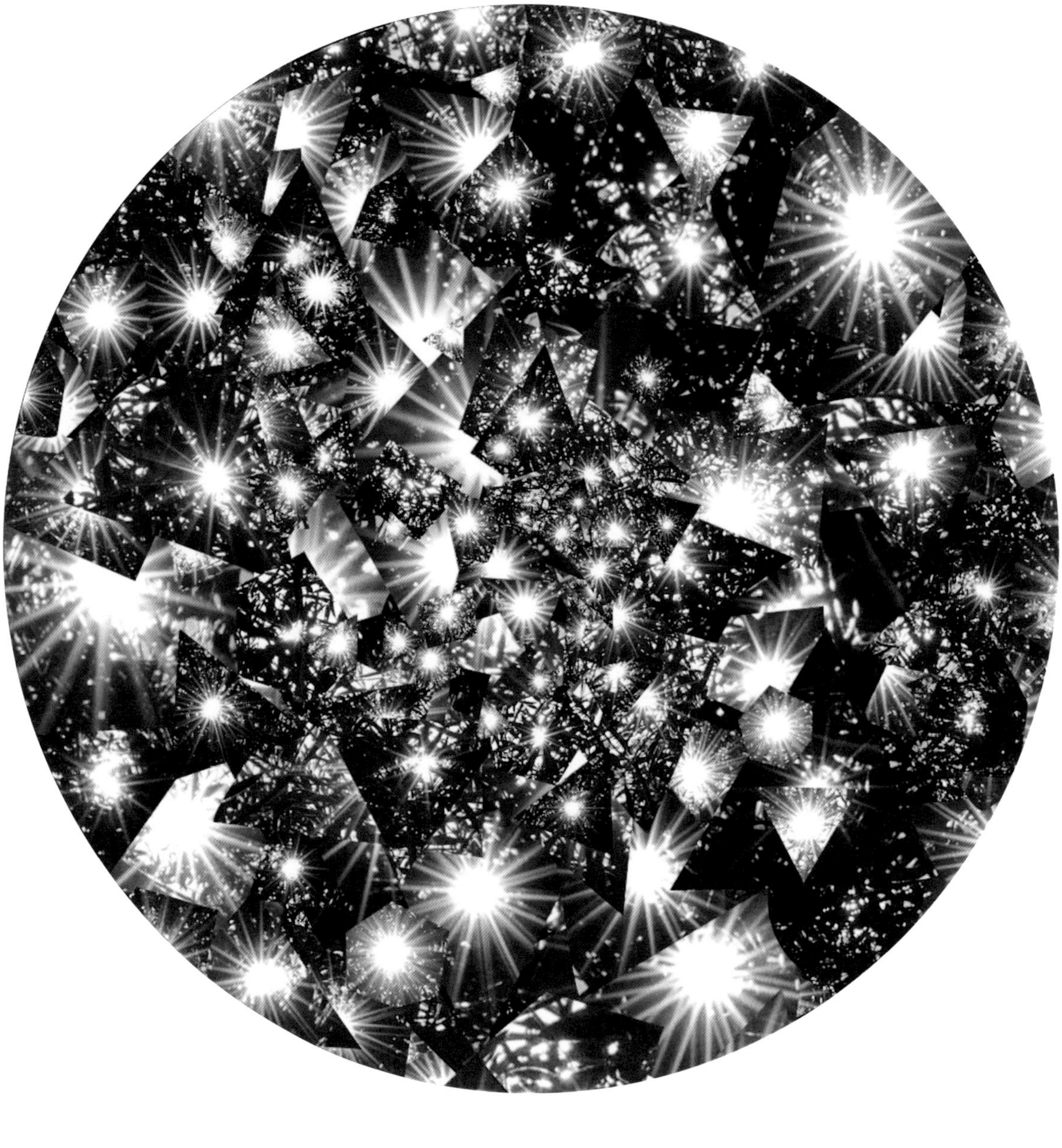

Jennifer Douzenel, *Poids du Soleil*, 2023 — video installation — 8' 38" in loop

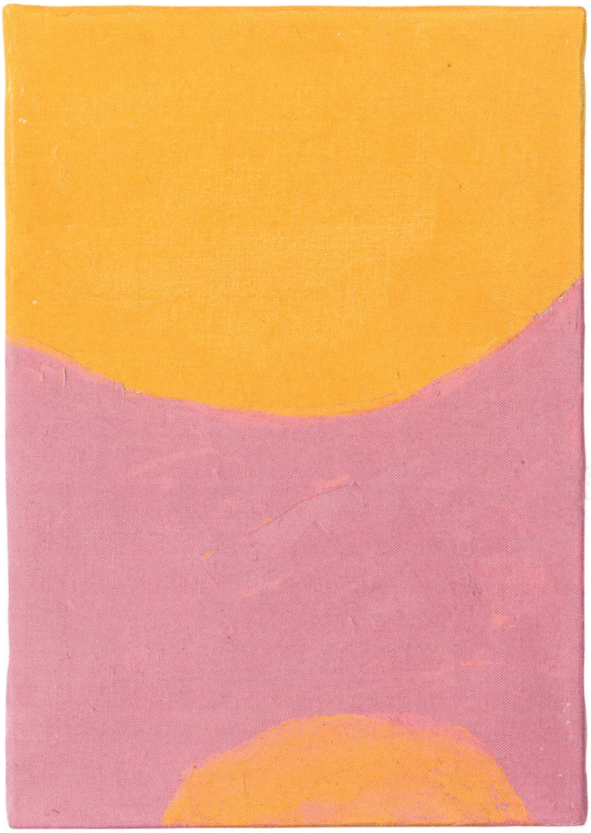

Etel Adnan, *Planète 20*, 2020 — oil on canvas — 33 × 22 cm

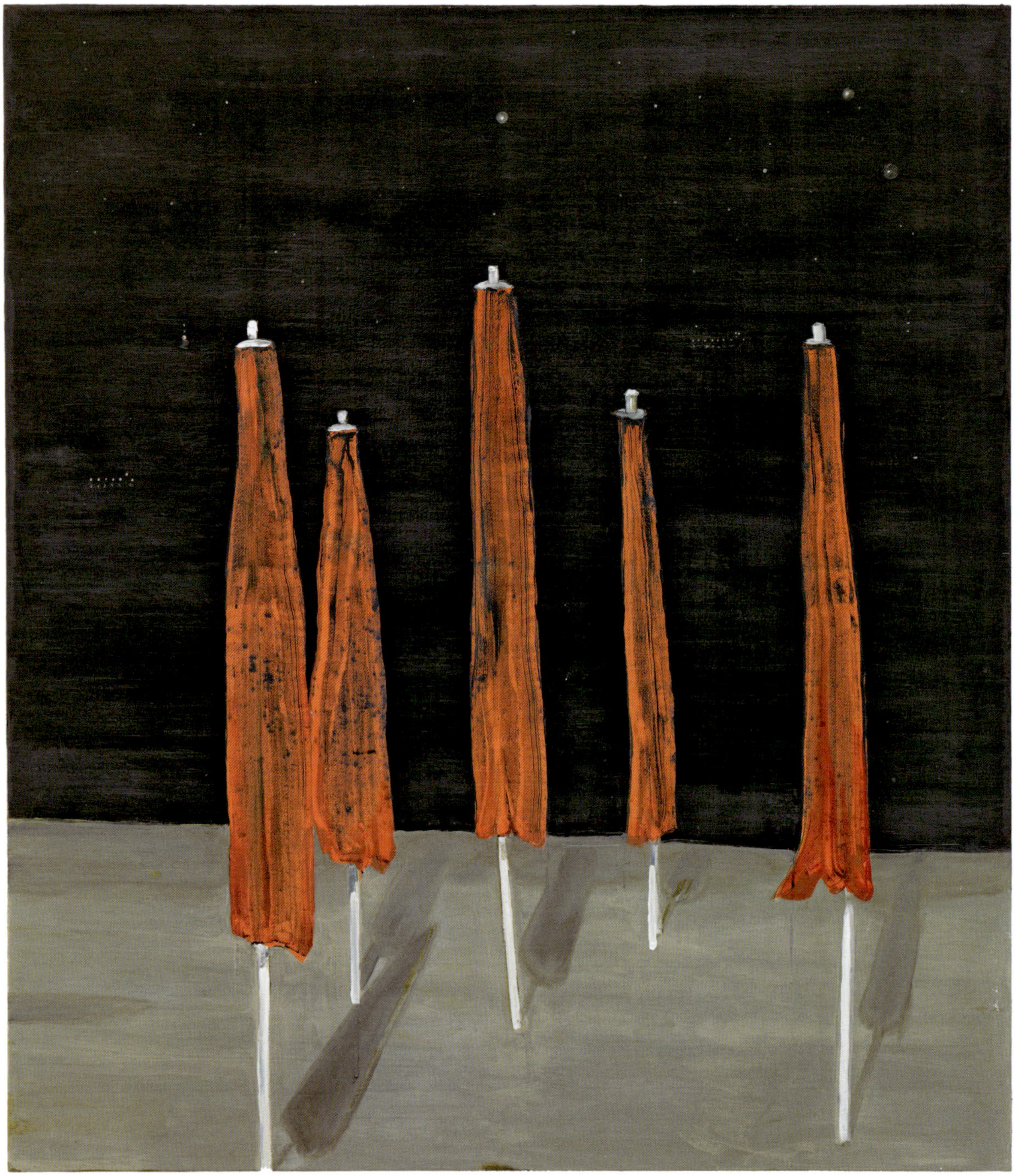

Norbert Schwontkowski, *Sopot*, 2010 — oil on canvas — 200 × 180 cm

NEITHER PLACE

NOR TIME

JMG Is it a sign of our time, which will soon be over? Contemporary painting, particularly figurative painting, seems to take great delight in past styles, blithely referencing certain historical avant-gardes as much through the content as the form, but whose radicality of the time has become today's order. The styles of the past are digested and suddenly re-emerge as answers to current questions, sometimes in a more political way than at first appears. They inventory neo-Romantics, orchestra conductors of anxious human confrontations within landscapes, paradises lost, or even universes with no human traces at all, even though the concept of *nature* is now inoperative due to anthropocentrism, and that of the *sublime* has now assumed an environmental connotation. Within today's dark dreams, neo-symbolists explore the signs of a bygone era or a post-apocalyptic future, travelling through time. Finally, the modernists are flourishing, since this term now has a classicist value: fauvists, fans of a *new* New Objectivity, targeting the shortcomings of the human species in crisis, or the disciples of a metaphysical painting that plays on the disorders of the present, sometimes at the risk of being described as reactionaries. These artworks fascinate and multiply to the point of forming a bona fide character trait of contemporary creation. In *Das entzweite Jahrhundert, 1750–1830*, the art historian Werner Hofmann analyses the extreme and striking variety in the artistic productions of that period in Europe (with its cardinal points being David, Goya, Friedrich, and Blake) as the result of several "disintegrations of sensibilities". The current period seems similar, except that the disintegrated sensibilities recompose themselves and converge towards the aesthetic of an art not situated within reality, all the while citing identified references: a *plausible* figuration loaded with references. The tensions and breakaways are no longer the same, but they have the same effects on the cultural production of humanity. We are torn by contradictory and intractable directions. So the artworks are increasingly open: we cannot situate the action in them, their genre, any recognisable geography, or any clear temporality – at least, visually, because the titles of the artworks

Norbert Schwontkowski's paintings resemble dreams and plunge the beholder (unless we are the ones beheld?) into a melancholy world, between naivety and sophistication. In *Sopot*, red parasols, the main subjects/characters of the painting, are artificially lit in front of a dark background, a nocturnal shore or cosmic void. They remind us of the fundamentally theatrical character of painting.

often paradoxically play with the idea of scales of time and memory. It is not a question of living in an atemporal world, but of circulating, imagining a future that resembles a past, and a past that resembles a future. Etel Adnan writes in her poem *Night*: "In its will to protect the living from the maddening effect of a constant present, nature created memory. An escape. A rest." Memory is the driver, the hybridisations and transplants are mechanisms that sustain this machine for creating new worlds.

YCT The anthropologist's dream (which, in a way, extended that of the explorer and the settler) was rooted in the belief that by moving within space – by visiting populations that they believed were isolated, and whose practices would have evolved at a different pace, in a different direction – they would also be travelling through time. Islands still bear the mark of this powerful anachronism that contradicts the idea of a global and monolithic evolution of culture. Anachronism relies on the freedom to occupy another time, or to combine times, to allow them to meet. Perhaps even cause them to vibrate together, to cause dissonance within a history that could be written in a more linear or harmonious way. But anachronism is not *achronic*, timeless or outside of time. Anachronism meets anarchism, in the sense that we could imagine a world undone by a central authority of time: each island is running on "island time". Islands are the agents of the liberation of time. Talking about islands within history means talking about appropriations, destructions, conquests, and colonisation. It also means talking about some of the *polychronic* powers of differentiation islands have, some of the temporal forks that they authorise. Islands alone – whether they are physical or mental – have the power to create the conditions for alternative timelines. Histories cross paths, freely, or don't, because they can also go their separate ways, without ever meeting, infinitely. Islands are *heterochronic* places, I believe: places in which it is possible to modulate one's time, to set the speed to one's own pace, and invent, definitively, one's own history.

I always feel I am a traveller, going somewhere and to some destination. If I tell myself that the somewhere and the destination do not exist, that seems to me very reasonable and likely enough.

VINCENT VAN GOGH
letter to his brother Theo, 6 August 1888

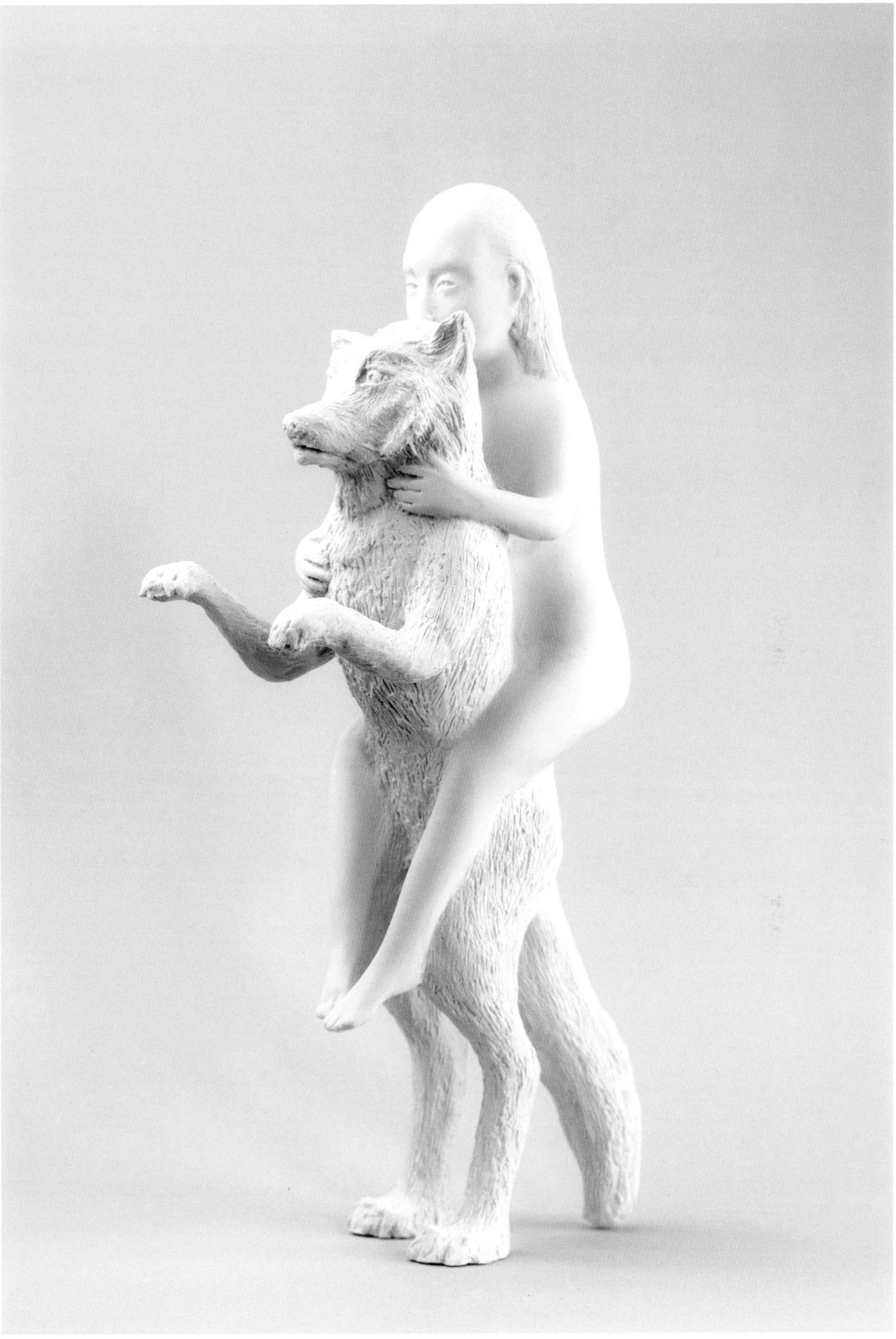

Kiki Smith, *Woman with Wolf,* 2003 — porcelain — 37 × 12 × 20 cm

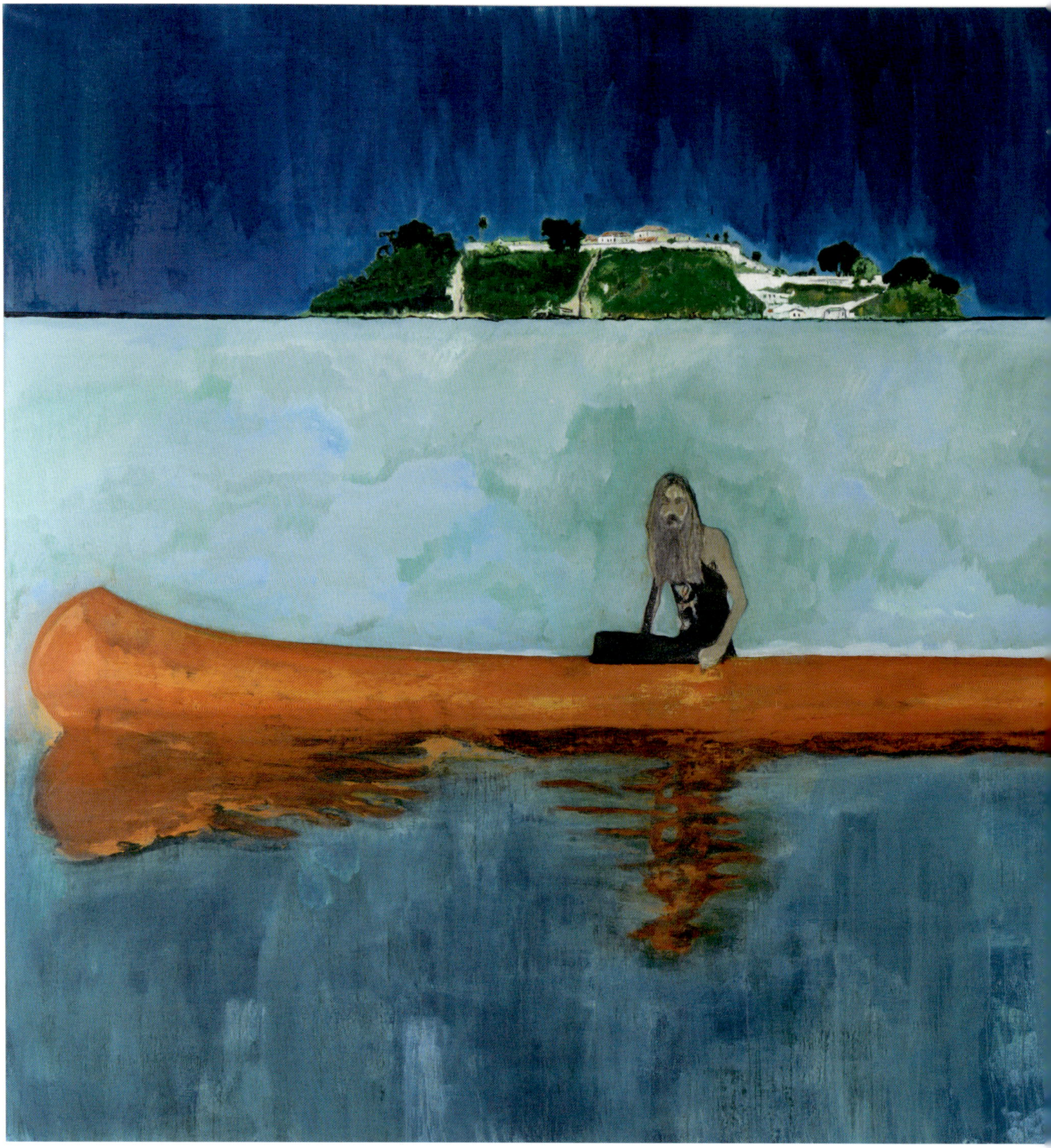

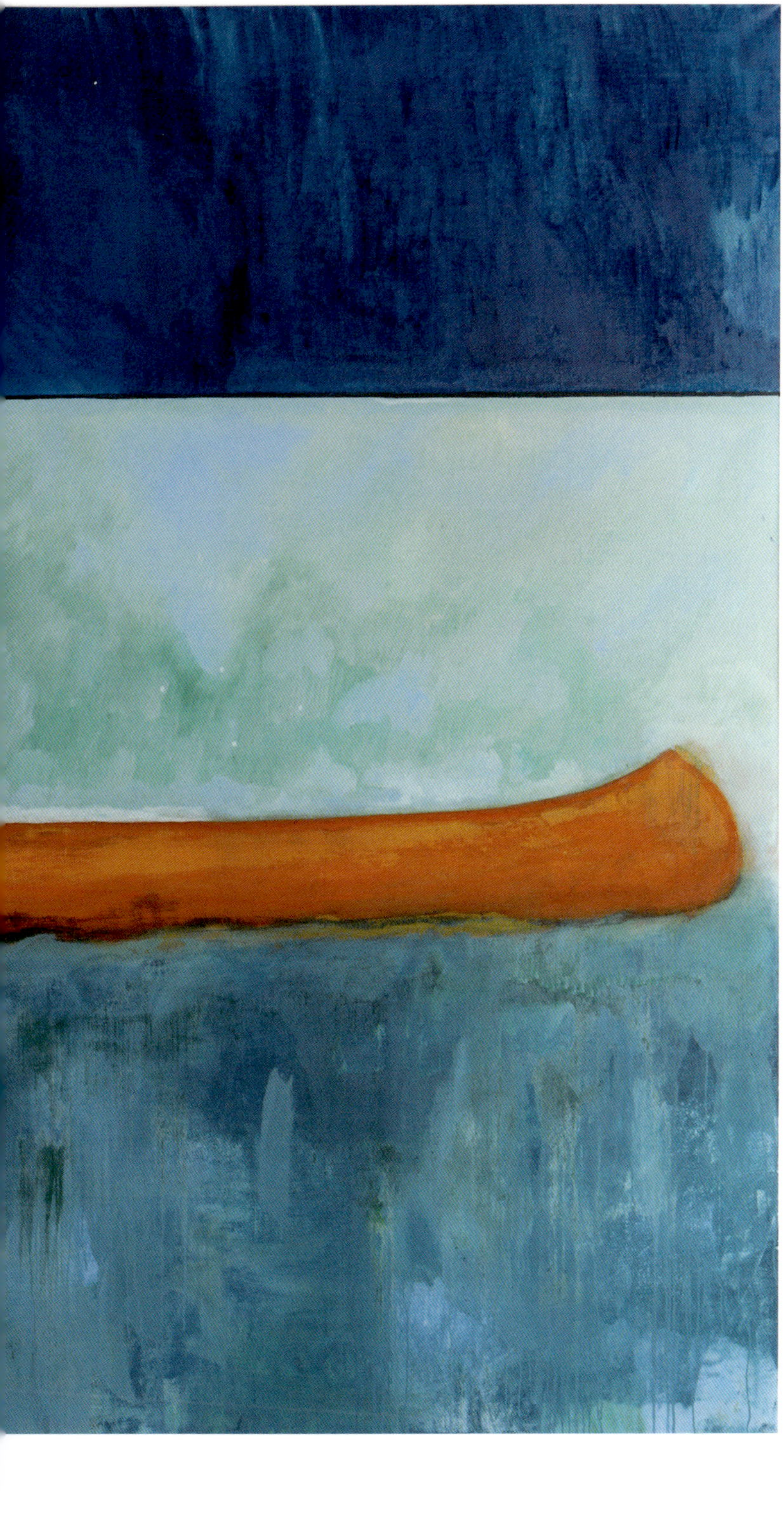

Peter Doig, *100 Years Ago (Carrera)*, 2001 — oil on canvas — 229 × 359 cm

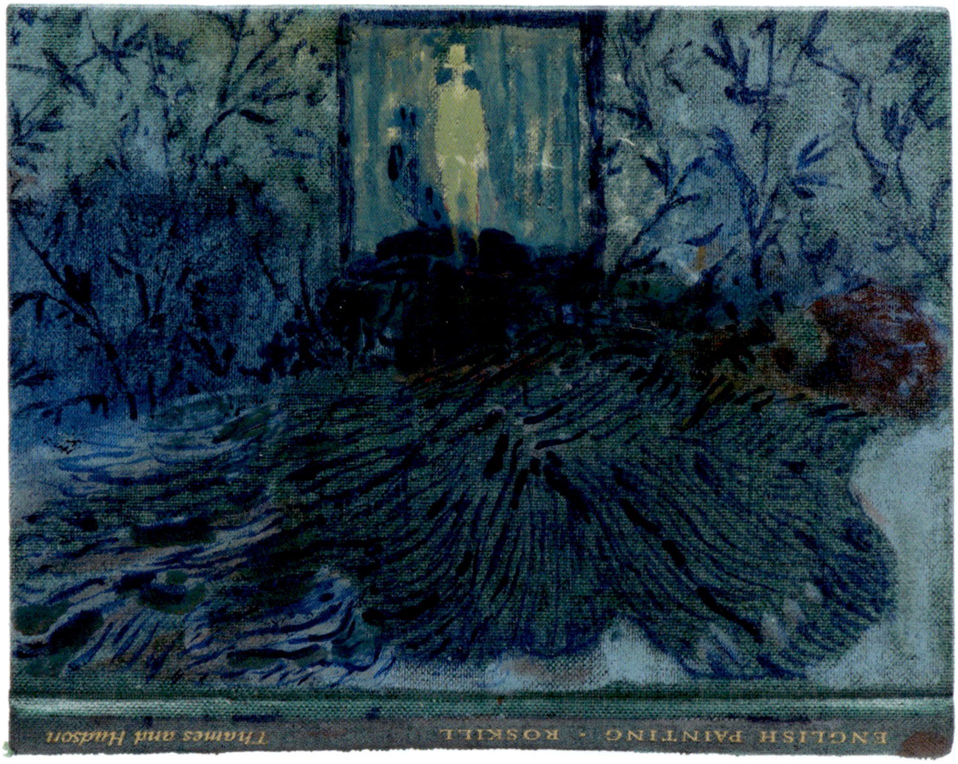

Andrew Cranston, *I Am More Comfortable,* 2017 — oil and varnish on cardboard book cover — 13 × 22 cm

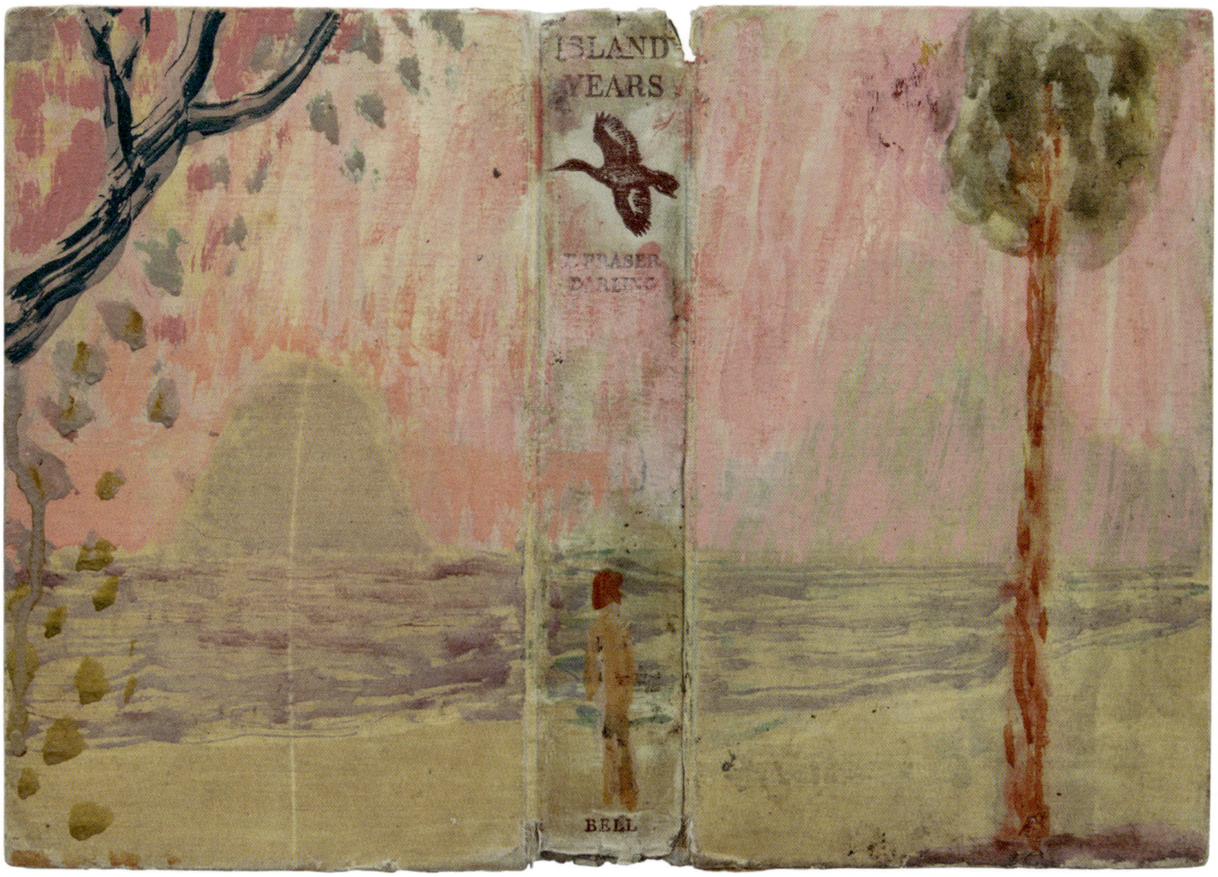

Andrew Cranston, *Island Years*, 2022 — pigment and gum arabic on cardboard book cover — 22 × 32 cm

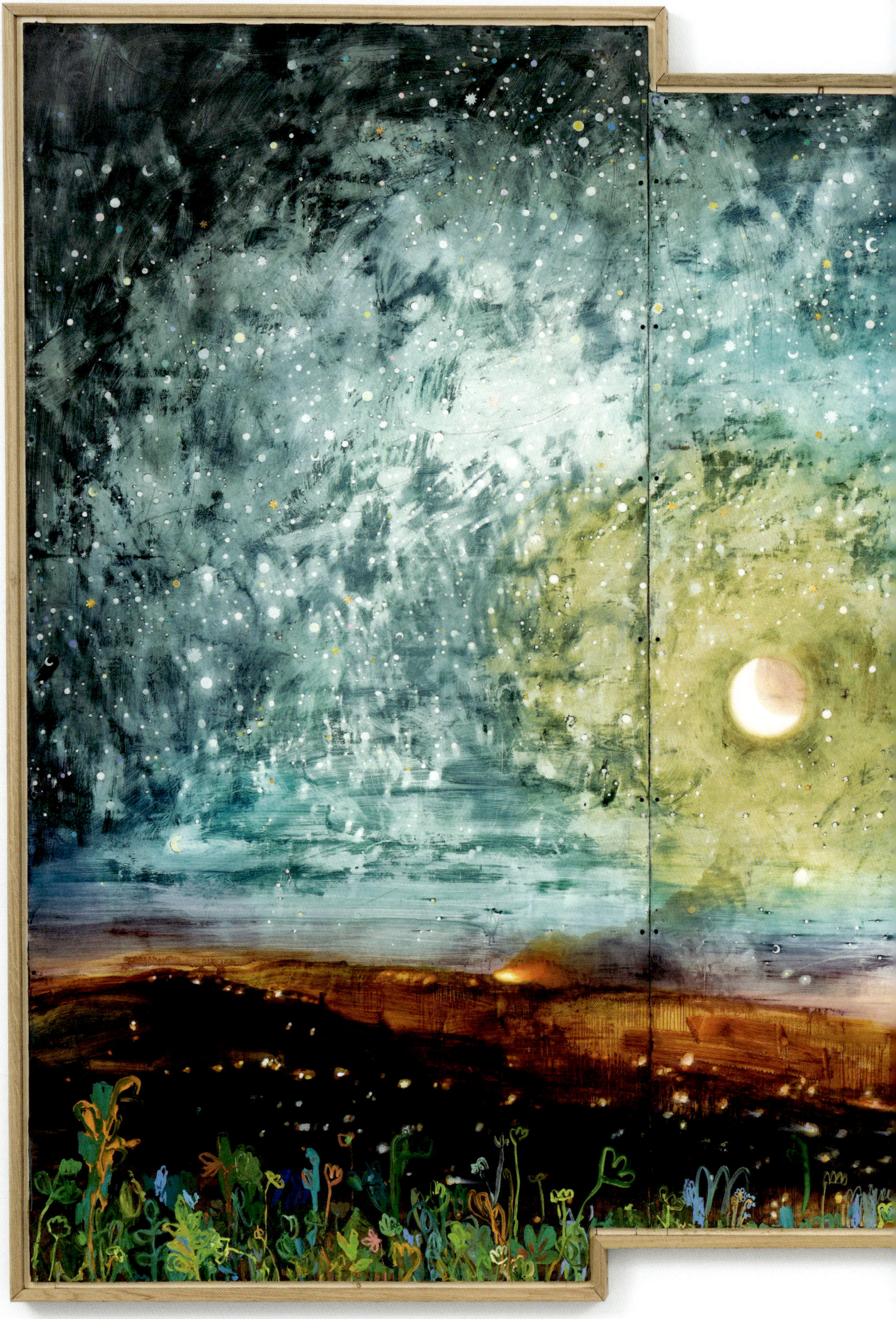

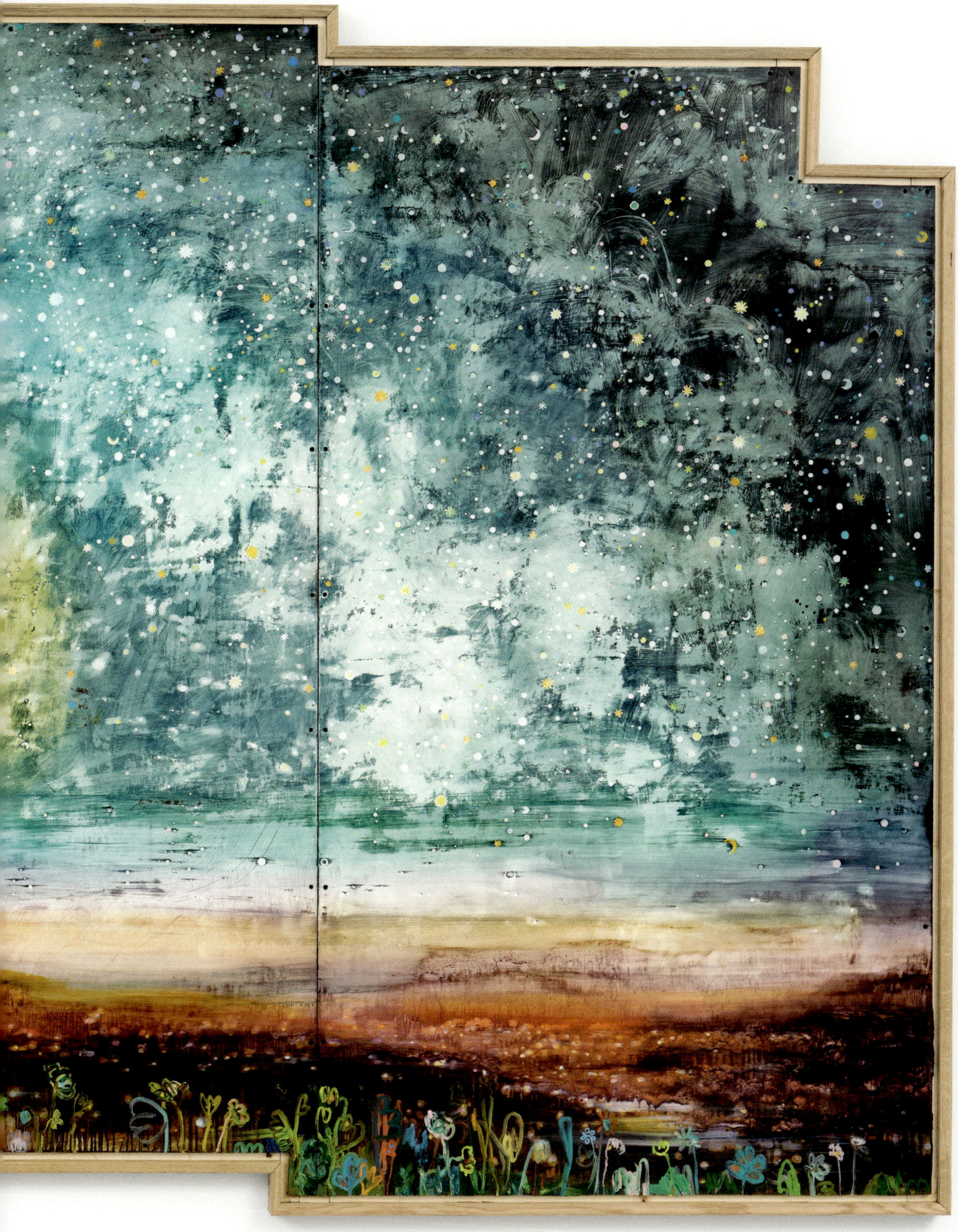

Tursic & Mille, *The Blue Landscape*, 2019 — oil on wood panel in an oak frame, in three parts — 246.3 × 373.7 cm

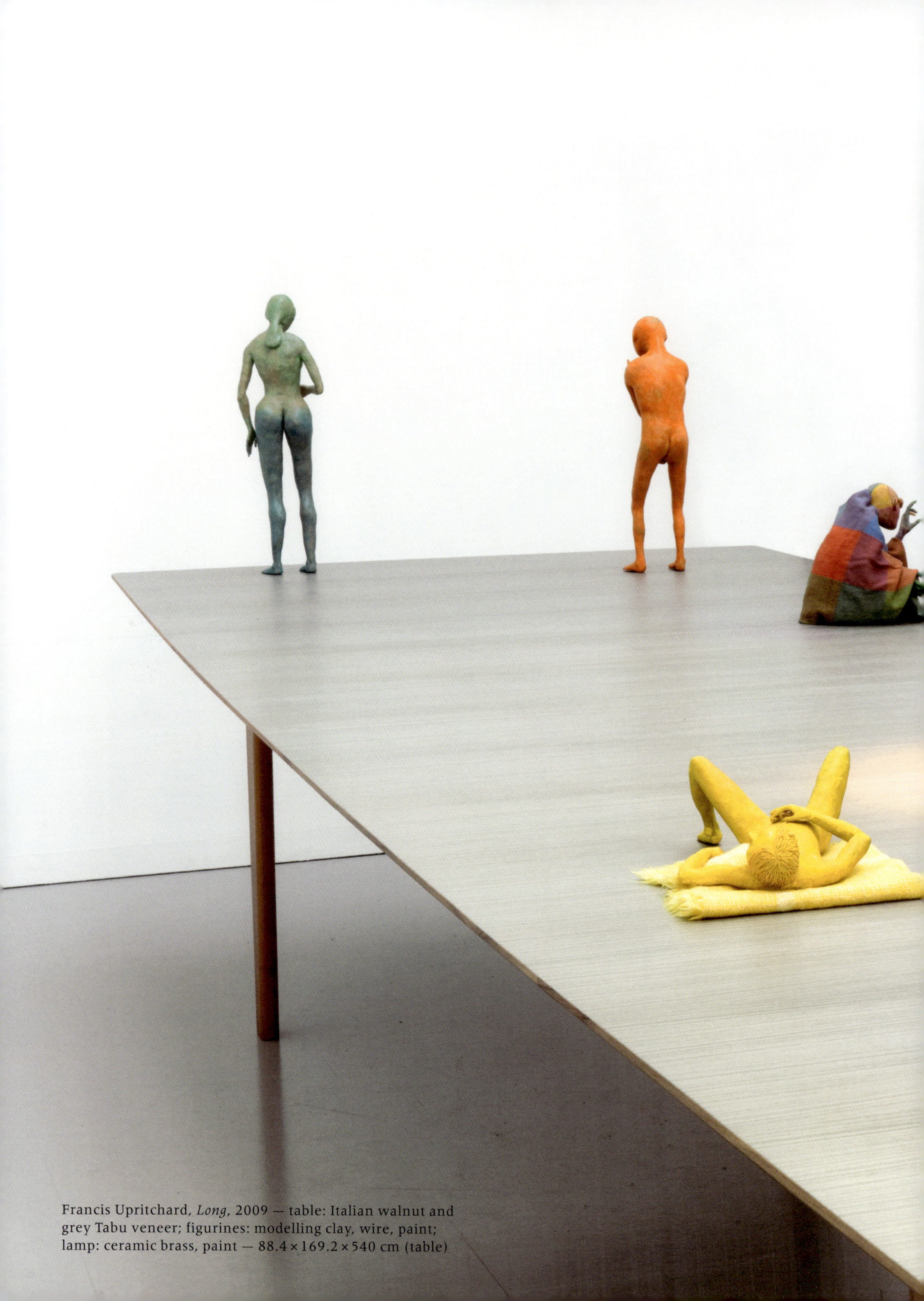

Francis Upritchard, *Long*, 2009 — table: Italian walnut and grey Tabu veneer; figurines: modelling clay, wire, paint; lamp: ceramic brass, paint — 88.4 × 169.2 × 540 cm (table)

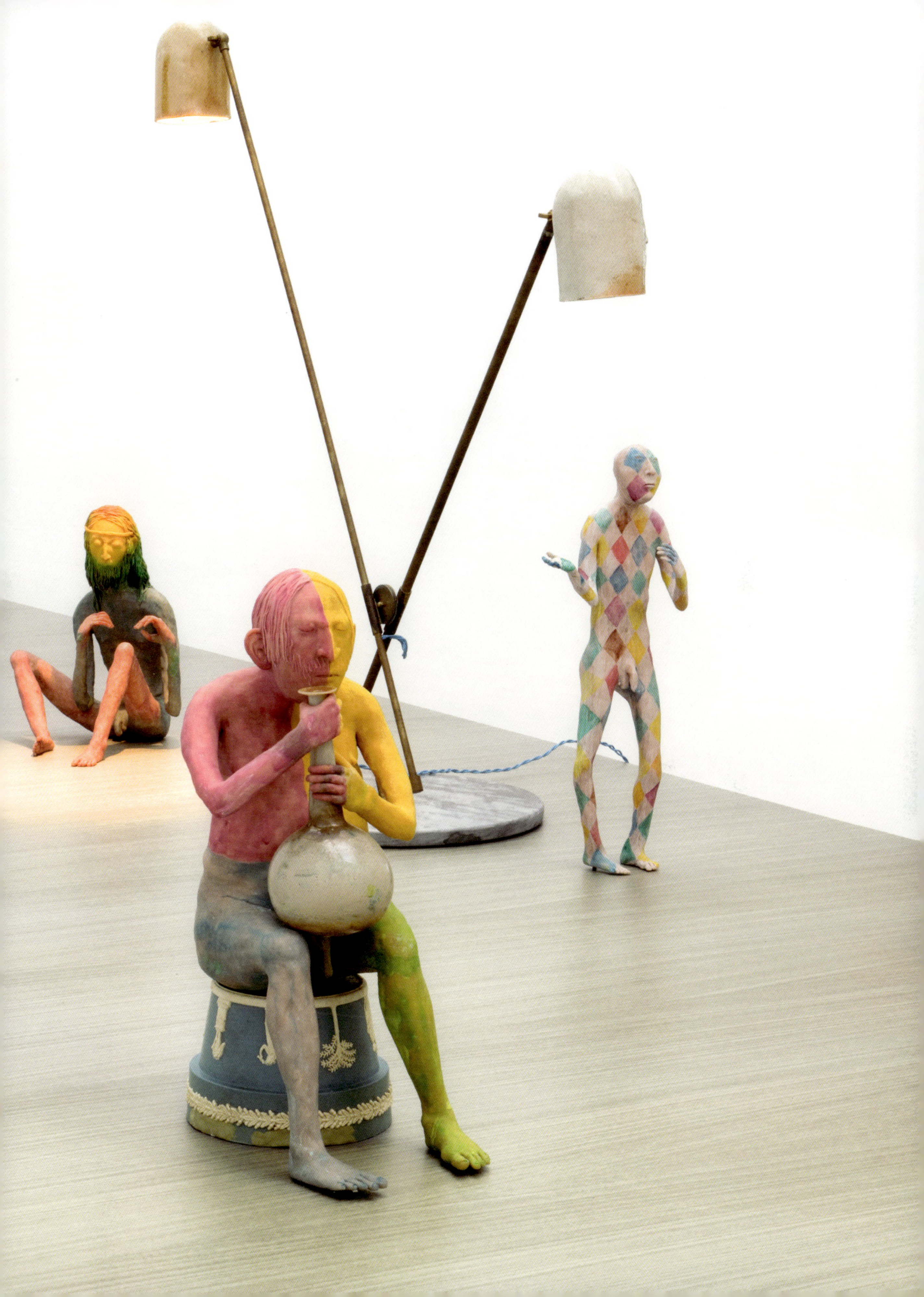

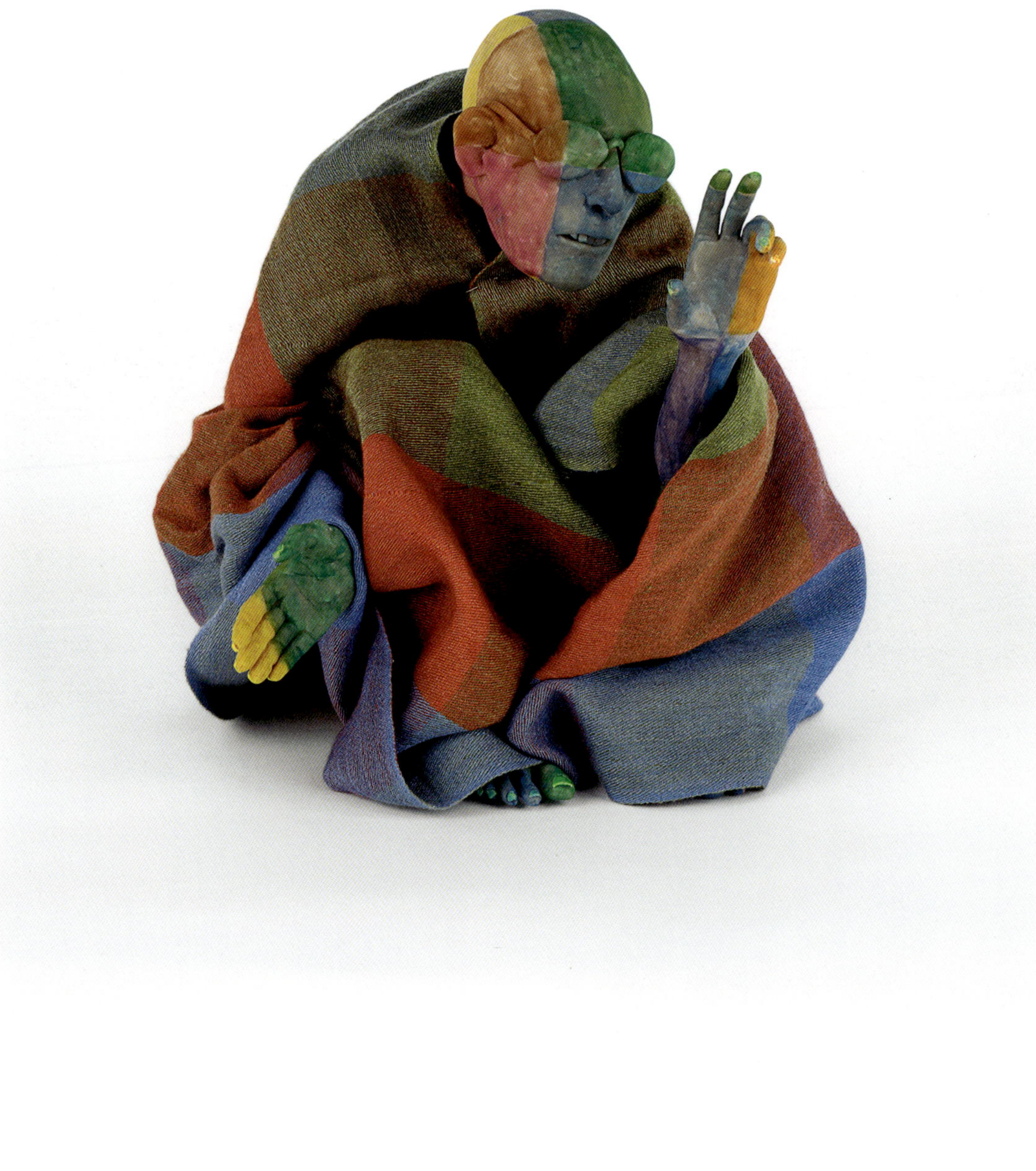

Francis Upritchard, *Richard*, 2008 — modelling material, foil, wire, paint, fabric — 26.5 × 19 × 14 cm

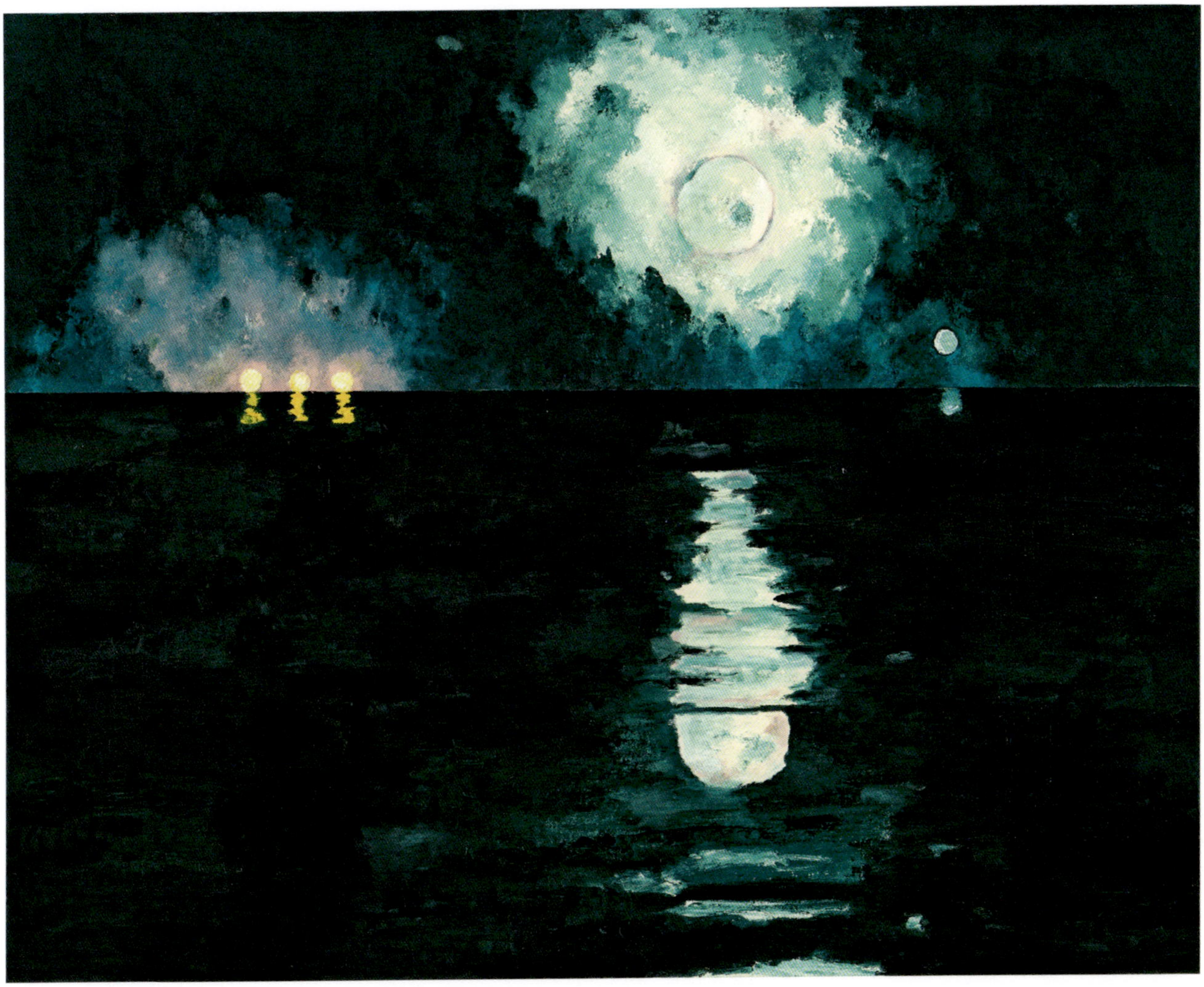

Harold Ancart, *Untitled*, 2022 — oil stick and pencil on canvas — 111.4 × 139.4 cm

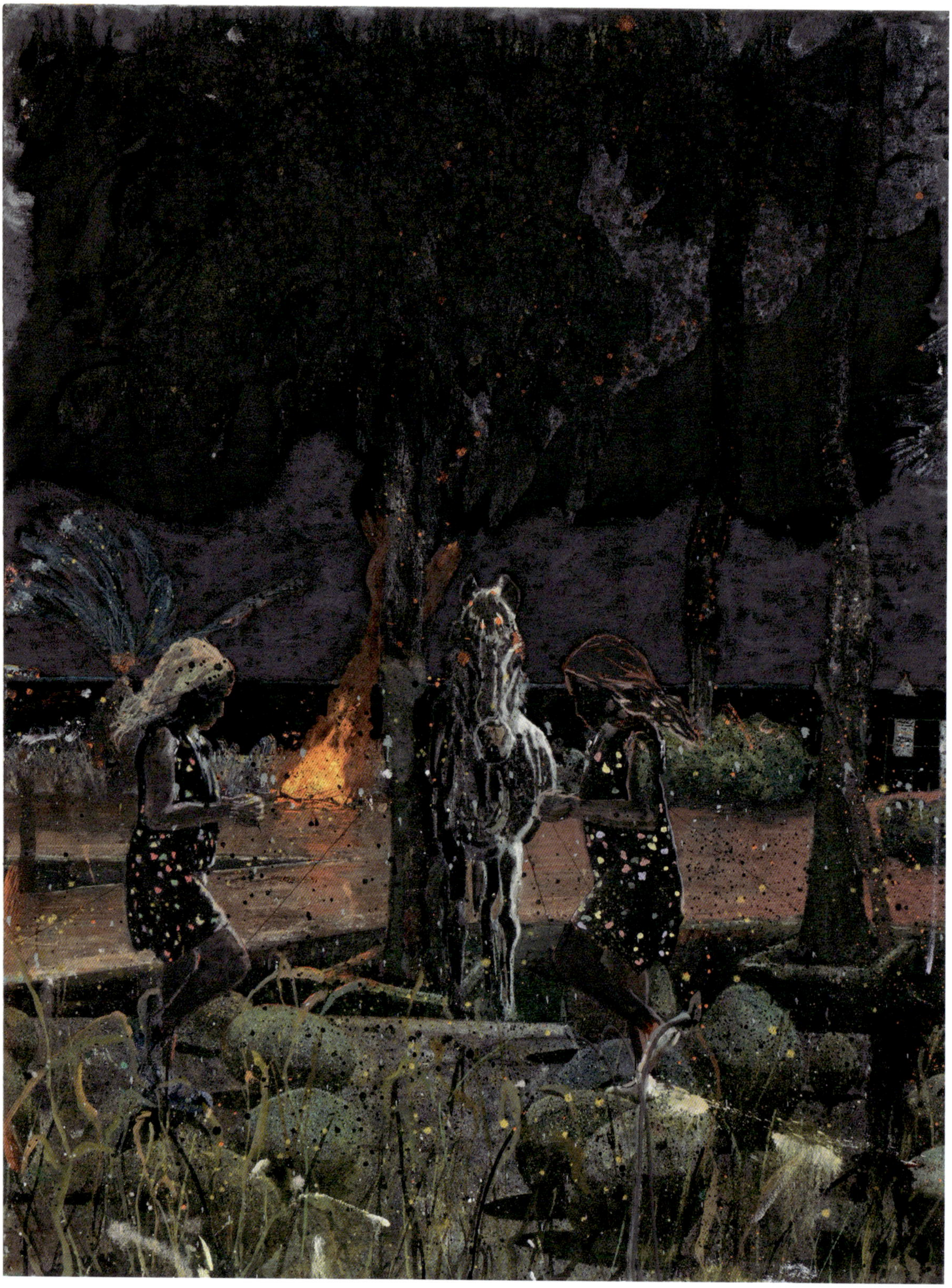

Marcus Cope, *Reflector*, 2021 — oil on jute — 170 × 130 cm

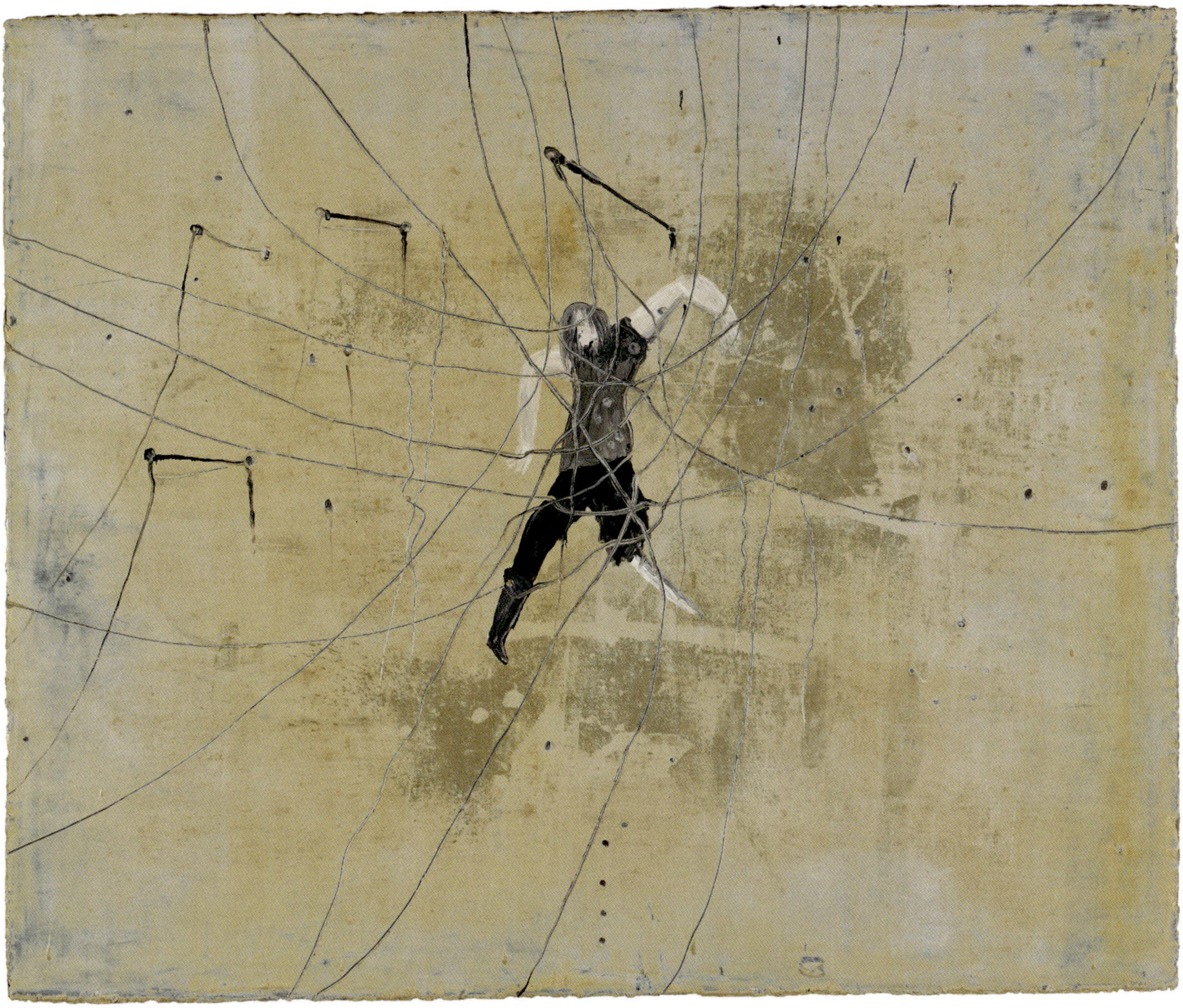

Norbert Schwontkowski, *Ohne Titel (AHAB)*, 2002 — oil and pigment on canvas — 132 × 160 cm

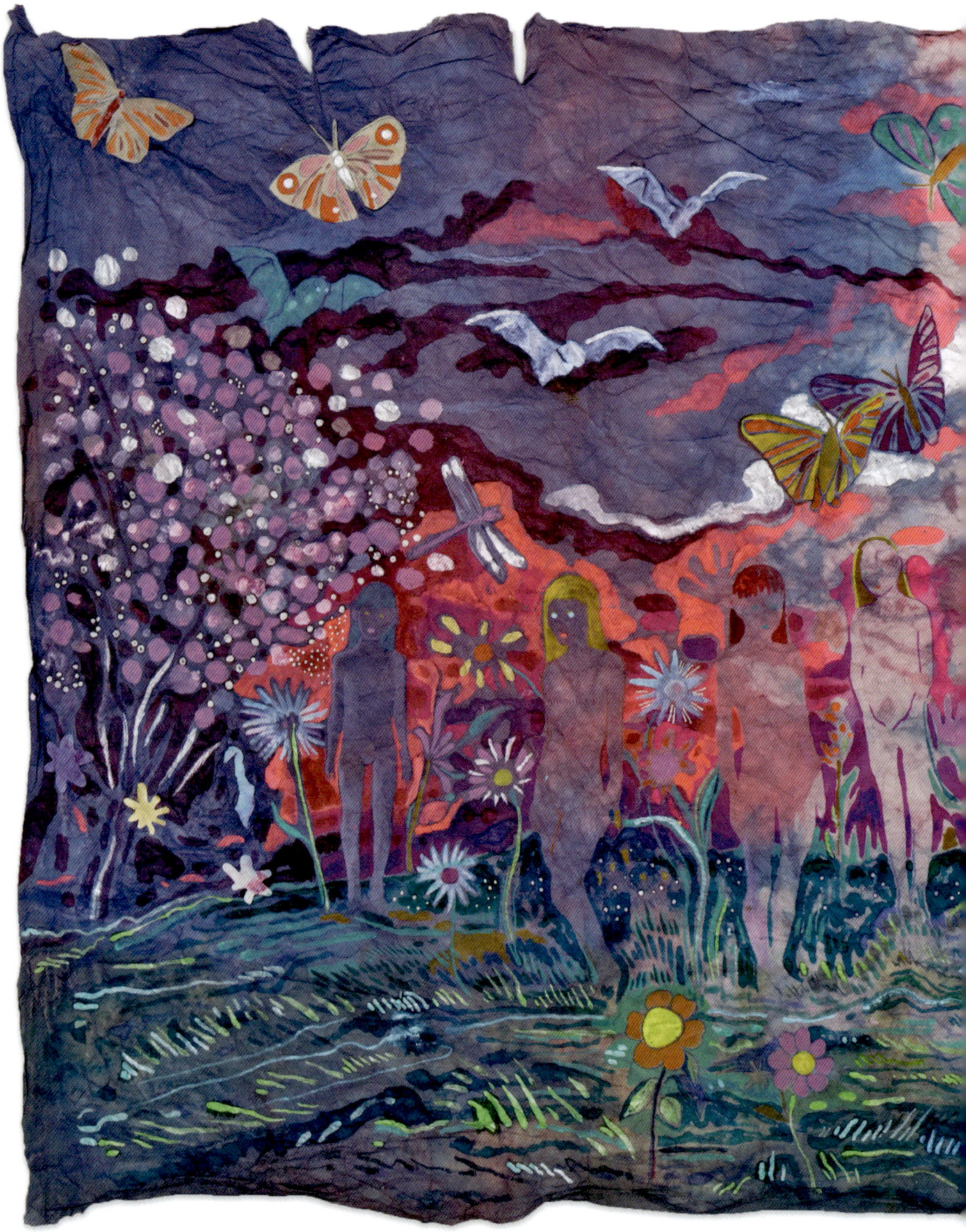

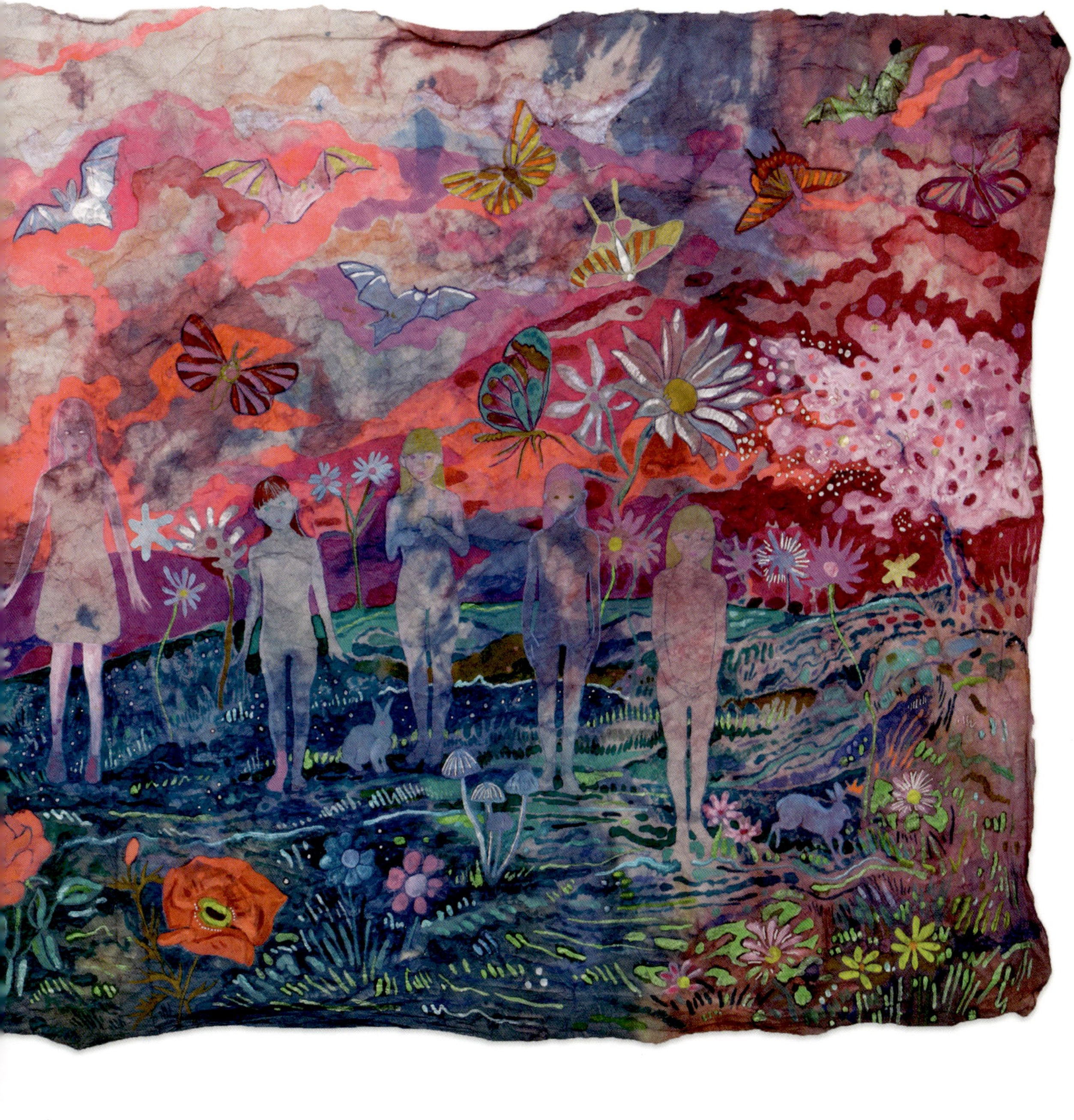

Marcella Barceló, *Pollination Syndrome*, 2021 — ink and watercolour on washi paper — 73 × 149 cm

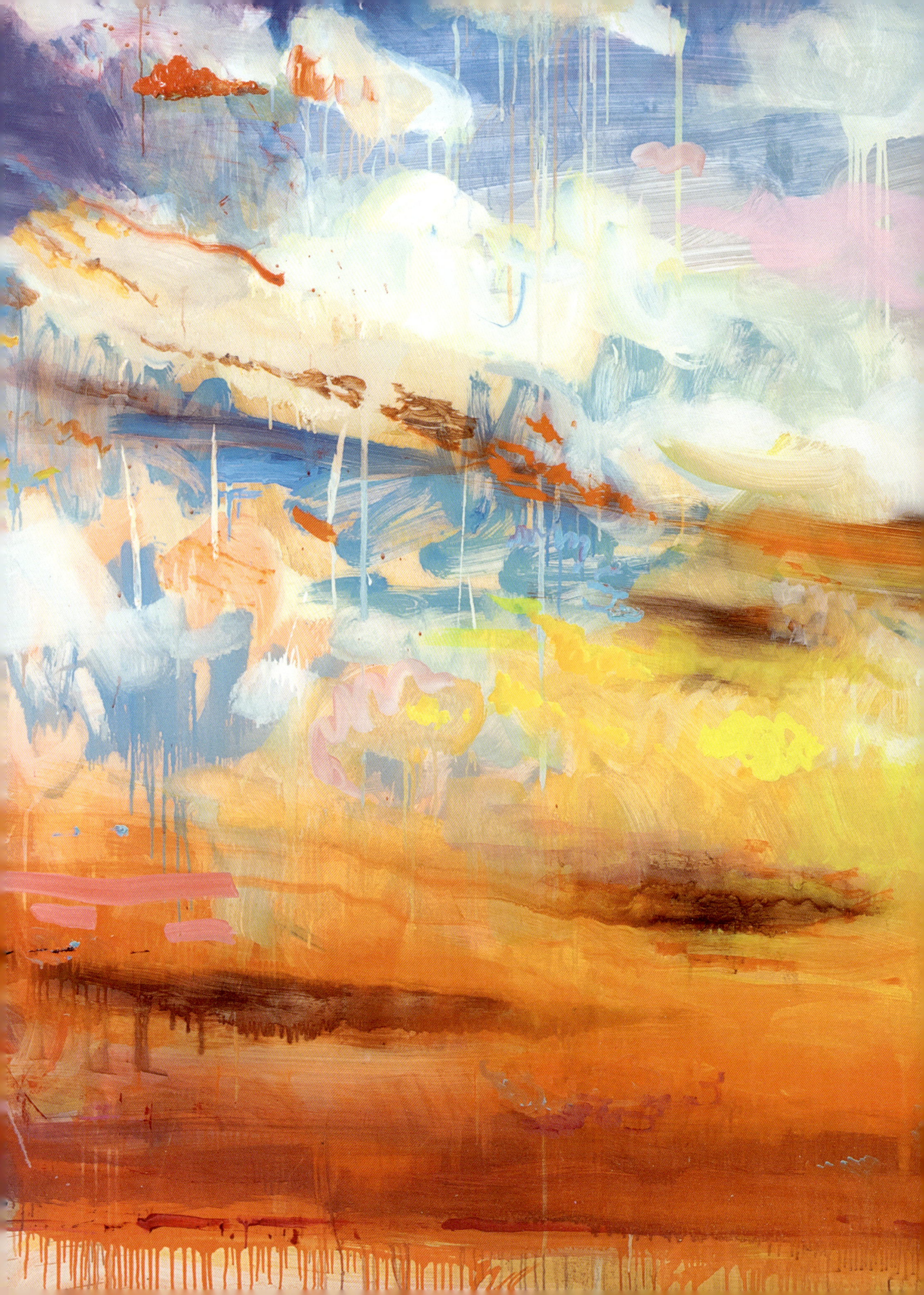

A WORLD UNTO ITSELF

There was a man who loved islands. He was born on one, but it didn't suit him, as there were too many other people on it, besides himself. He wanted an island all of his own: not necessarily to be alone on it, but to make it a world of his own.

D. H. LAWRENCE
The Man Who Loved Islands, 1927

JMG If painting is central to this idea of an art detached from reality (although it is not isolated), it is because it naturally keeps things at bay: it blurs vision in a similar way to memory. Incidentally, it is *not* vision. It falls within a different image regime, which, despite its very well acknowledged materiality, can have the same subtlety and volatility as dreams, memories, clouds, wind, or shadows. In this respect, paintings themselves are inner islands.

YCT There are inner islands, and then there is the interior of islands. In Barbet Schroeder's film *The Valley*, the centre of the island is a black spot, a *terra incognita*, a mysterious *paradise* from which no one has ever returned. For Édouard Glissant, the hinterland of colonial and post-colonial Martinique is a "terrifying" area, consisting of impenetrable, entangled mangroves and remote sites of resistance. On Porquerolles, the interior forest also hides its secrets, its dark side, whether it is "untouched" or humanised, untamed, domesticated, privatised, or even militarised.

JMG During the Renaissance, books about islands were circulating within the Mediterranean (*insularium* in Latin, *isolario* in Italian), which were colourful atlases, inspired by portolan nautical charts. They brought together poems, historical and mythical stories, and accounts of explorations, forming a kind of illustrated literary

Tursic & Mille,
Melancholic Sunset (detail), 2018
oil on wood panel in an
oak frame, in three parts,
64 Heineken bottles
214 × 372 cm

and geographical guide. Much has been written about them, because they proposed a new system of representation of the maritime space. These were not purely scientific books – in other words, they were books stemming from a period in which science was also considered with myths. The *insularium* came about at a time when geography was still in its infancy and did not necessarily correspond to reality. Some artworks operate in this way: they are based on a piece of our world, then heighten, adorn, and transform it. They detach this fragment of reality from a continent to transform it into a little "portable" island.

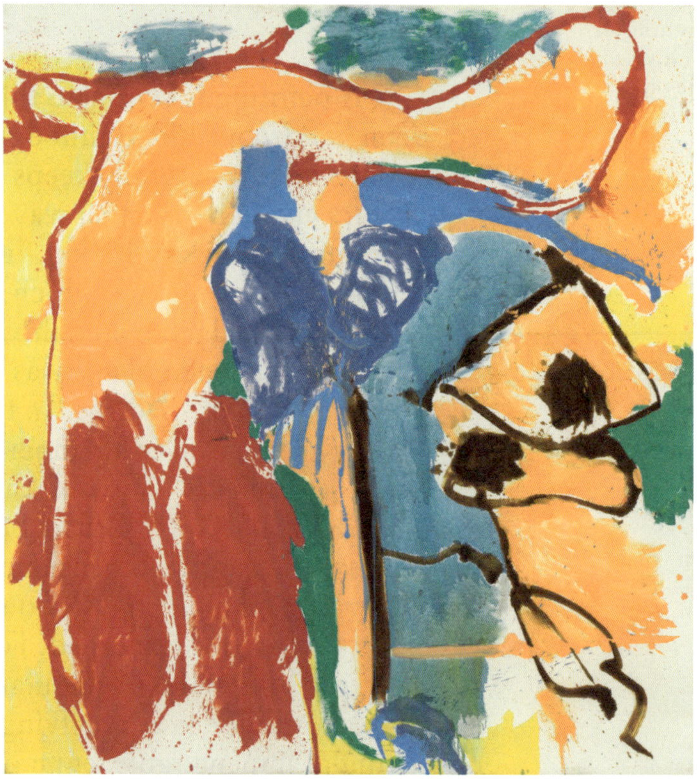

HELEN FRANKENTHALER
Mediterranean Thoughts, 1960, oil on canvas, glued and primed, 256.5 × 237.5 cm

YCT I've noticed that I am increasingly living lost and adrift in the middle of an ocean, but it is an ocean of data. The structures of my world have become liquid. The foundations, the bearings are disappearing, submerged, engulfed beneath waves of uncertainty, new layers of information. I try to read, caught up in currents that capture and carry my attention off into the distance. I strive to decipher, but my vision is impaired. I am tempted at times to isolate myself, to seal off my mind. To become my own island.

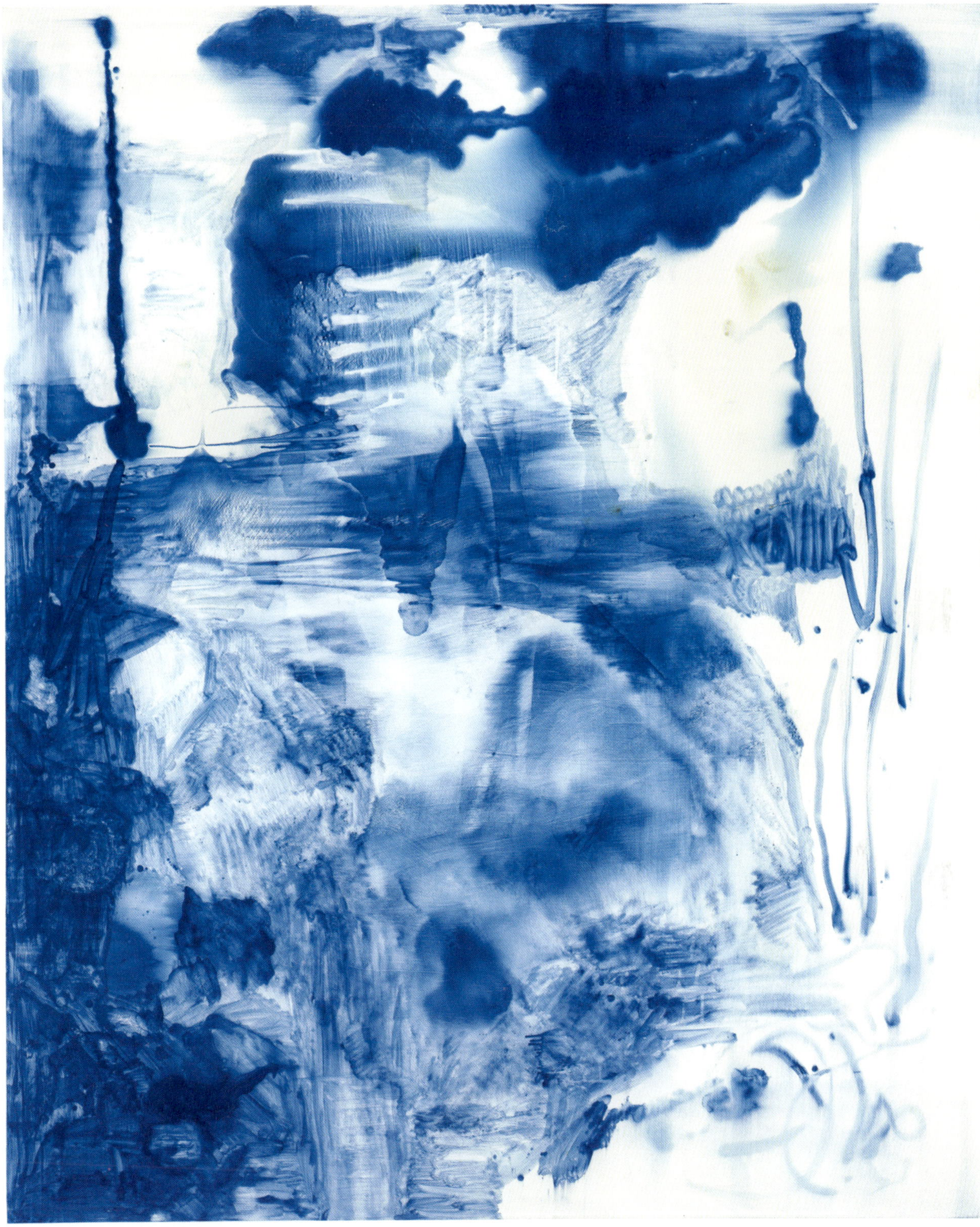

Sigmar Polke, *Untitled (Lapis-Lazuli)*, 1998 — pure lapis lazuli pigment and resin on canvas — 240 × 200 cm

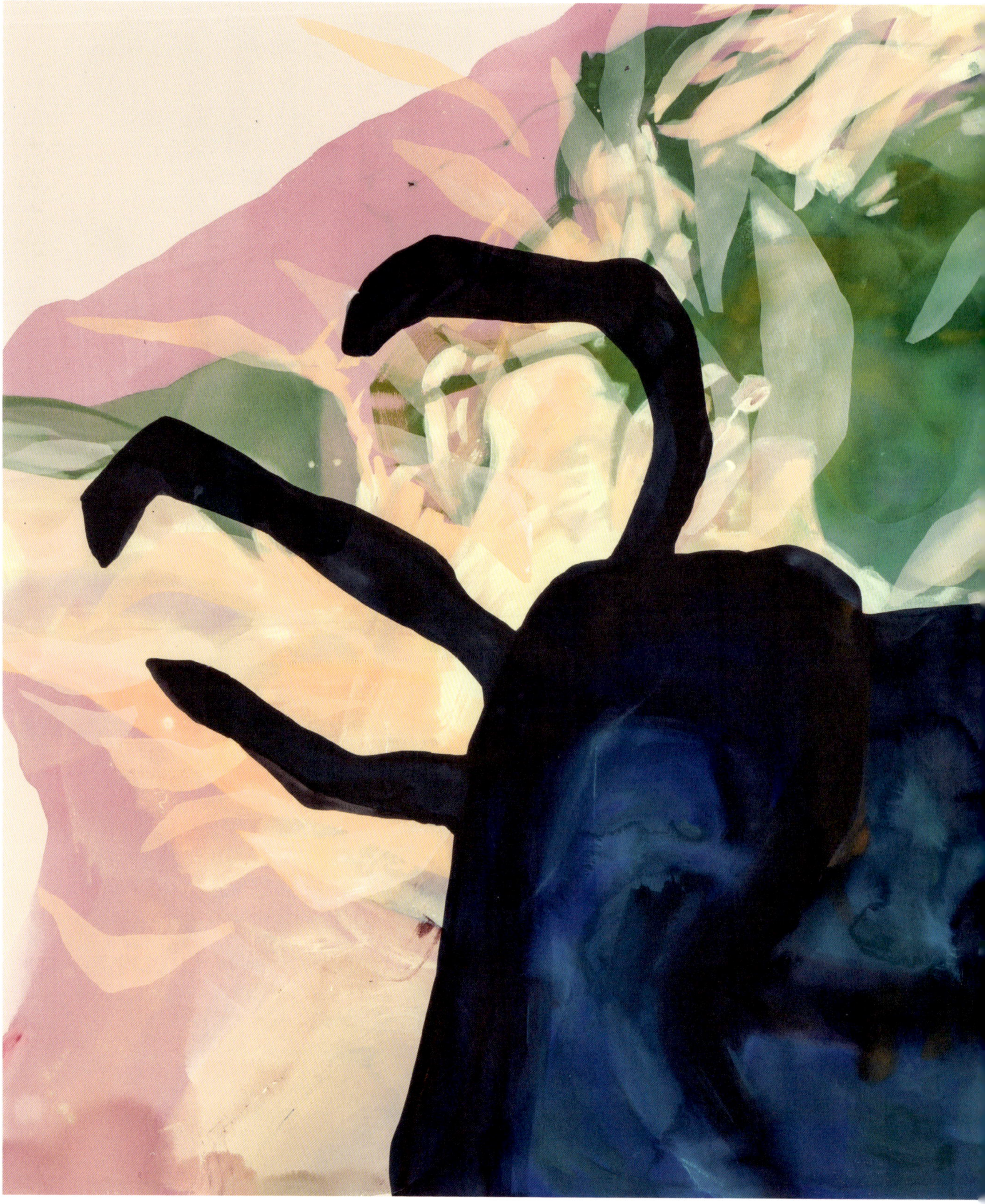

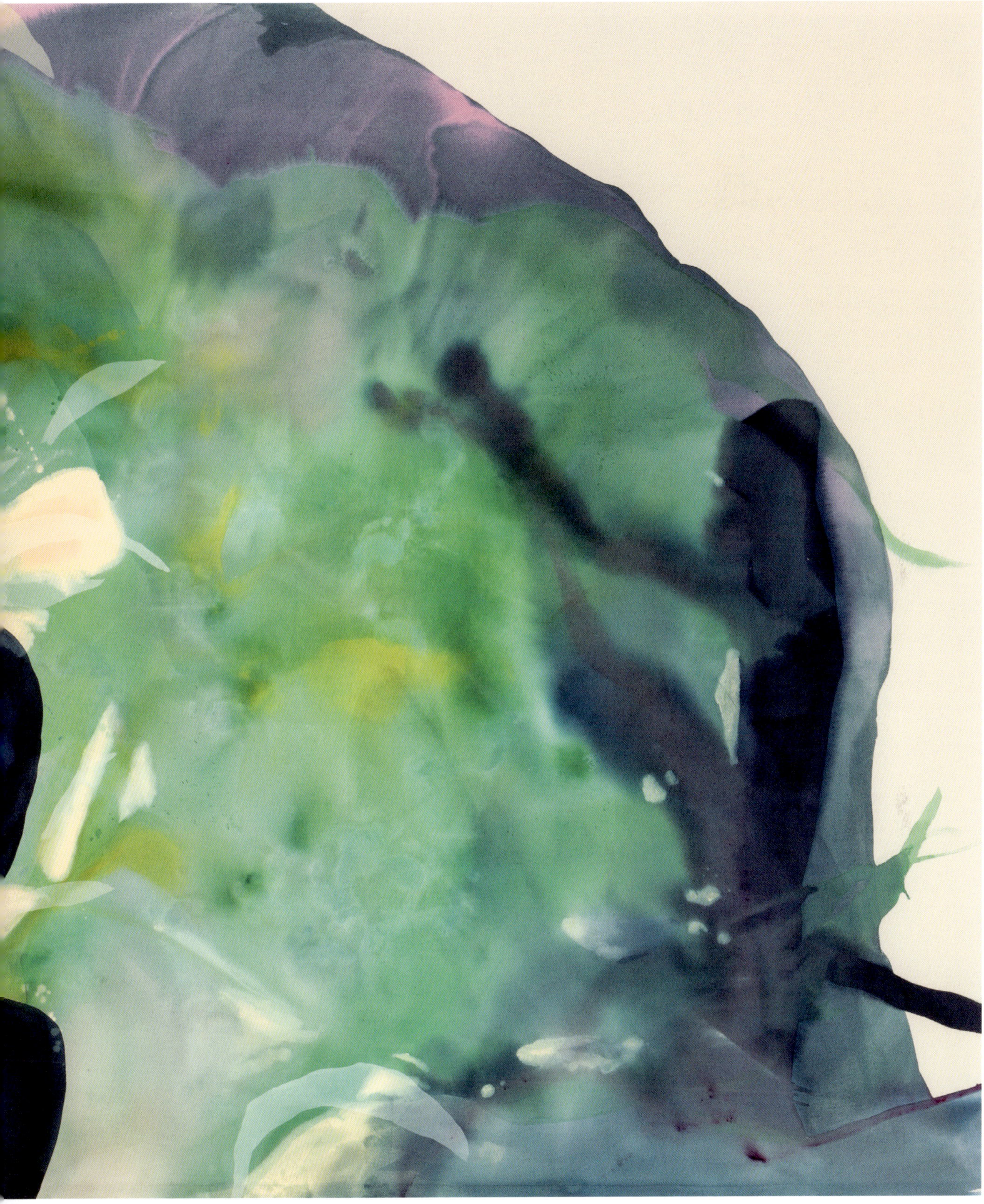

Ragna Bley, *La Belle Époque*, 2022 — acrylic on canvas — 215 × 375 cm

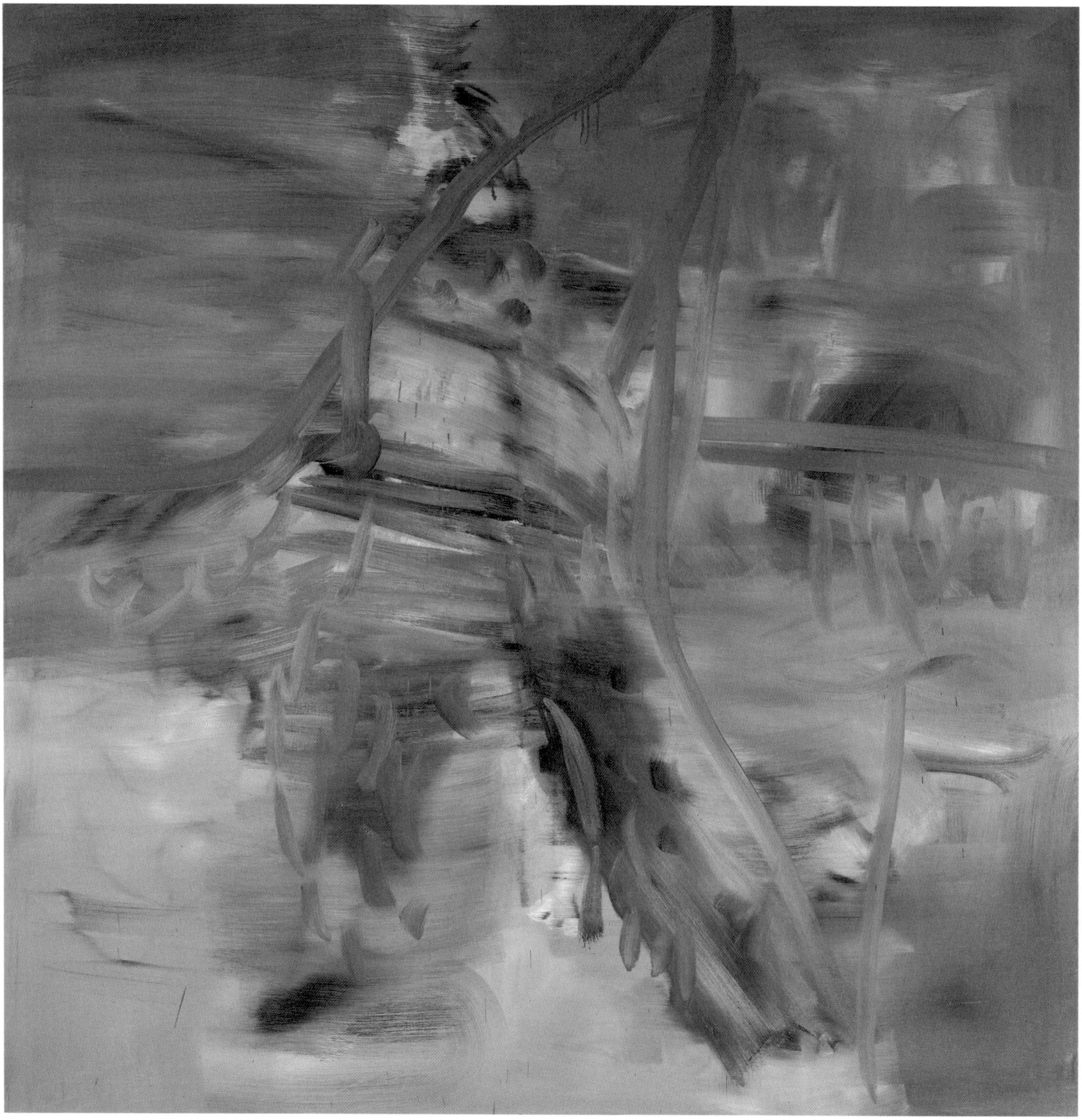

Albert Oehlen, *Symbol*, 1997 — oil on canvas — 200 × 200 cm

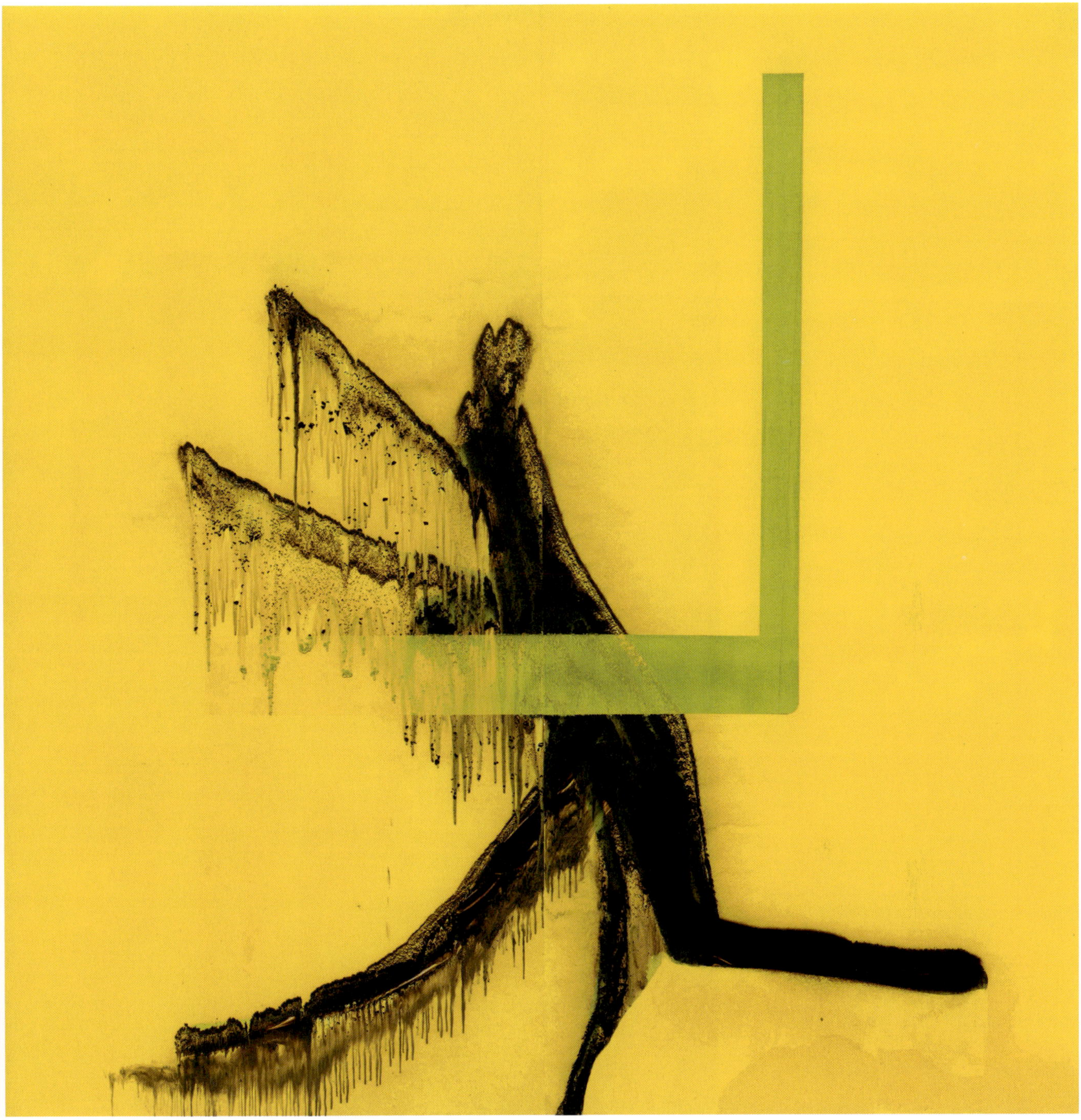

Albert Oehlen, *Hill and Gully Rider*, 2018 — lacquer and oil on aluminium plates — 260 × 260 cm

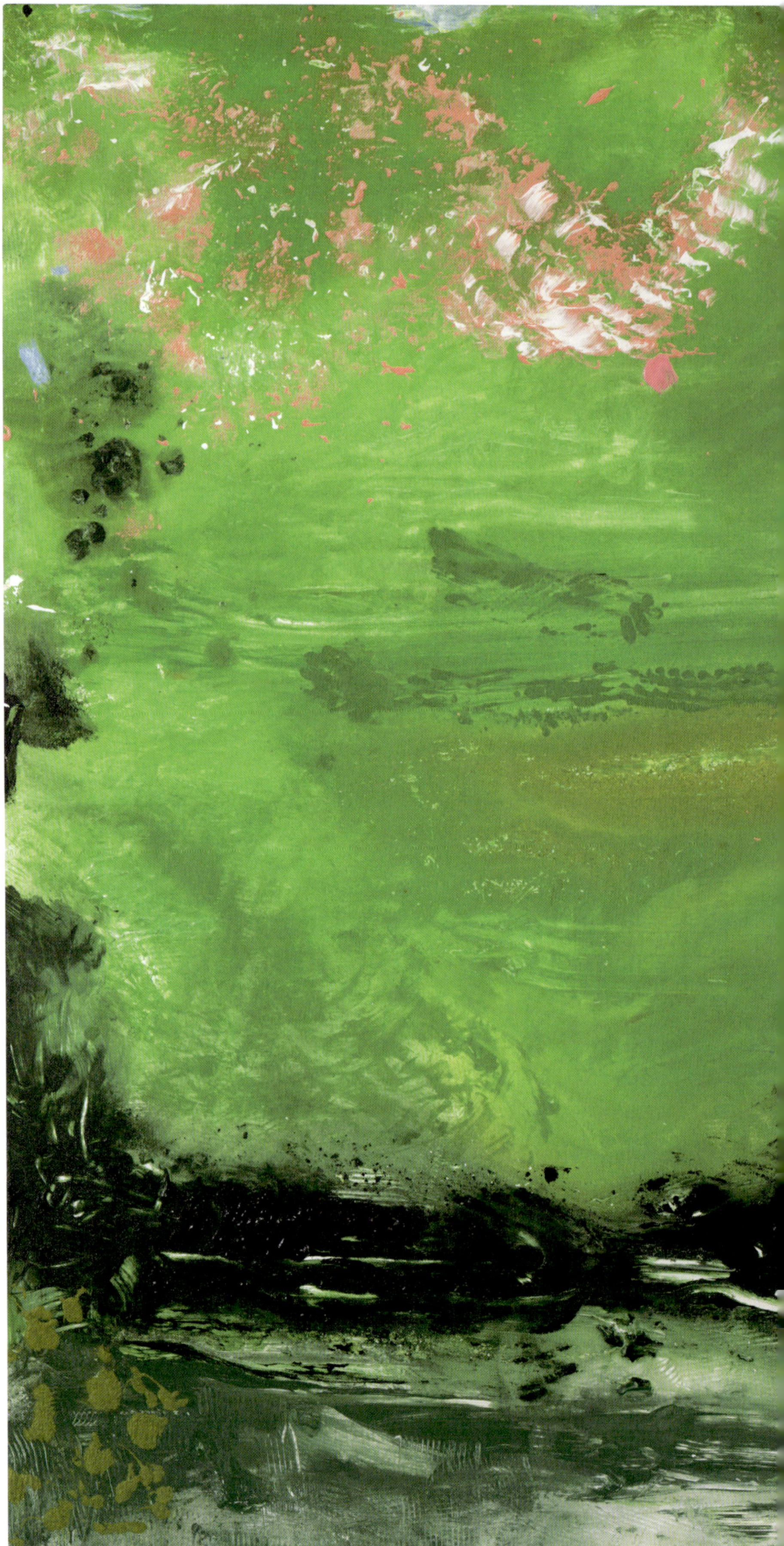

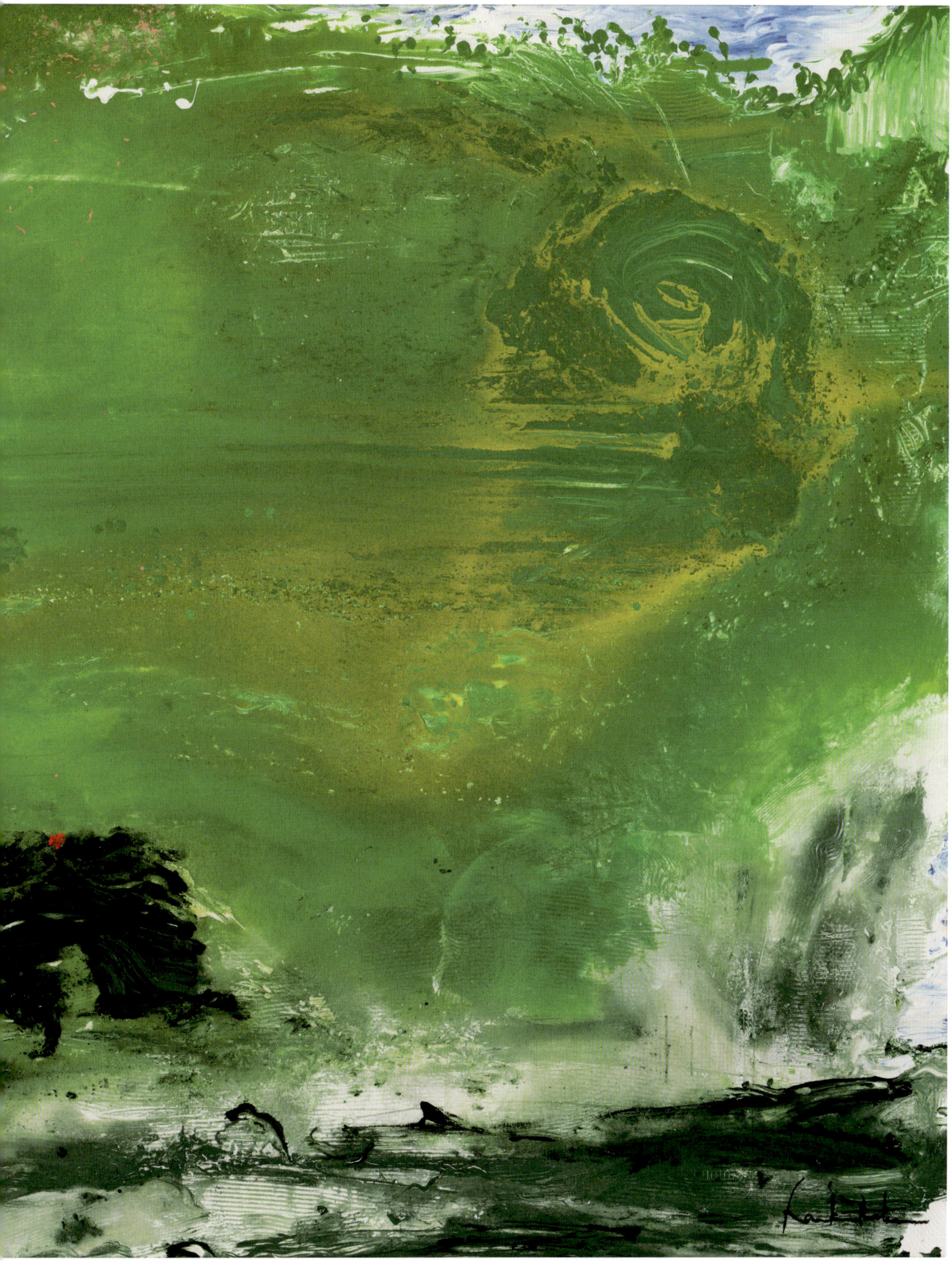

Helen Frankenthaler, *Overture*, 1992 — acrylic on canvas — 177.8 × 238.8 cm

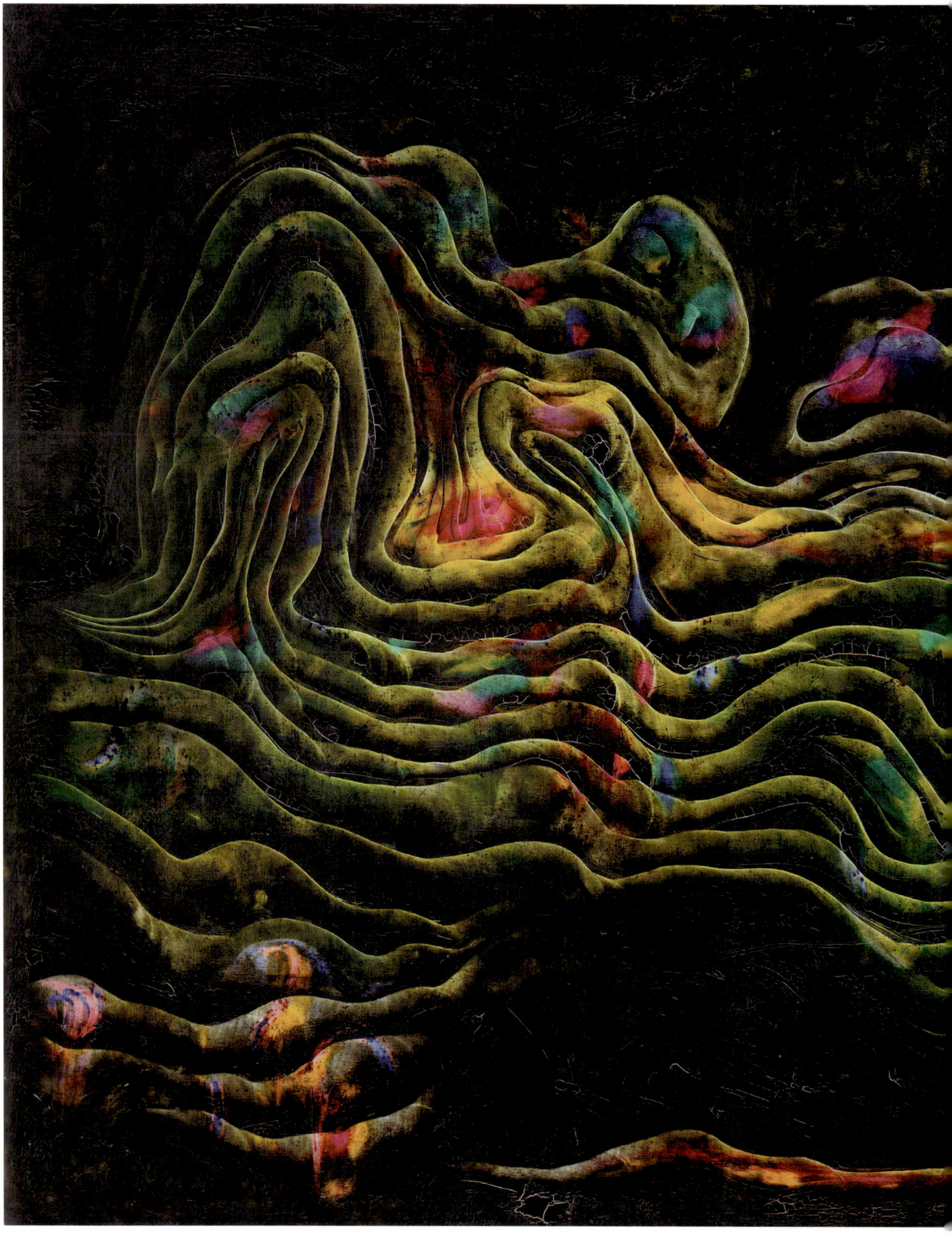

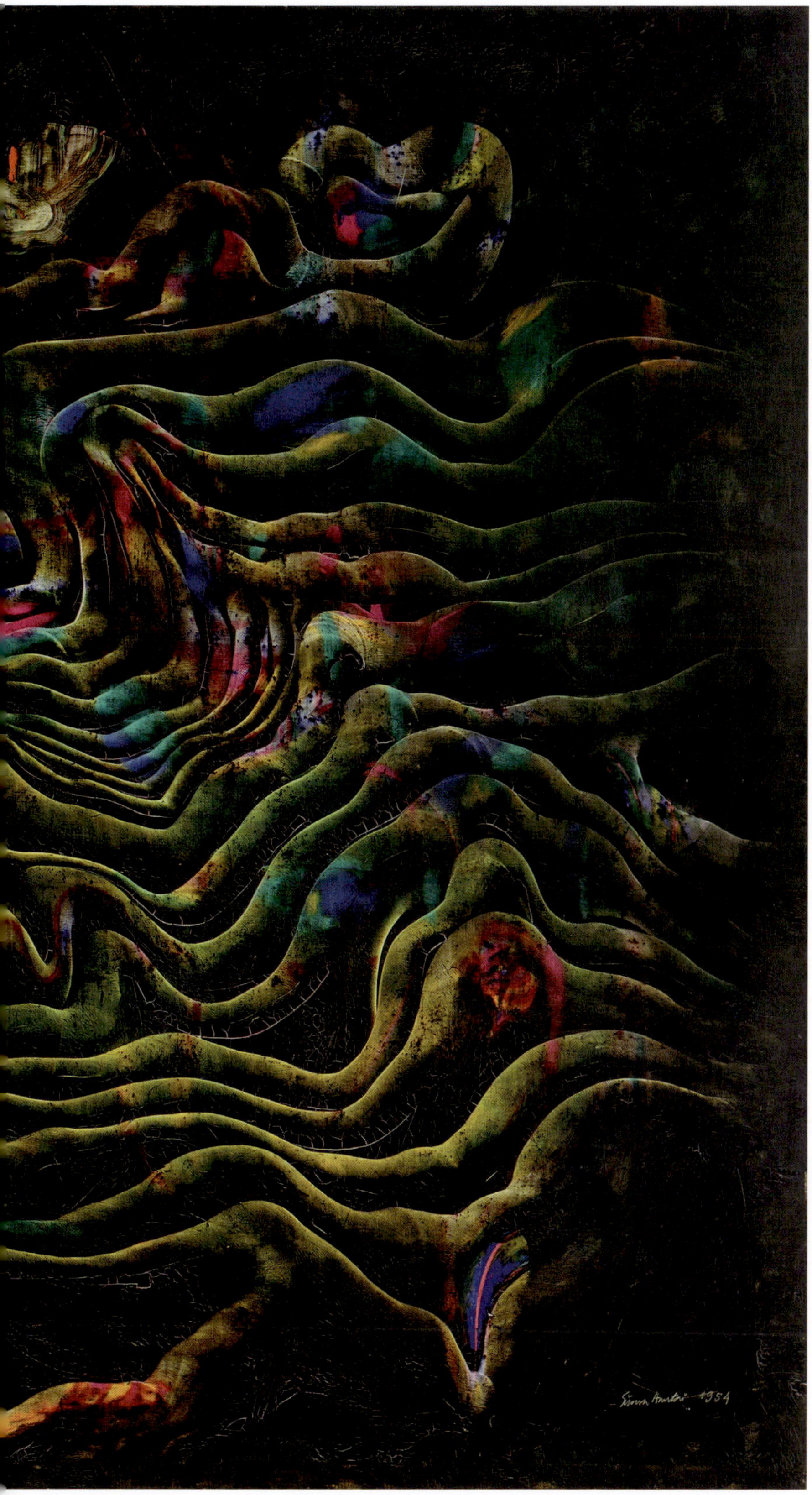

Simon Hantaï, *Sans titre*, 1954 — oil on canvas — 155 × 220 cm

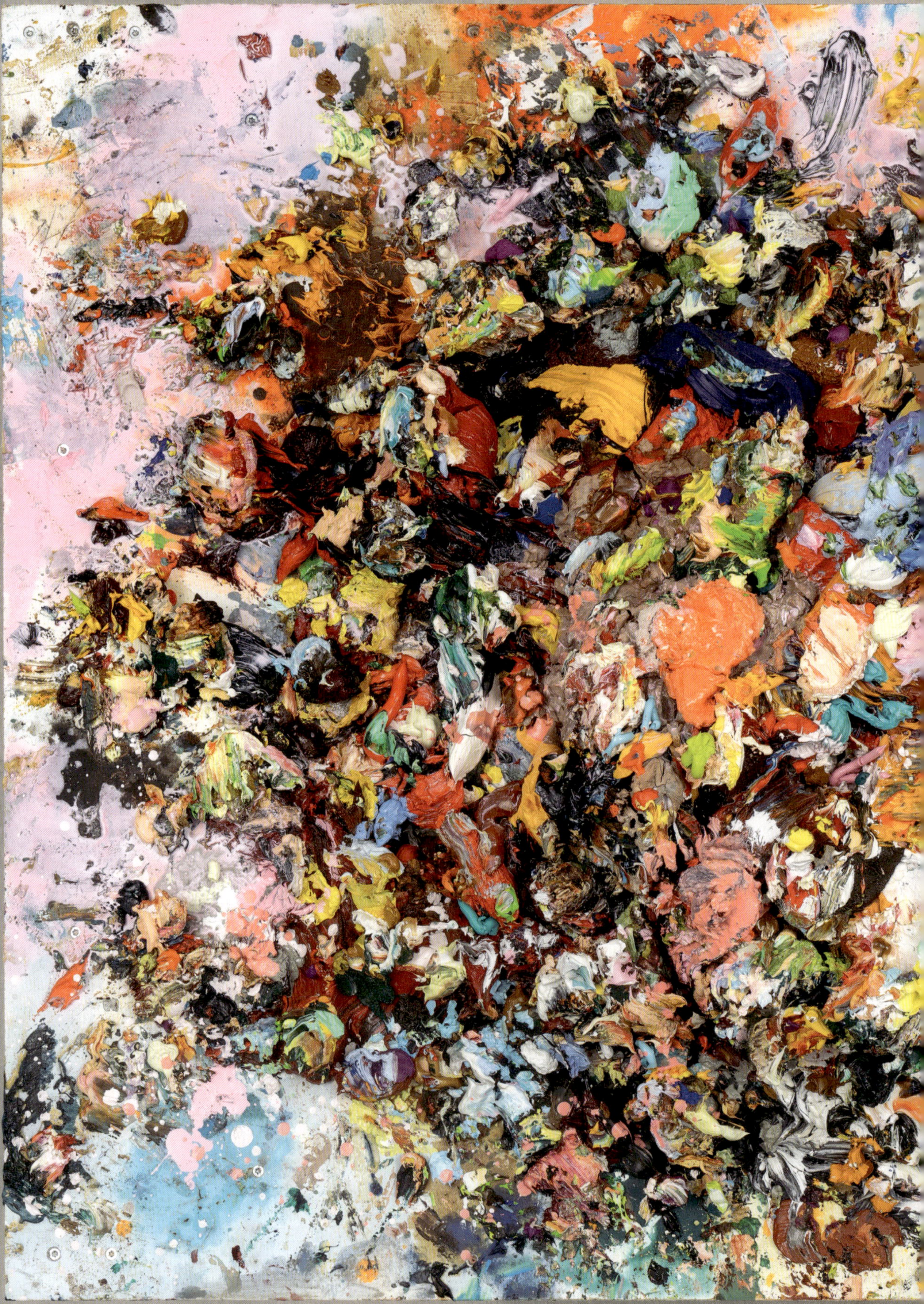

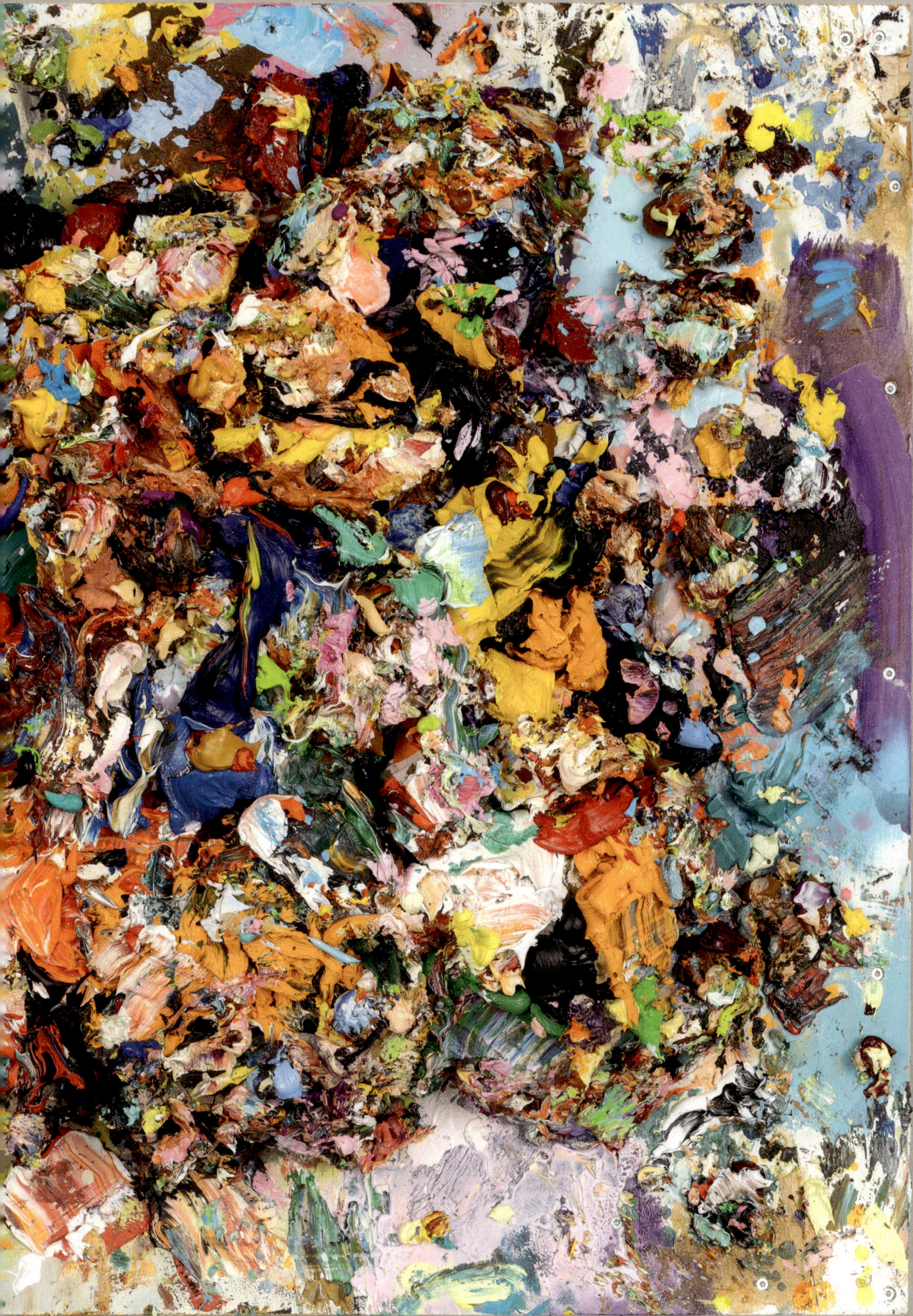

Tursic & Mille, *Sisyphe (Time Mass)*, 2016–2023 — oil on panel, oak base — 97 × 120 × 80 cm

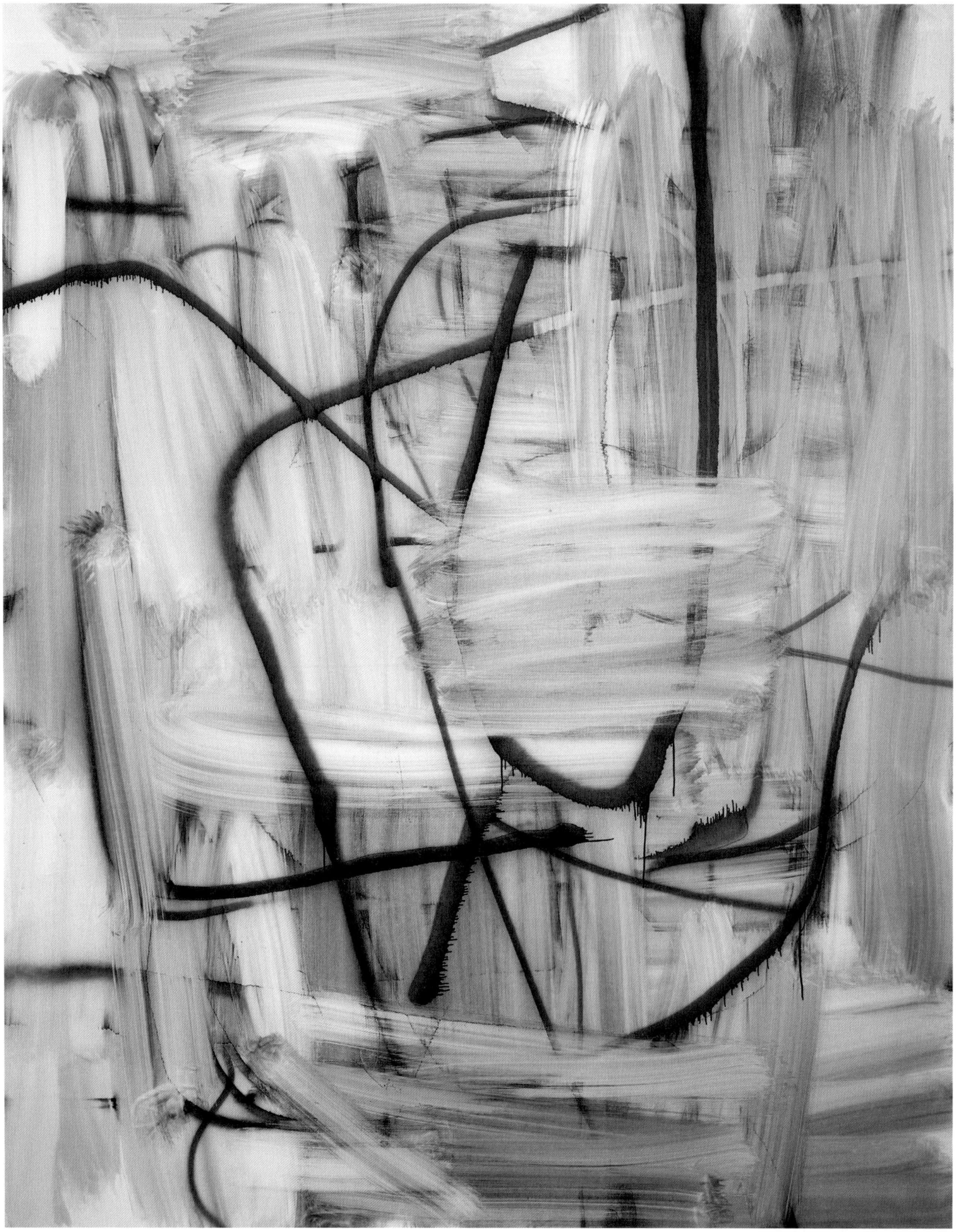

Christopher Wool, *Untitled*, 2007 — enamel on linen canvas — 304.4 × 243.8 cm

But that belies the insular environment, which is in fact open, porous, and composite. Diverse. Making one's brain an island: why not? But in reality, the island is already a fluid and amphibian brain. Becoming an island, today, in fact, would mean rebuilding a base for oneself, a mountain in the middle of the magma, and allowing a hybrid milieu to sprout there. What do islands think about? The paintings of Simon Hantaï, Sigmar Polke, or Ragna Bley may provide an answer. They are fragmentary, speculative maps of these new mental geologies.

JMG In Hantaï, forms that evoke a biomorphic relief are the result of successive gestures revealing the older layers of the painting. Diving into an inner island means embarking on an exploration in the manner of an islander. Exploring, turning around a painting wrapped up in itself, discovering its history and strata. Albert Oehlen also plays on layering, and enters into competition with the machine as much as with nature to give rise to an abstract composition (unless it isn't?). Through Sigmar Polke's alchemical approach or Christopher Wool's successive coats and erasures, painting affirms its inherent and autonomous life. It is deployed with the most passion and *disquiet* in Helen Frankenthaler's work, whose canvas *Overture* illuminates the room through the multitude of events and agitation occurring on the surface or within the green depths of the painting. The gentle and aquatic forms of Swedish painter and sailor Ragna Bley have lost any relationship to scale and drown their referents. The world that we share is no more than an impulse. Everything here becomes liquid matter, an enveloping substance that brings the body into the painting. A cosmos.

For every human Creature can create an Immaterial World fully inhabited by Immaterial Creatures, and populous of Immaterial subjects, such as we are, and all this within the compass of the head or scull; nay, not onely so, but he may create a World of what fashion and Government he will, and give the Creatures thereof such motions, figures, forms, colours, perceptions, &c. as he pleases, and make Whirl-pools, Lights, Pressures, and Reactions, &c. as he thinks best; [...] And since it is in your power to create such a World, What need you to venture life, reputation and tranquillity, to conquer a gross material World?

MARGARET CAVENDISH
The Blazing World, 1666

INTERSECTION

> The more I meditate on our
> capacity for self-deception, the more
> my certainties crumble, slipping
> through my fingers as fine sand.
> And when this meditation becomes
> a feeling that clouds my mind,
> then the whole world appears
> to me as a mist made of shadows,
> a twilight of edges and corners,
> a fiction of the interlude, a dawn
> that never becomes morning.
>
> FERNANDO PESSOA
> *Book of Disquiet*, 1913-1935

JMG The centre of *The Inner Island* is synonymous with the return of solar light and forms a second zenithal breakthrough after Jennifer Douzenel's installation. These rays are filtered by a slim layer of water floating above our heads, reacting to the wind. On the walls, cryptic indications are the result of the collaboration between an artificial intelligence and ideograms from the Palaeolithic, which are the oldest remains of human signs or proto-writing found in Europe and Asia, dated between 40,000 and 10,000 BCE. The artificial intelligence created by artist Agnieszka Kurant digested all of the images of these traces identified by palaeontologist Genevieve von Petzinger so as to invent new ones, rather than attempting to decipher them. The idea was to imagine some of the potential developments of these drawings, which may be discovered one day. These signs only appear when the sun illuminates them. If the centre of the exhibition is in the shade, the walls fall silent once again. Past and future intersect, just as yesterday's science fiction has become our present.

YCT According to geologists, the level of the sea is rising by fifty to sixty centimetres every one hundred years. This equates to saying that many islands, including Porquerolles, will almost

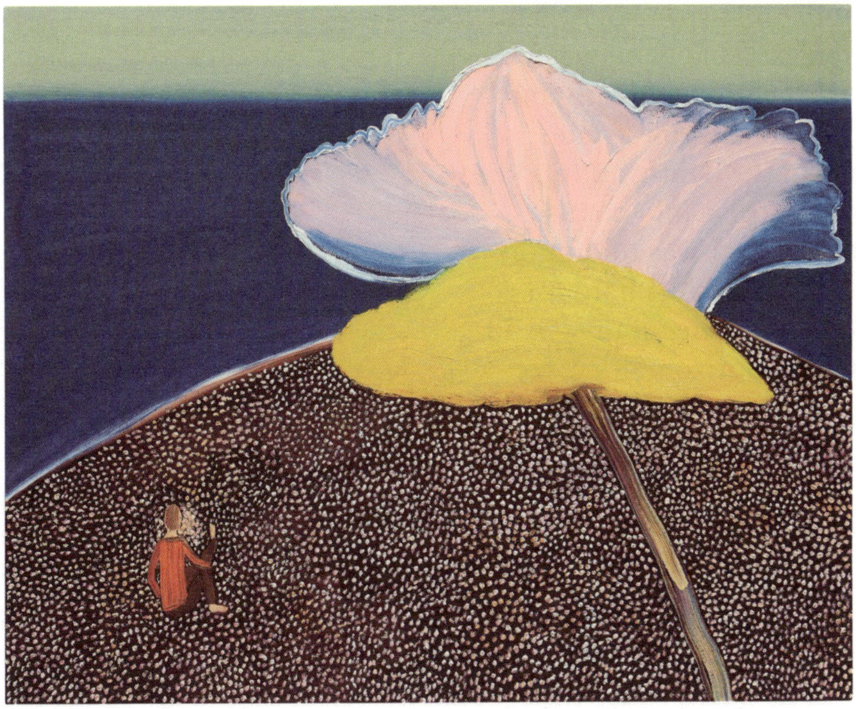

MATTHEW WONG
Pink Wave, 2017,
oil on canvas, 121.9 × 152.4 cm

no longer be visible within the relatively short term. In other words, at a historical distance comparable to that which separates us from the oldest artworks in the exhibition, the island will no longer exist on the surface of the Mediterranean, but will be engulfed. To try to imagine what this landscape of the island will look like under the sea, what will remain, how other lifeforms will take possession of it, we can settle in opposite Miquel Barceló's artwork, and plunge into the depths of an aquatic future.

JMG Six colourful, fragile, and venerable mounds landed in the centre of *The Inner Island*: they are the result of a collaboration between Kurant and termite colonies, insects that are among the most socially developed. While the scale of these mounds was reduced to that of humans, building these sculptures – whose internal complexity no one can fathom – would amount to building a cathedral or a pyramid. Hundreds of thousands of termites allocated themselves distinct roles to achieve this. The work was organised. By collaborating with entomologists, the artist made colourful materials available to these insect societies for their constructions. An artificialisation took place naturally. The intersection is an indistinct space between the habitual hierarchies, namely between the aquatic and terrestrial worlds, humans and non-humans, and liquid and solid states. We are cephalopods of the depths; our bodies are ready to metamorphosise into corals.

YCT One of the first things that I was told upon arrival on Porquerolles, was that it is hard for a mainlander to understand how life on the island makes social relations more horizontal, more supportive, and the connections between beings stronger and more intimate as well. The scale of an island allows us to feel how these interdependent relationships extend to the scale of the environment as a whole. We could not find a better example of the interconnectedness of living organisms than through Otobong Nkanga's *Tied to the Other Side*. The connections are both symbolically represented and physically manifested. They hold the woven work together, which is itself a bond. The plant (trees, plants), animal (wool, the viewers), and geological (earth) entities are intertwined and form networks. A myriad of multiplied relationships, animating the surface of the work, a condensed image of vital, multifarious exchanges, in all dimensions, which construct life and are constructed by it.

What would a human be without elephants, plants, lions, cereals, oceans, ozone or plankton? A human alone, much more alone even than Robinson Crusoe on his island. Less than a human. Certainly not a human.

BRUNO LATOUR
Politics of Nature: How to Bring the Sciences into Democracy, 1999

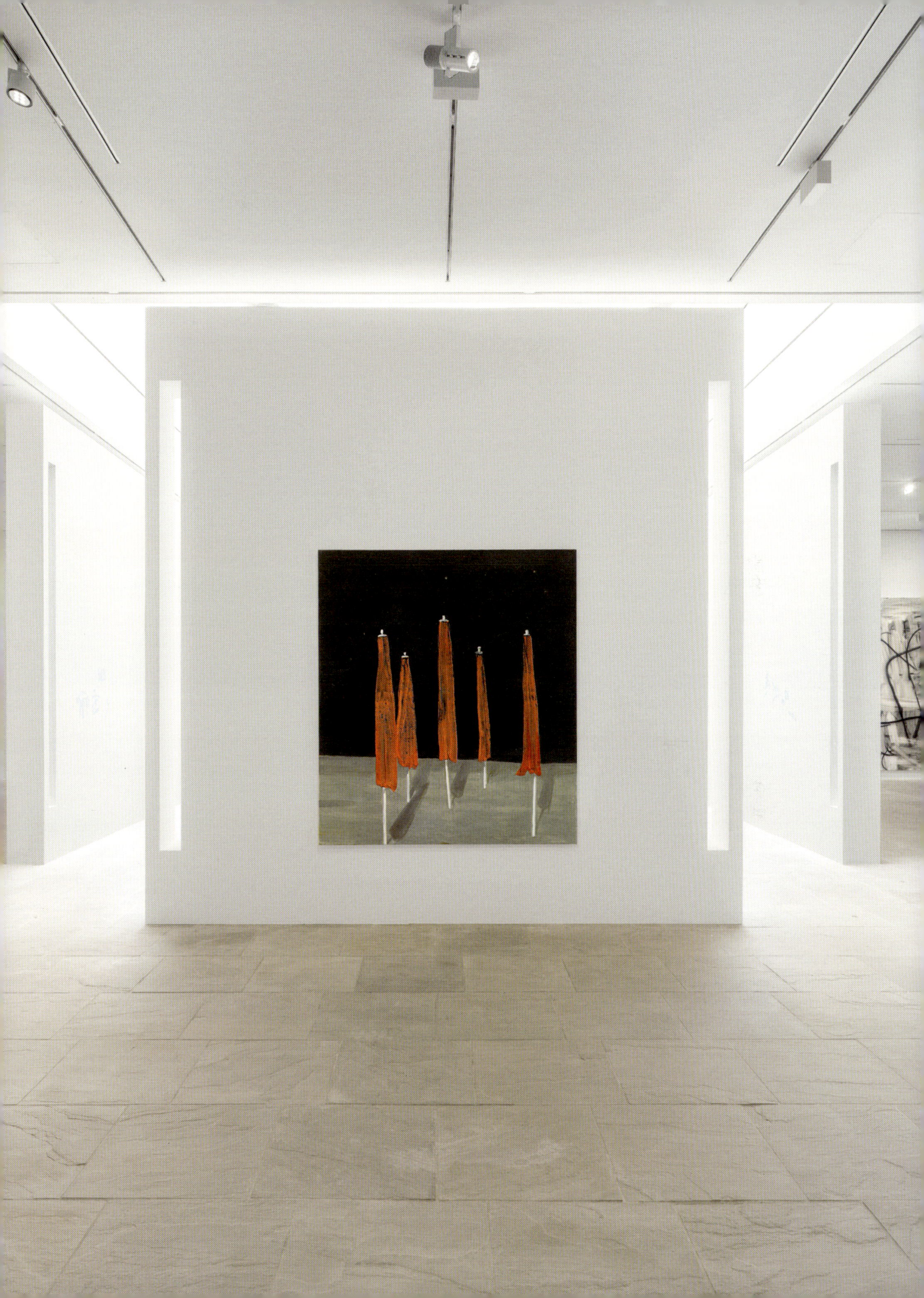

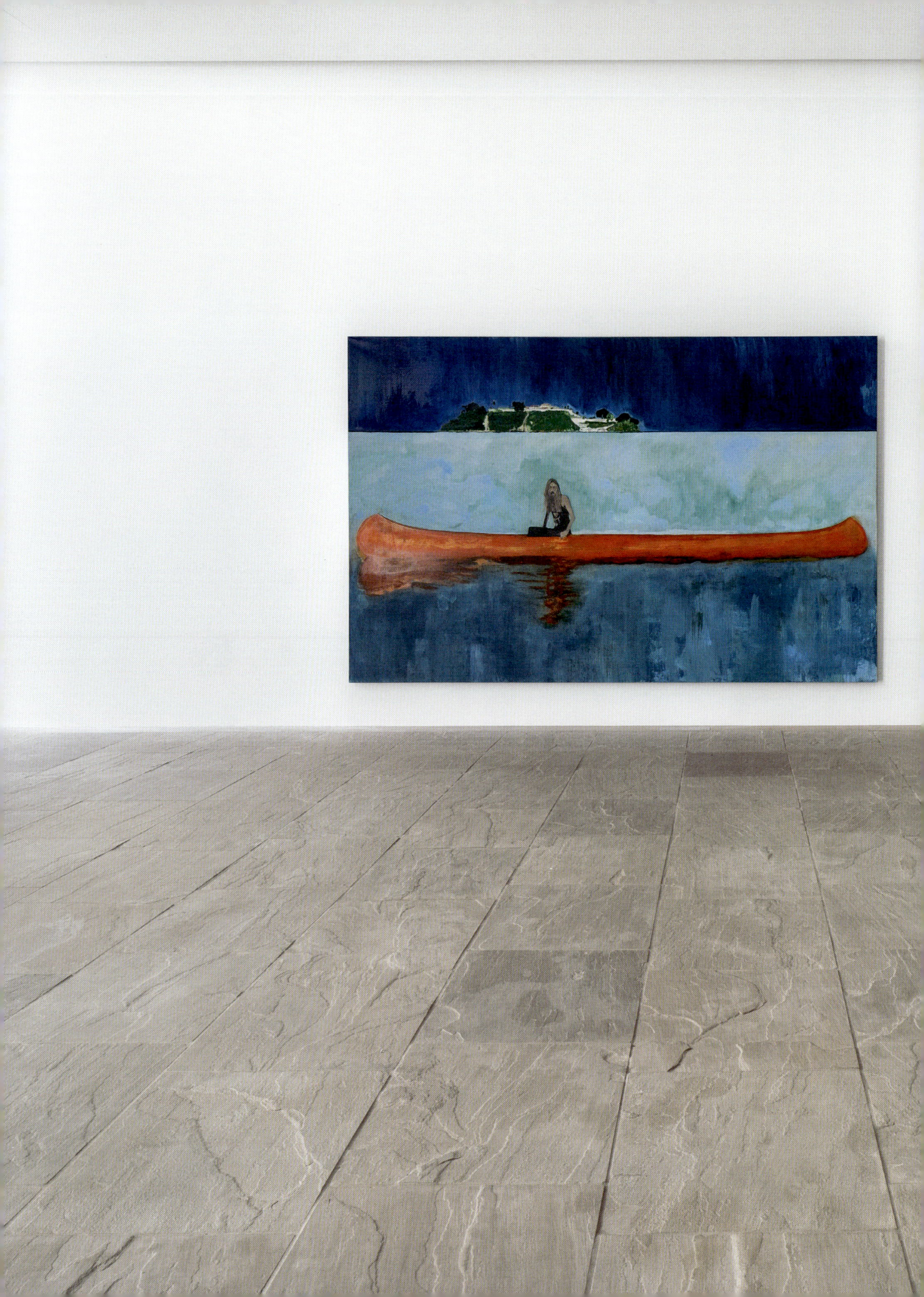

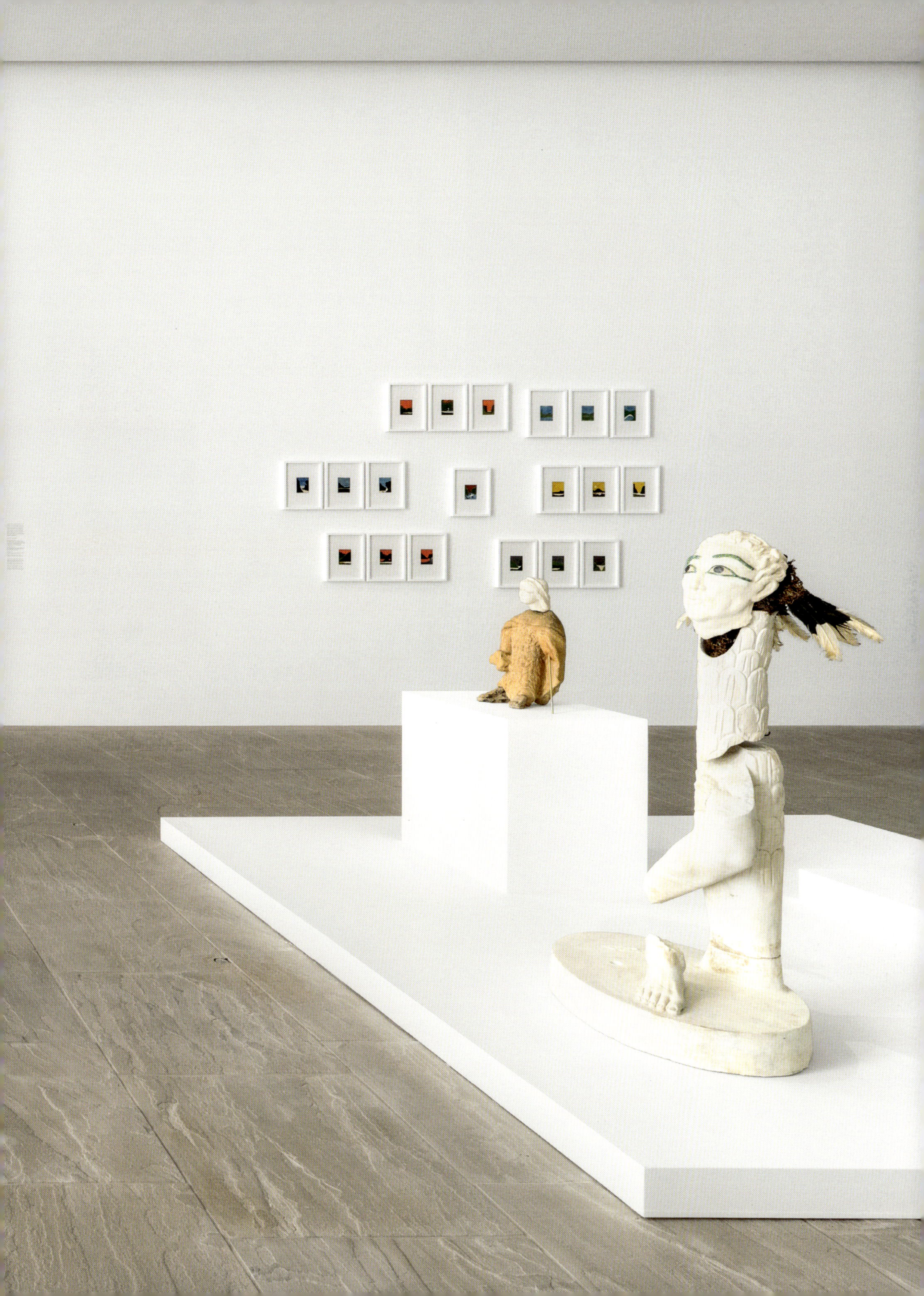

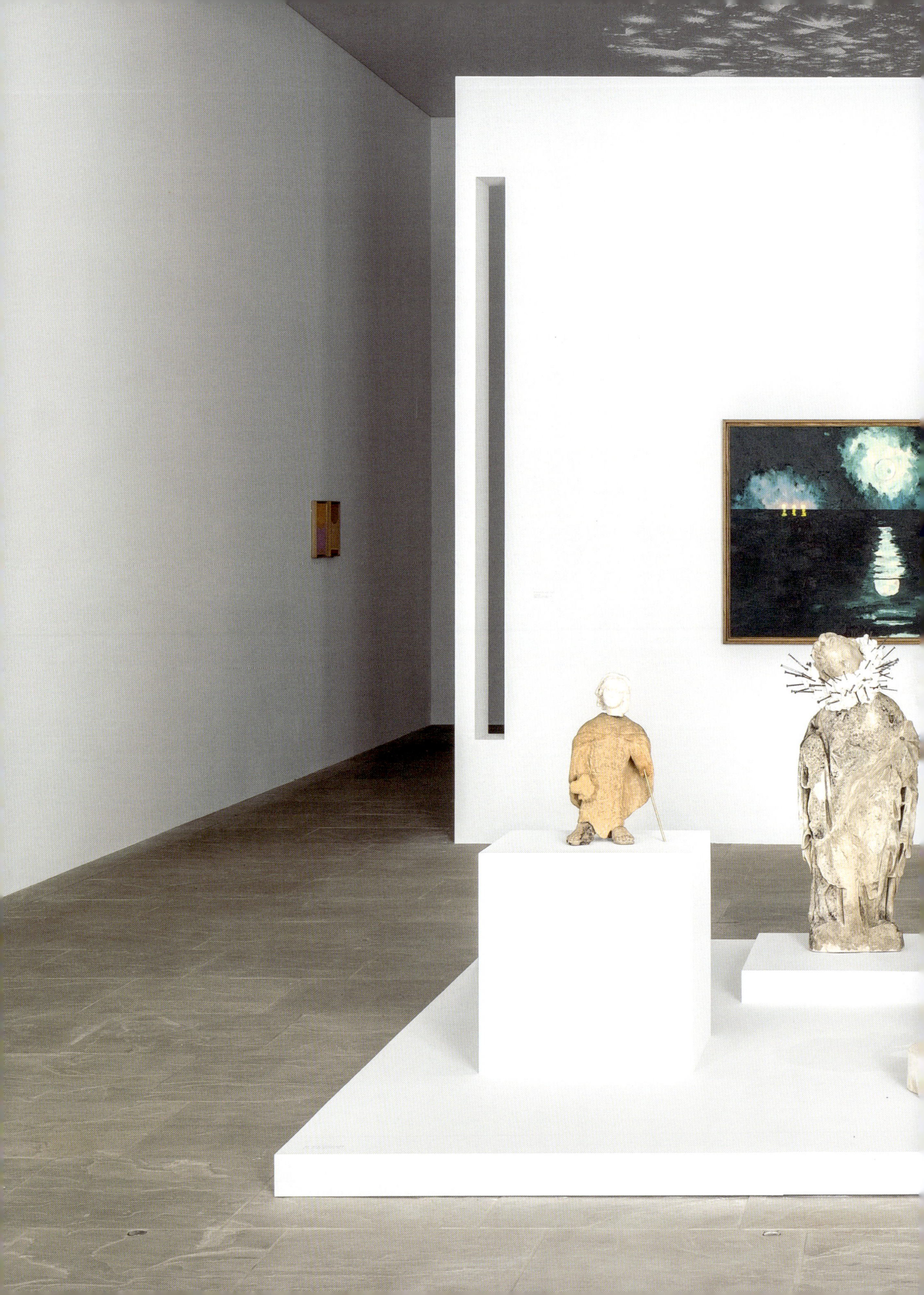

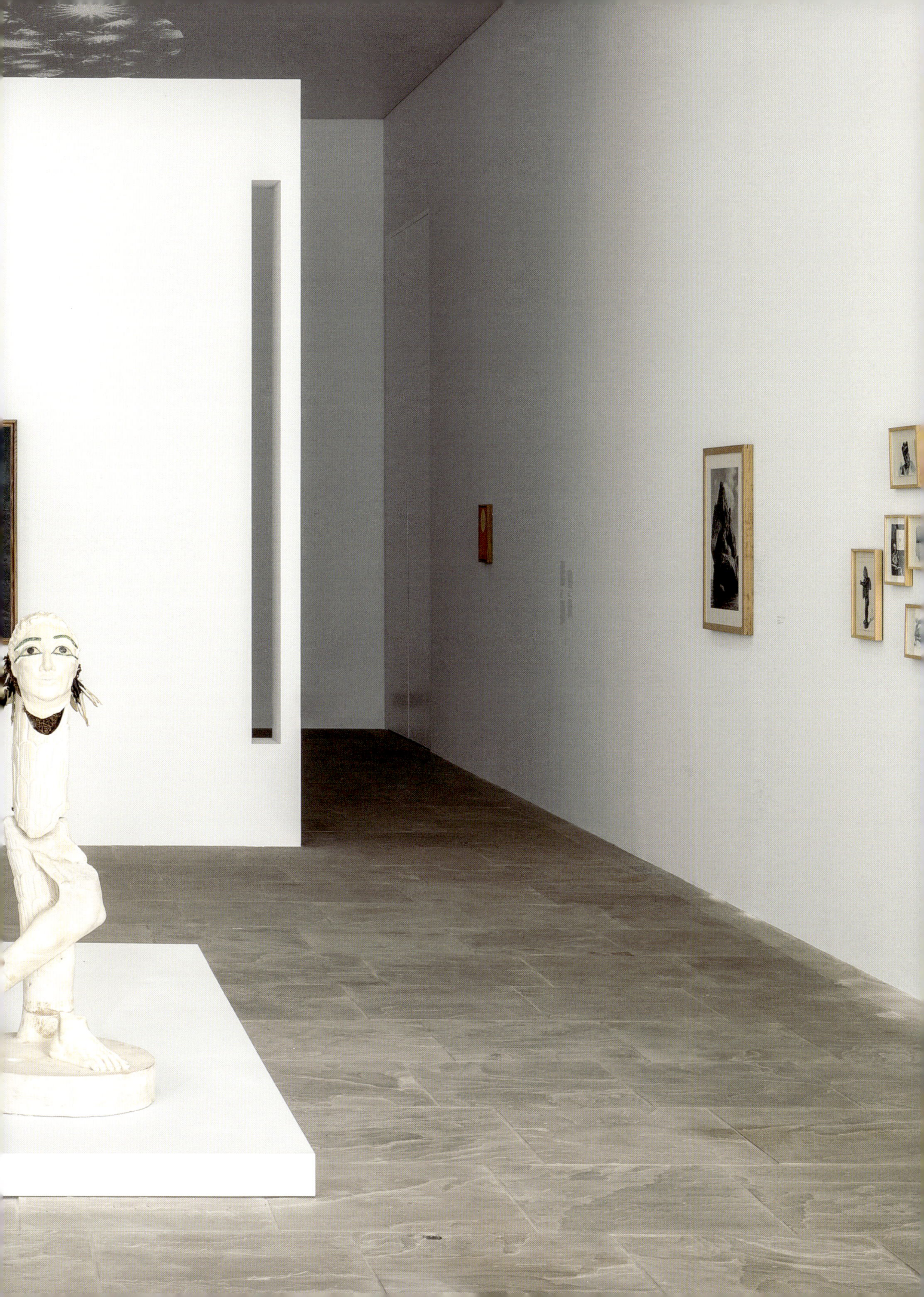

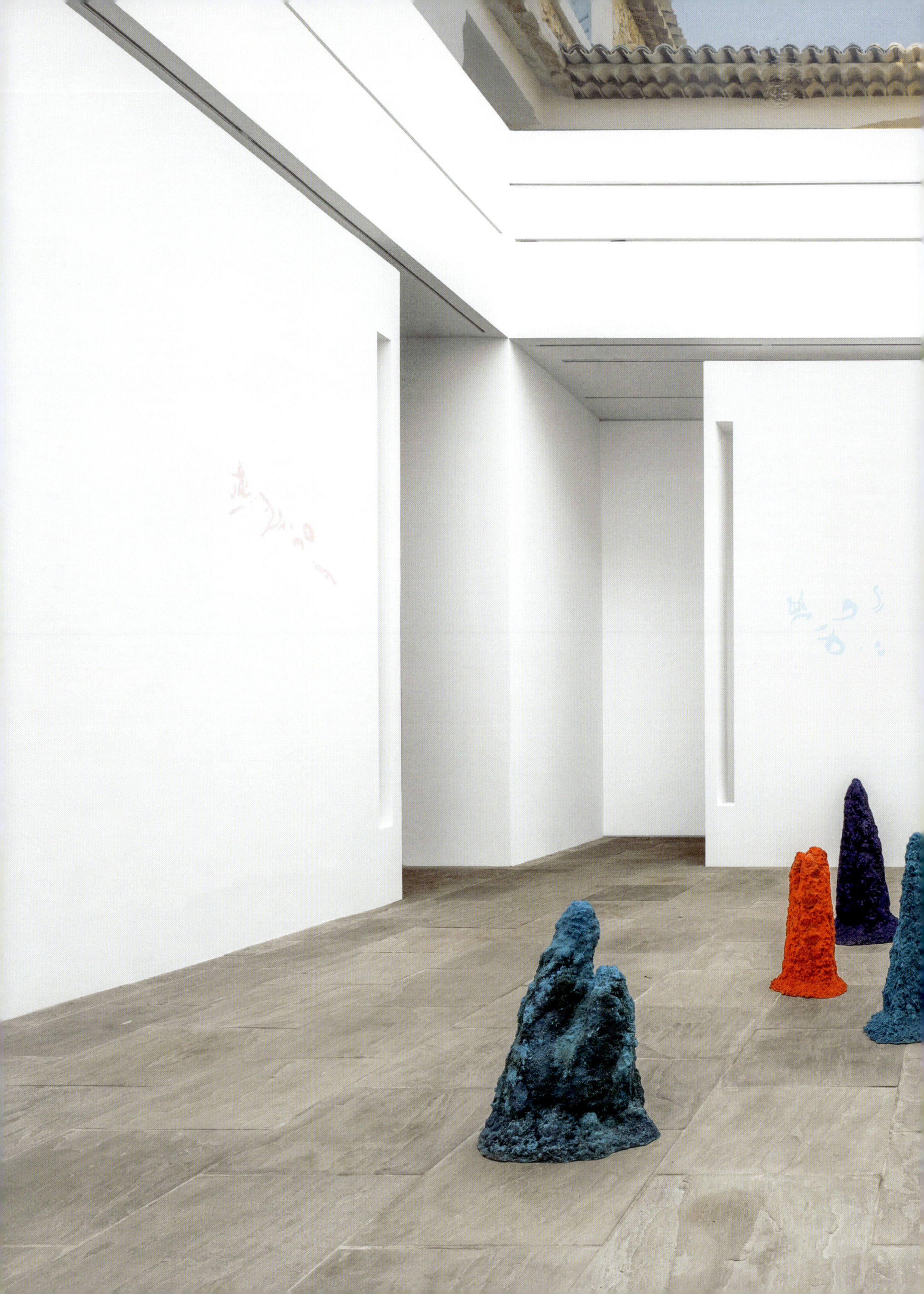

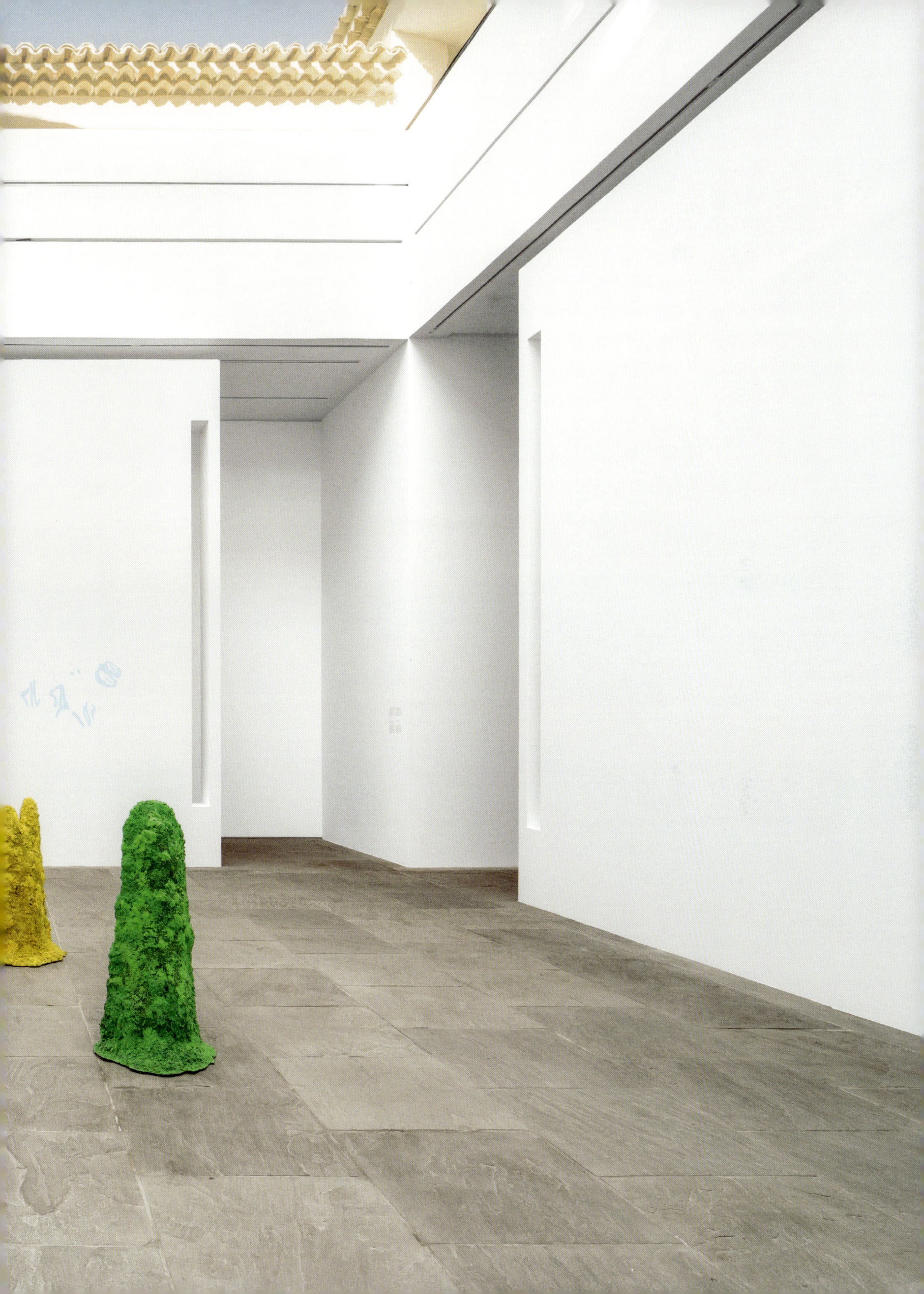

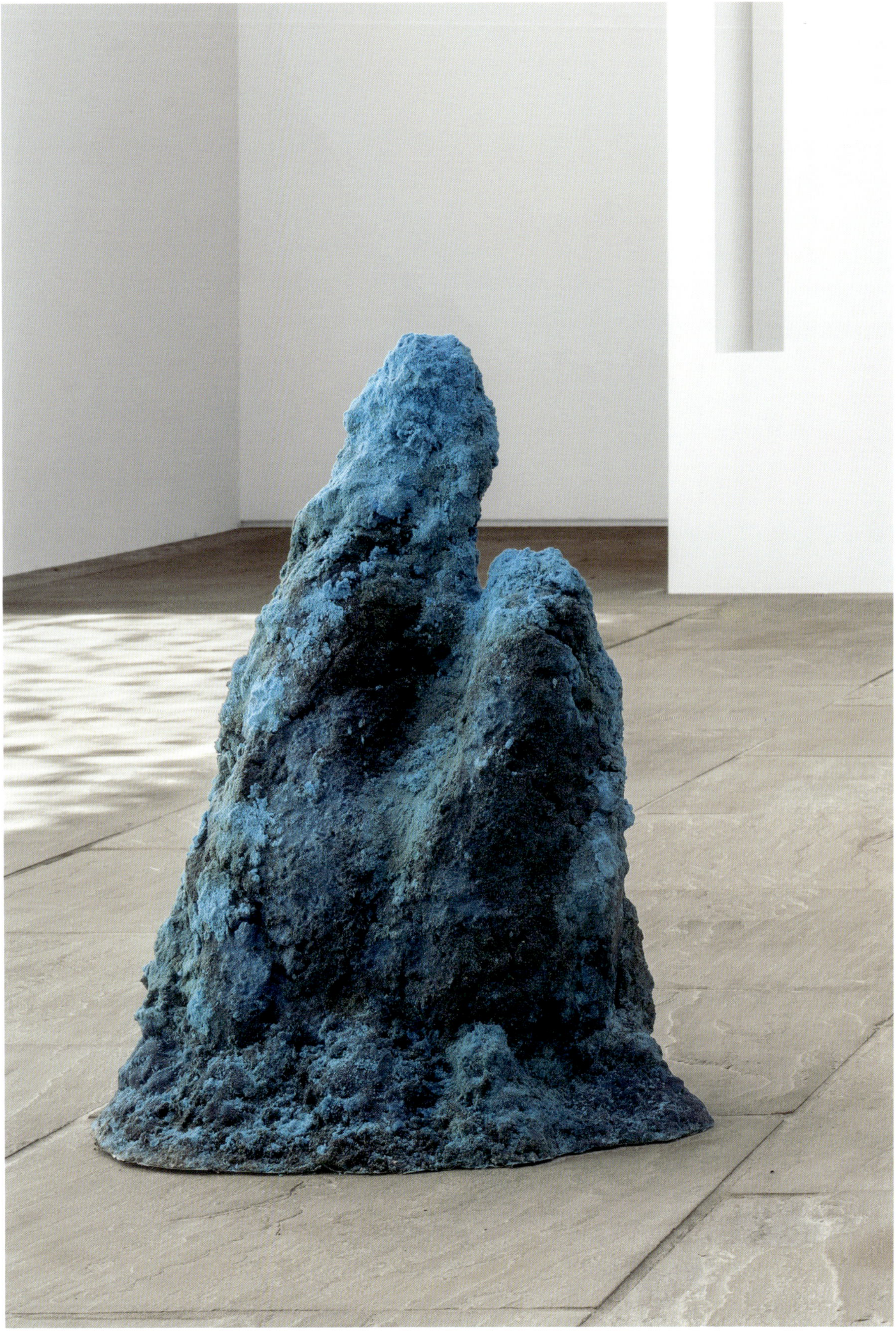

Agnieszka Kurant, *A.A.I. 15*, 2017 — termite mound made of coloured sand, gold, glitter, and crystals — 68.6 × 61 cm

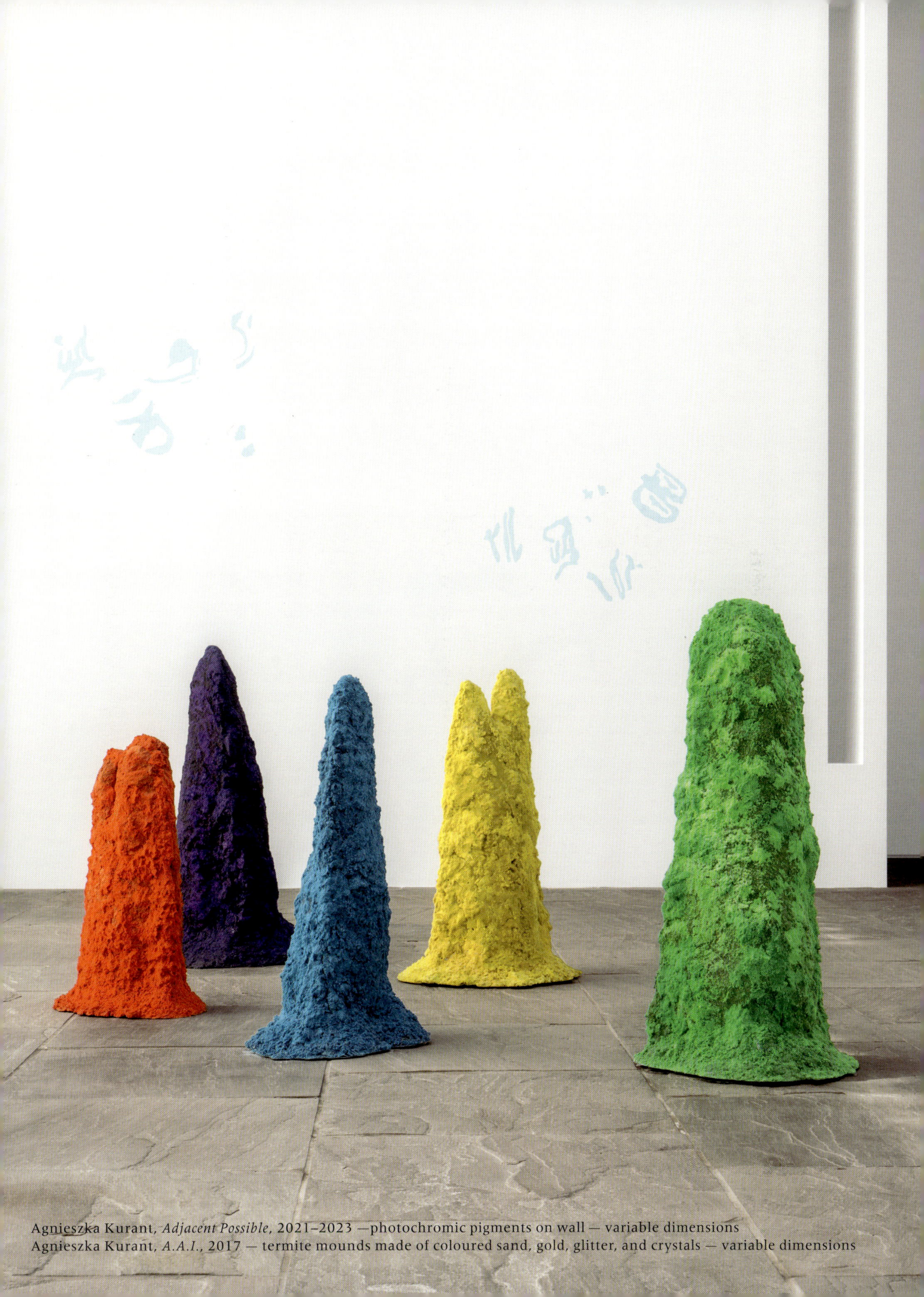

Agnieszka Kurant, *Adjacent Possible*, 2021–2023 —photochromic pigments on wall— variable dimensions
Agnieszka Kurant, *A.A.I.*, 2017 — termite mounds made of coloured sand, gold, glitter, and crystals — variable dimensions

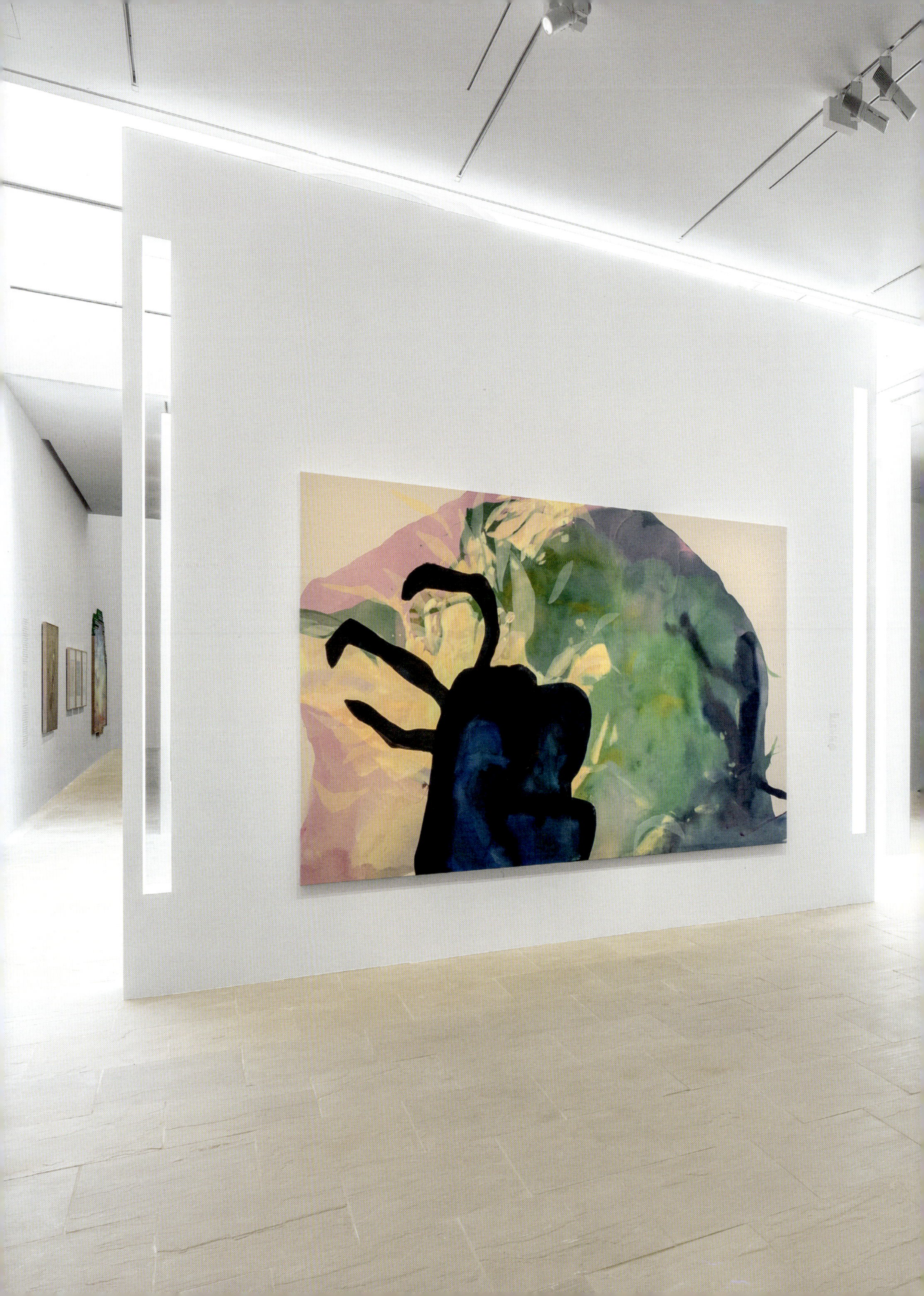

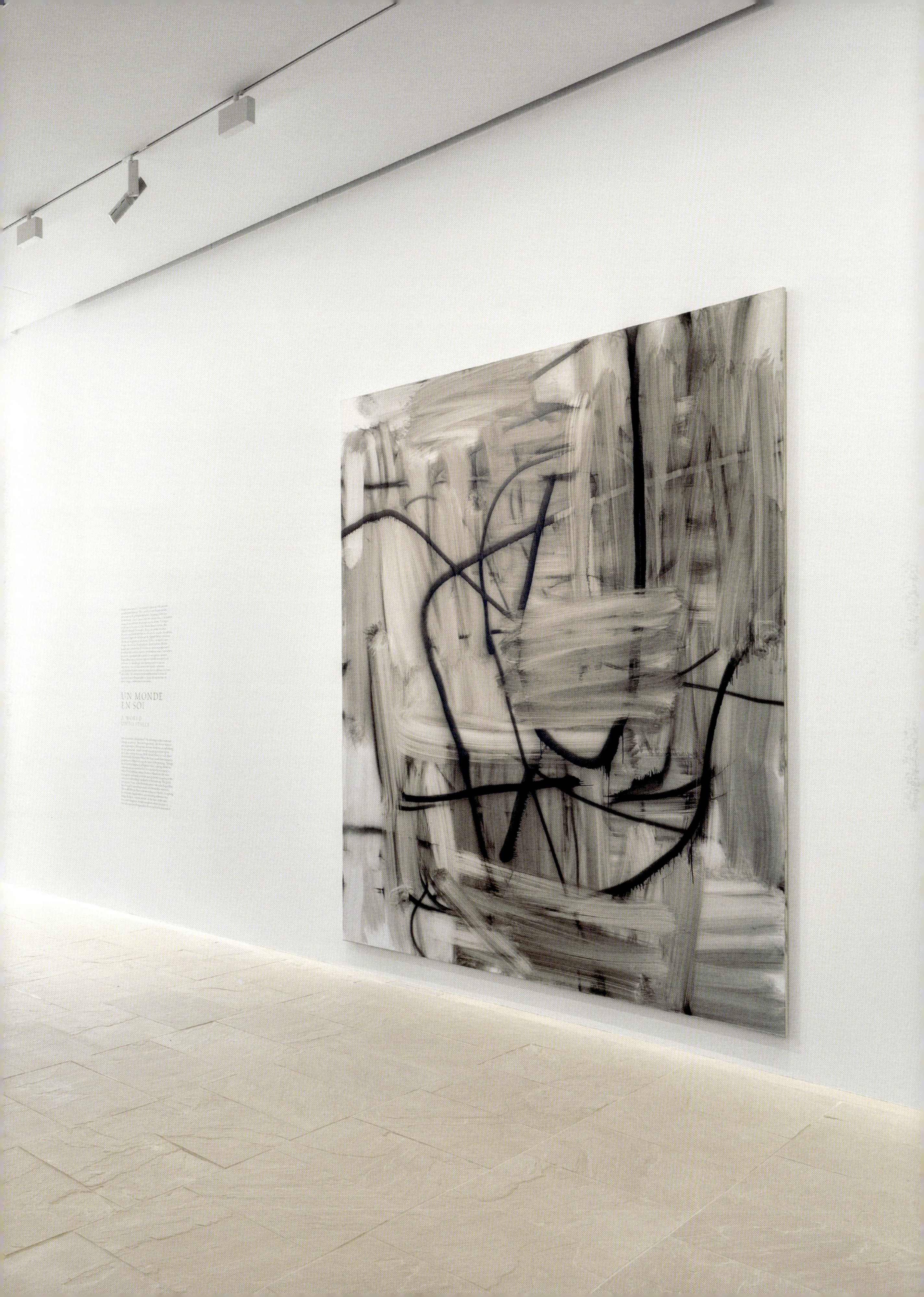
UN MONDE
EN SOI

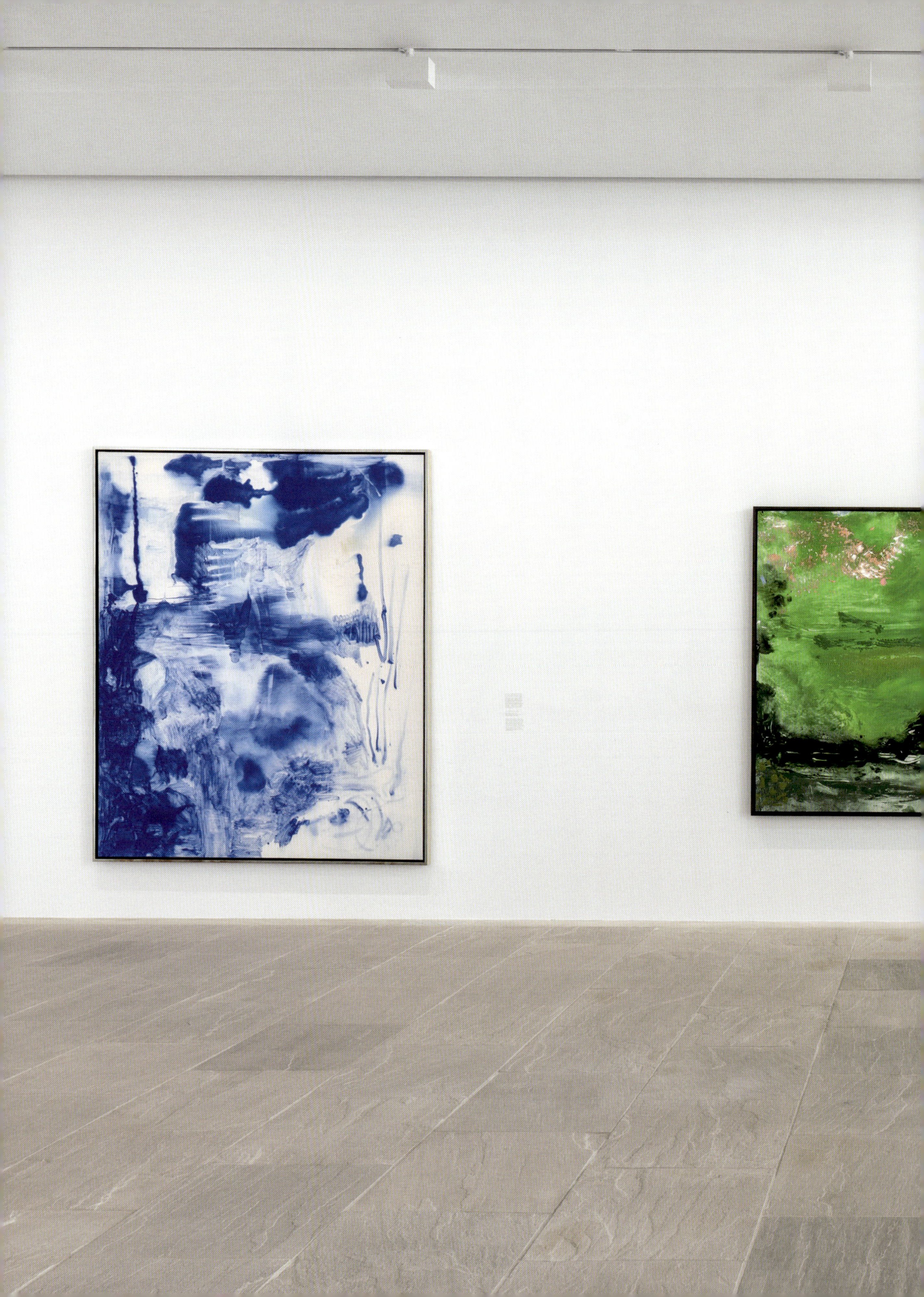

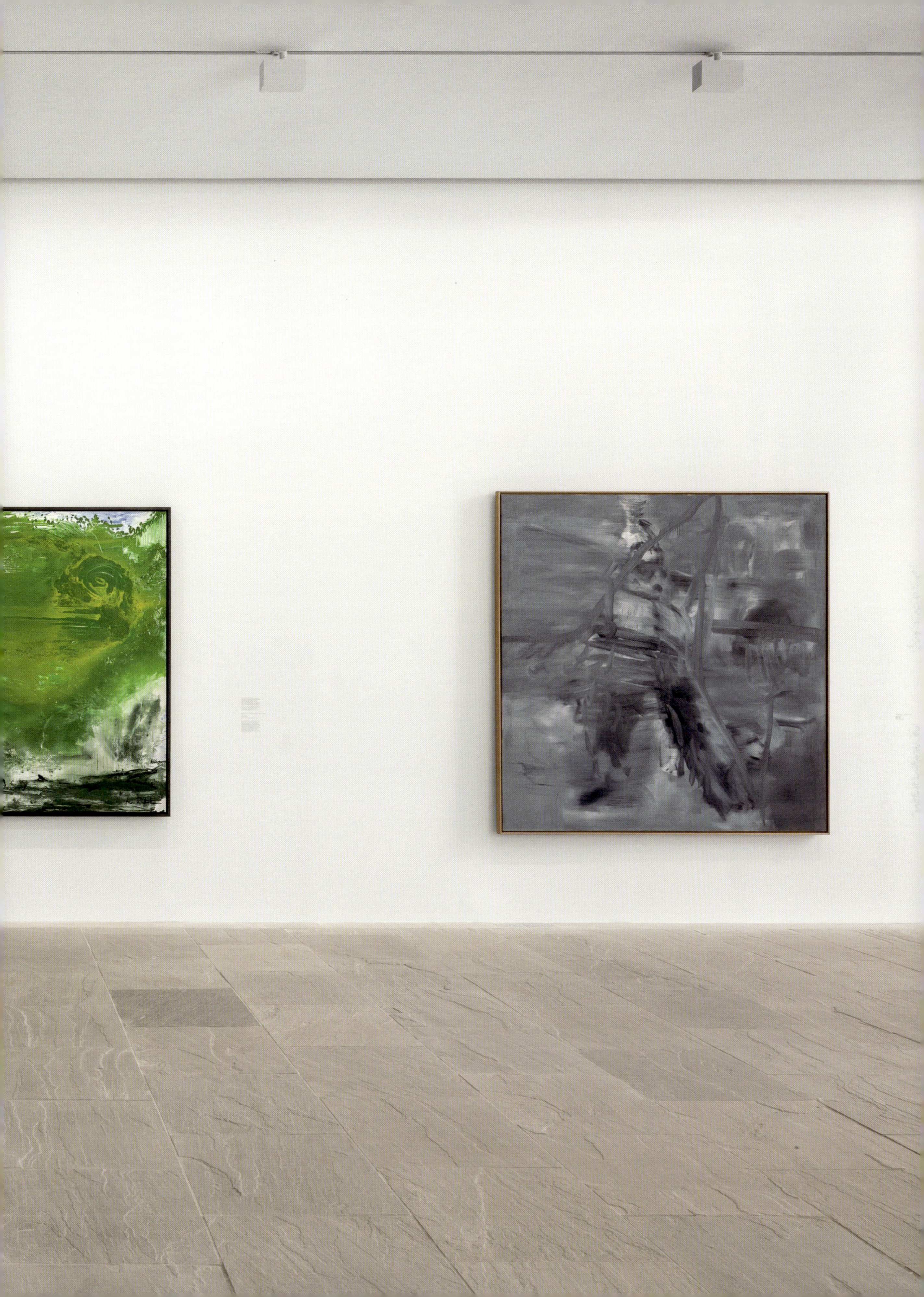

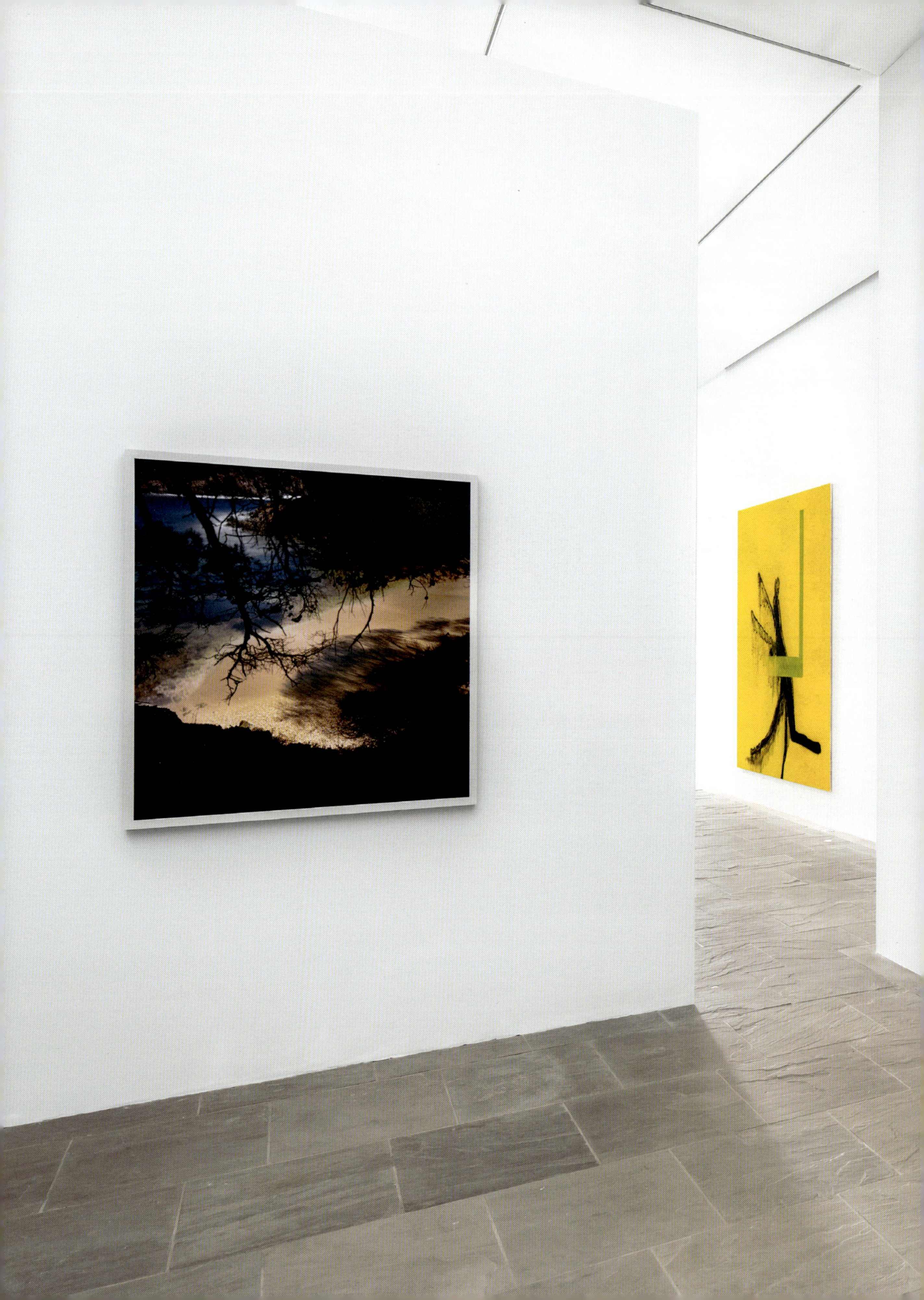

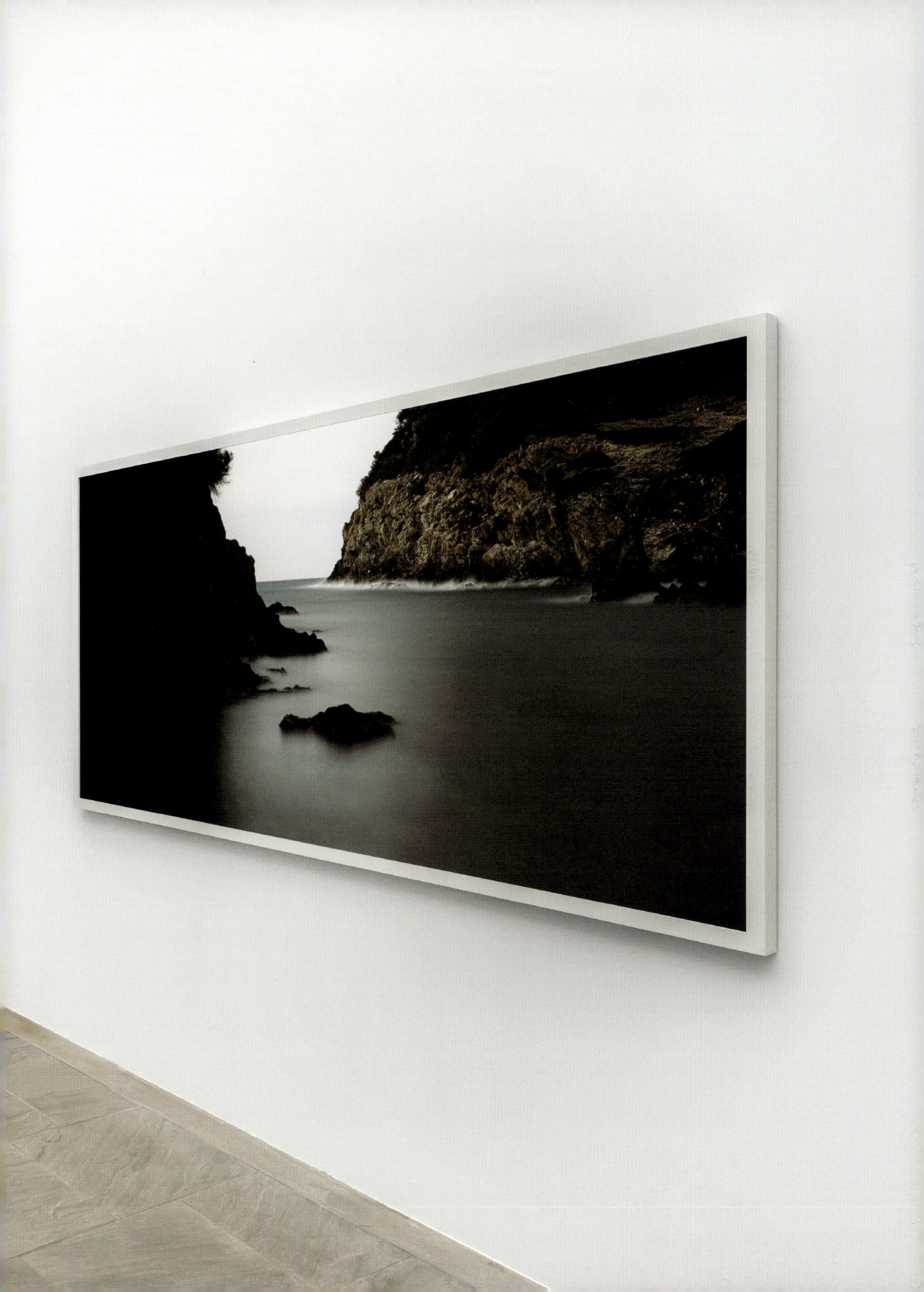

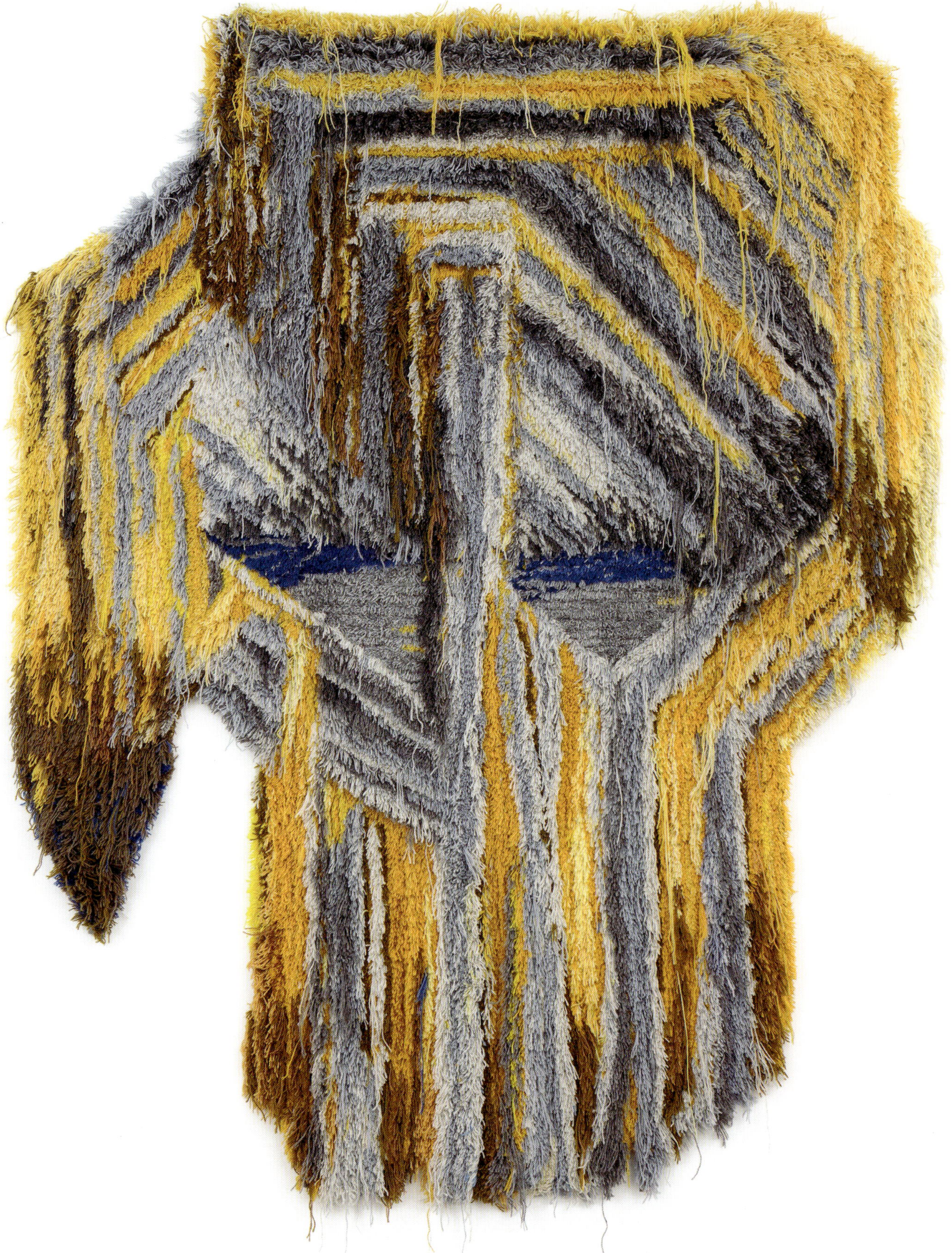

Caroline Achaintre, *Brutus*, 2016 — hand-tufted wool — 223 × 180 cm

MYTHOLOGICAL RETURNS

Just as man's first speech was poetic before it became utilitarian, so man first built an idol of mud before he fashioned an ax. Man's hand traced the stick through the mud to make a line before he learned to throw the stick as a javelin. [...] The God image, not pottery, was the first manual act. It is the materialistic corruption of present-day anthropology that has tried to make men believe that original man fashioned pottery before he made sculpture. [...] The artistic act is man's personal birthright.

BARNETT NEWMAN
The First Man Was an Artist, 1947

JMG The further into *The Inner Island* we delve, the more numerous the apparitions become. In the last room of the exhibition, characters, faces of creatures, or entities seem to watch us: they confront us. Up until now, very few figures have broached the visitor directly, only the man with the long hair on Peter Doig's canoe turned to us, silently. The sculptures and all the other bodies were absorbed, into a world, in a dream or a landscape, like Jill Mulleady's image reader, the self-conscious silhouette of Norbert Schwontkowski, or the many sleepers. In *Macedonia Road* by Verne Dawson, an artwork with the look of a lost paradise, one of these characters conversed with a bird placed on his arm (we should also ponder the role of birds, insects, and primates in contemporary art). *The Inner Island* inevitably convokes some of the founding myths and a primordial spirituality.

YCT The separated, encircled island is the ultimate site of community, the invention of different relationships and new rituals. Philosopher Gilles Deleuze reminds us that many ancient myths see islands as the site of reinvention, distance, and togetherness – as in the communities of women of Circe and Calypso. Beings that form a bond with water, which protects and isolates them, in a privileged relationship whose ghosts or ancestral shadows we might perceive in Marcella Barceló's painting, *Pollination Syndrome*. During the deluge, the water, this time destructive, spared an island. And it was from this last place on Earth still submerged – a "circular and sacred place" – that everything began again. But Deleuze insists in *The Desert Island* on the fact that this creation is based on a movement in two phases, for which the island apparently serves as the model. As in dreams, on the island, the creation of worlds is always a re-creation. From whence, probably, feelings oscillate between familiarity and strangeness all at once, when facing figures introduced in the works of Verne Dawson, Kiki Smith, or Francis Upritchard. Reinvention – product of "the second origin" Deleuze speaks of – authorises reprisal and repetition, imitation, or even parody. But above all it allows reproduction, and a navigation heading backwards through time, as the philosopher theorises in a surprising way: on the island "there is in the ideal of a new beginning something that precedes the beginning itself, which

Geographical map of paradise: see the other side. Once a year, the man must go back there for his own good. He does as follows: travels to Hyères, from there by bus to Giens, from there, a boat – 20 mins = 5 FF – to the island. You are hereby cordially invited. Yours, Hannah Stern.
– poste restante!
Island of Porquerolles (Var).

HANNAH ARENDT,
Postcard (representing a map of the island of Porquerolles) sent to Walter Benjamin, 1937

starts over in order to delve deeper and withdraw into time". Stories within stories, not a mechanism to ascend *to* the origin, but *the origin* itself. And to recreate it each time, with each artwork.

JMG Strolling among these hybrid figures, animal, divine, human... gives the impression of being observed and not having control of the situation. Francis Upritchard's supernatural characters are distant and seem absent,

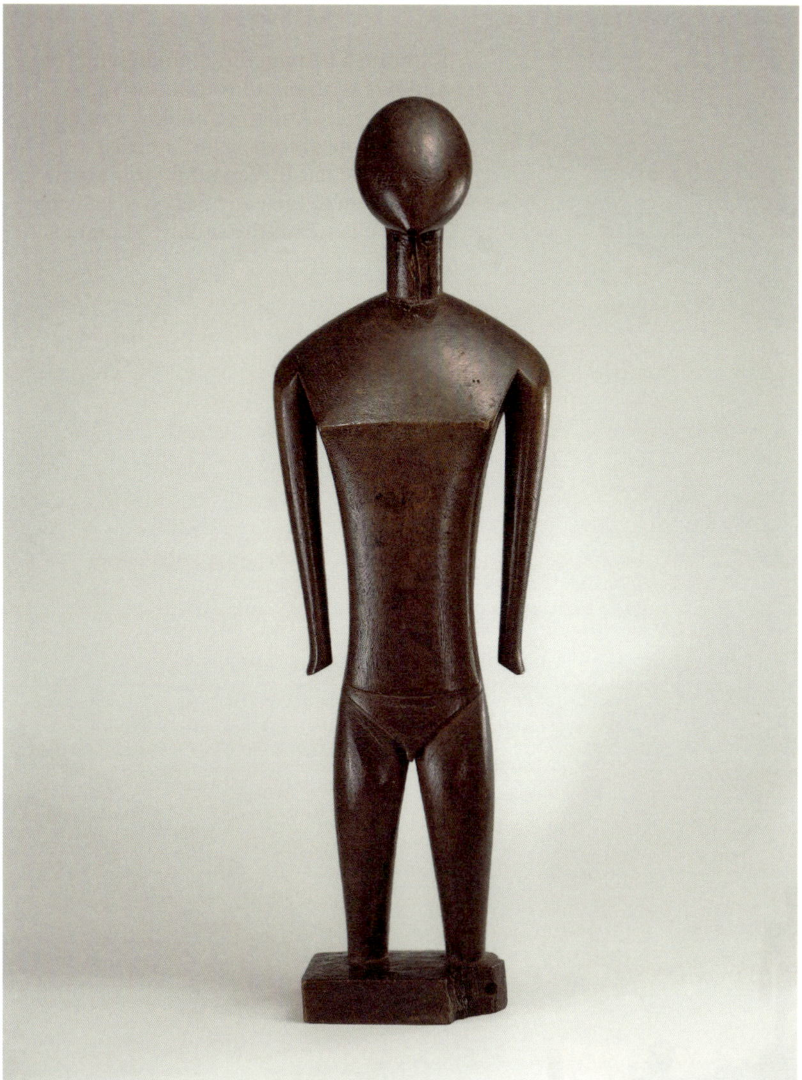

Deity (dinonga eidu), early nineteenth century, wood, H: 58.4 cm, Nukuoro (Caroline Islands)

like the very real (and rare) ones of Giulia Andreani. Those of Marcus Cope indulge in rituals, around a fire that could be a zoom into the incandescent landscape of Tursic & Mille. That is what happens on the horizon, beyond the cliché of the sunset: a crossing between two worlds. In *The Inner Island*, pagan divinities and fantastical forces, references to mythical or sacred creatures, such as the spirits of Beninese Vodun in Jeremy Demester's work, find an appropriate setting. In this last room, they confront us, the gazes are direct and the figures strident. It is the other hidden heart of the inner island.

I'll build a heaven out of hidden hopes
And live without your luminosity.
We dreamers know we hold within our
souls divine secrets, a lost eternity.
My temple has no room for your cruel
light. I aim to bury the past you revealed
And live beneath the canopy of night.

NAZIK AL-MALA'IKA
Revolt Against the Sun, 8 July 1946

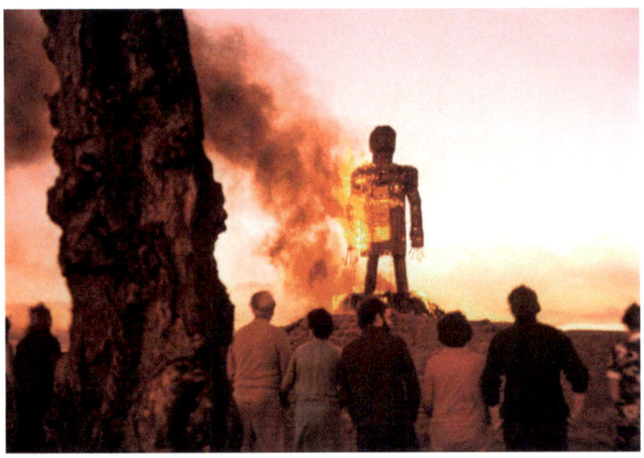

ROBIN HARDY (director),
The Wicker Man (1973)

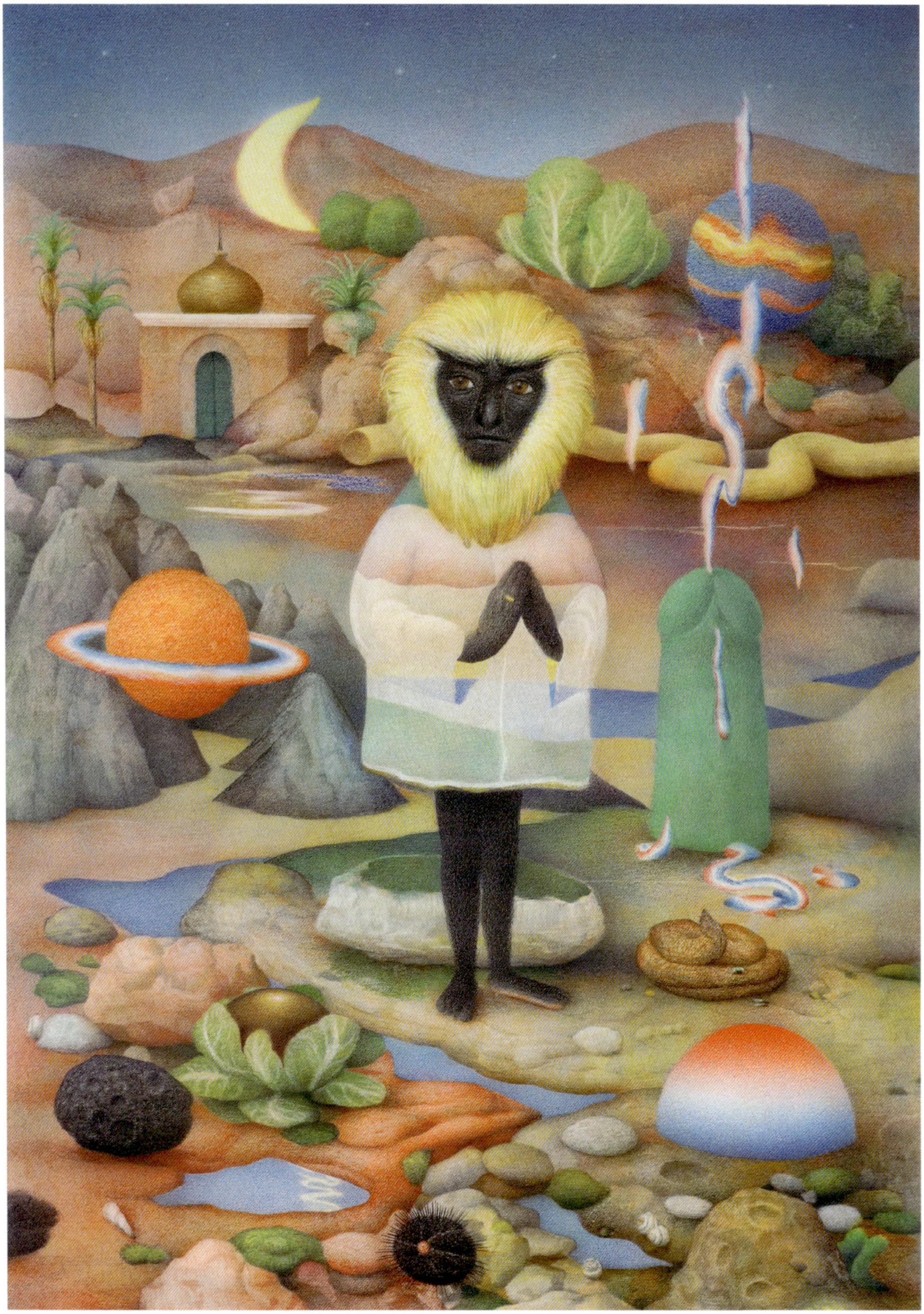

Corentin Grossmann, *Un doute intersidéral*, 2019 — graphite, dry pastel, and coloured pencils — 155 × 113 cm

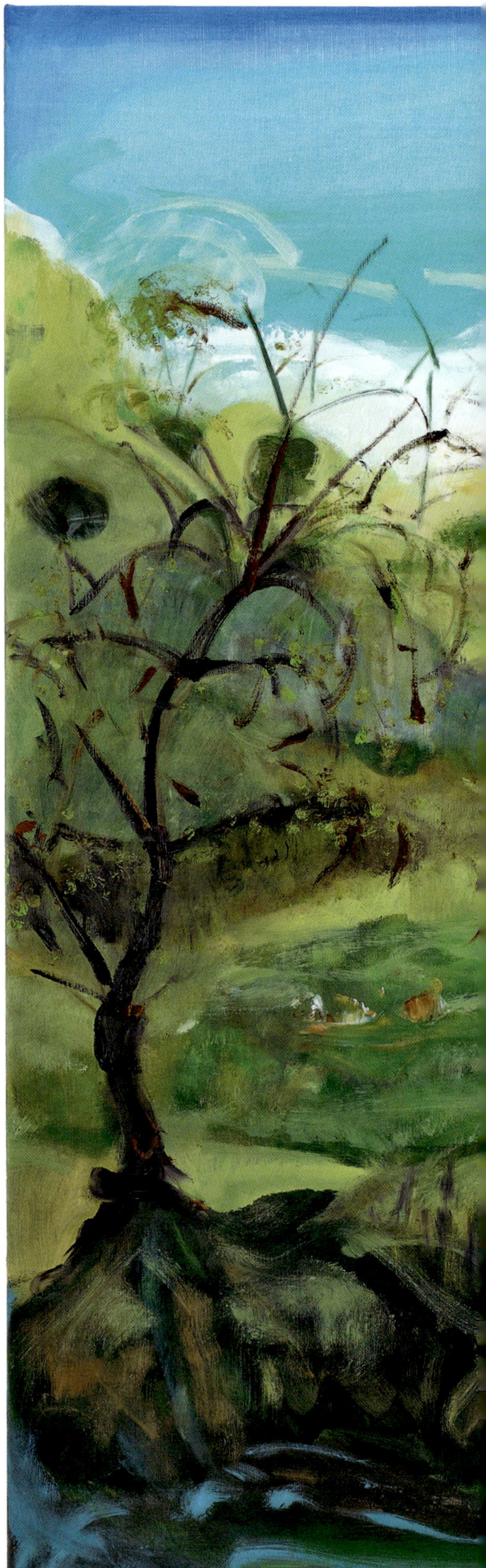

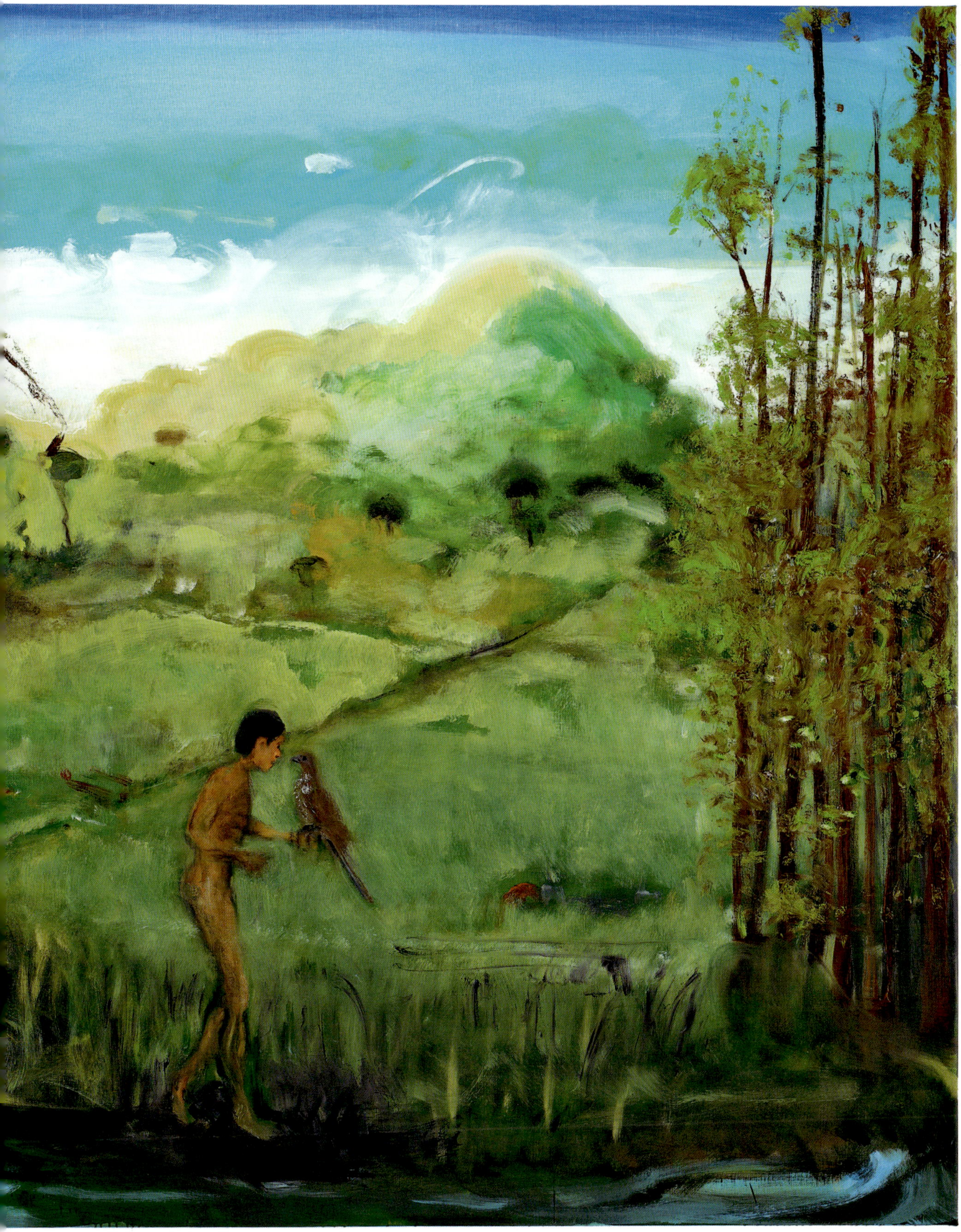

Verne Dawson, *Macedonia Road*, 2013 — oil on linen canvas — 182.9 × 213.4 cm

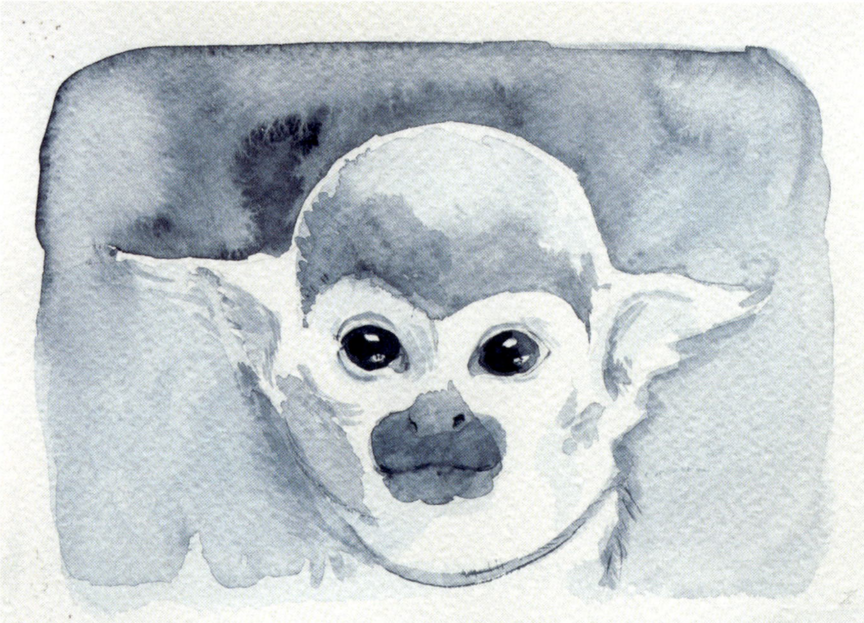

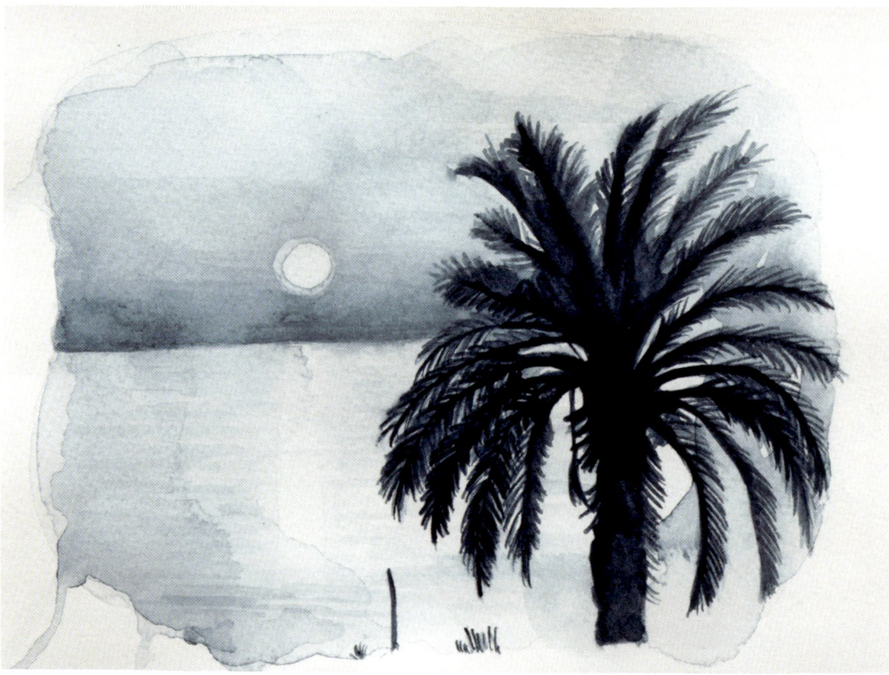

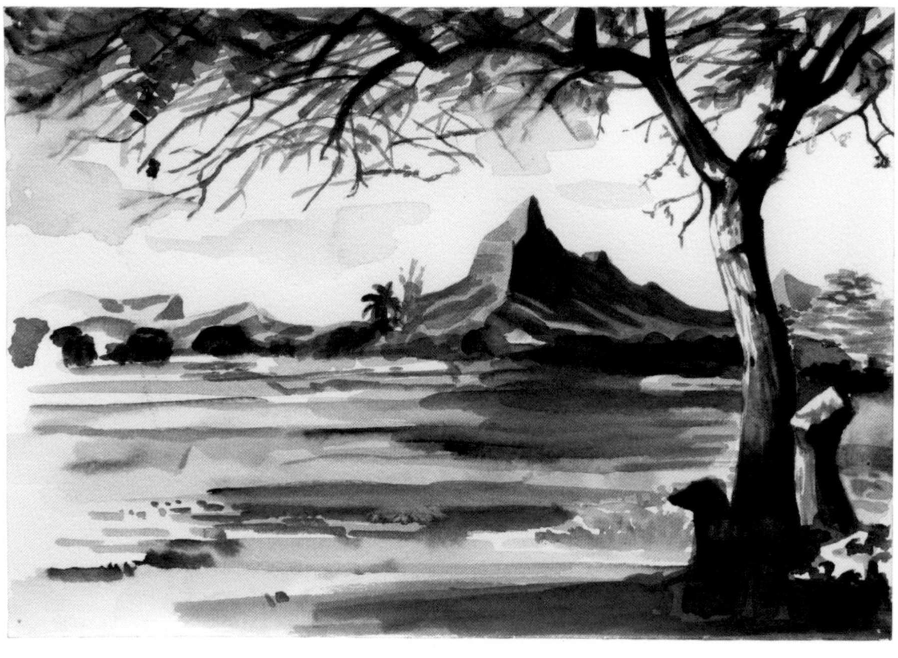

Giulia Andreani
XV (ape), 2011 — watercolour on paper — 12.5 × 18 cm
Crépuscule, 2013 — watercolour on paper — 12.5 × 18 cm
Le Rempart, 2015 — watercolour on paper — 18 × 12 cm

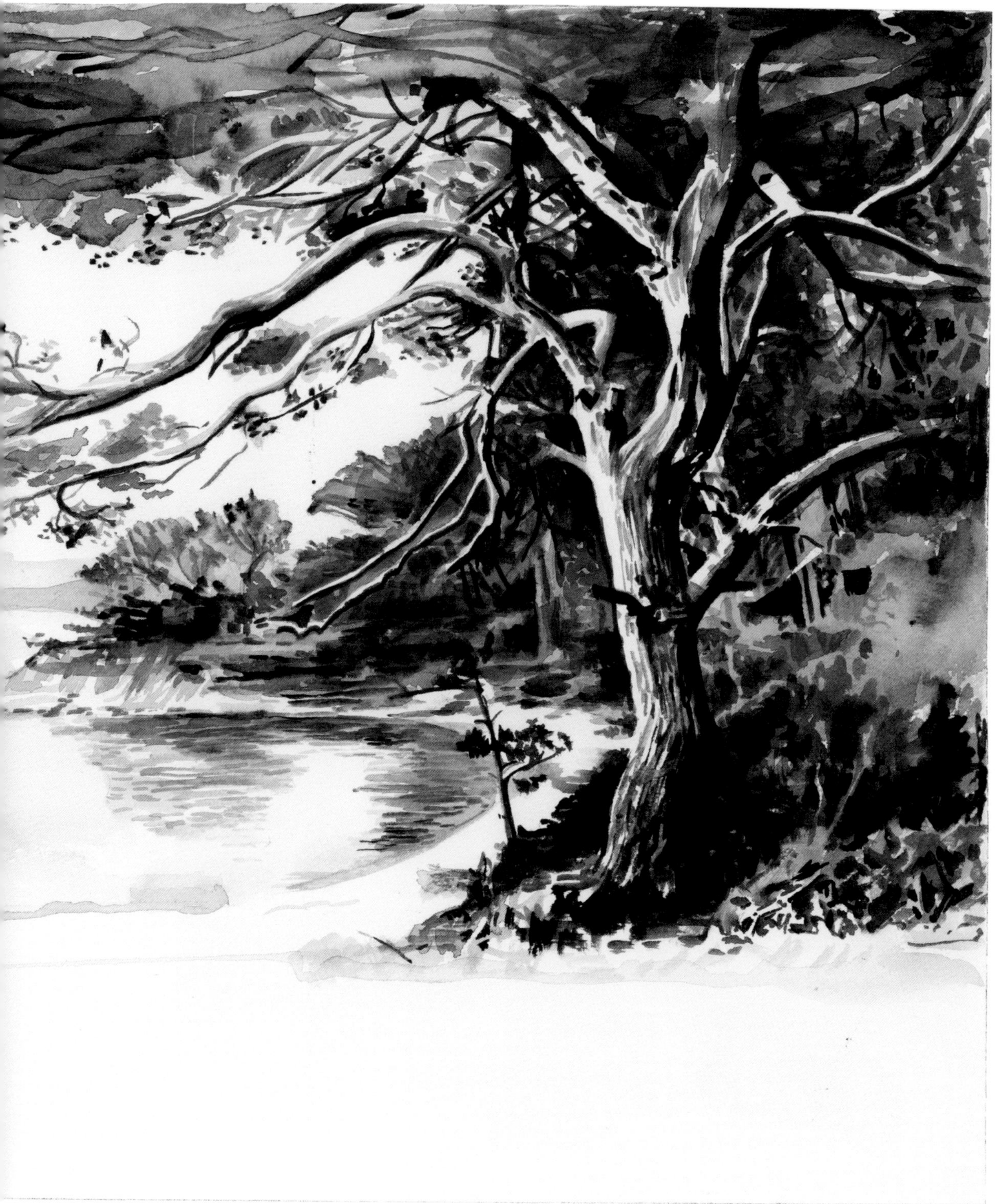

Giulia Andreani, *Faoucado*, 2023 — watercolour on paper — 36 × 51 cm

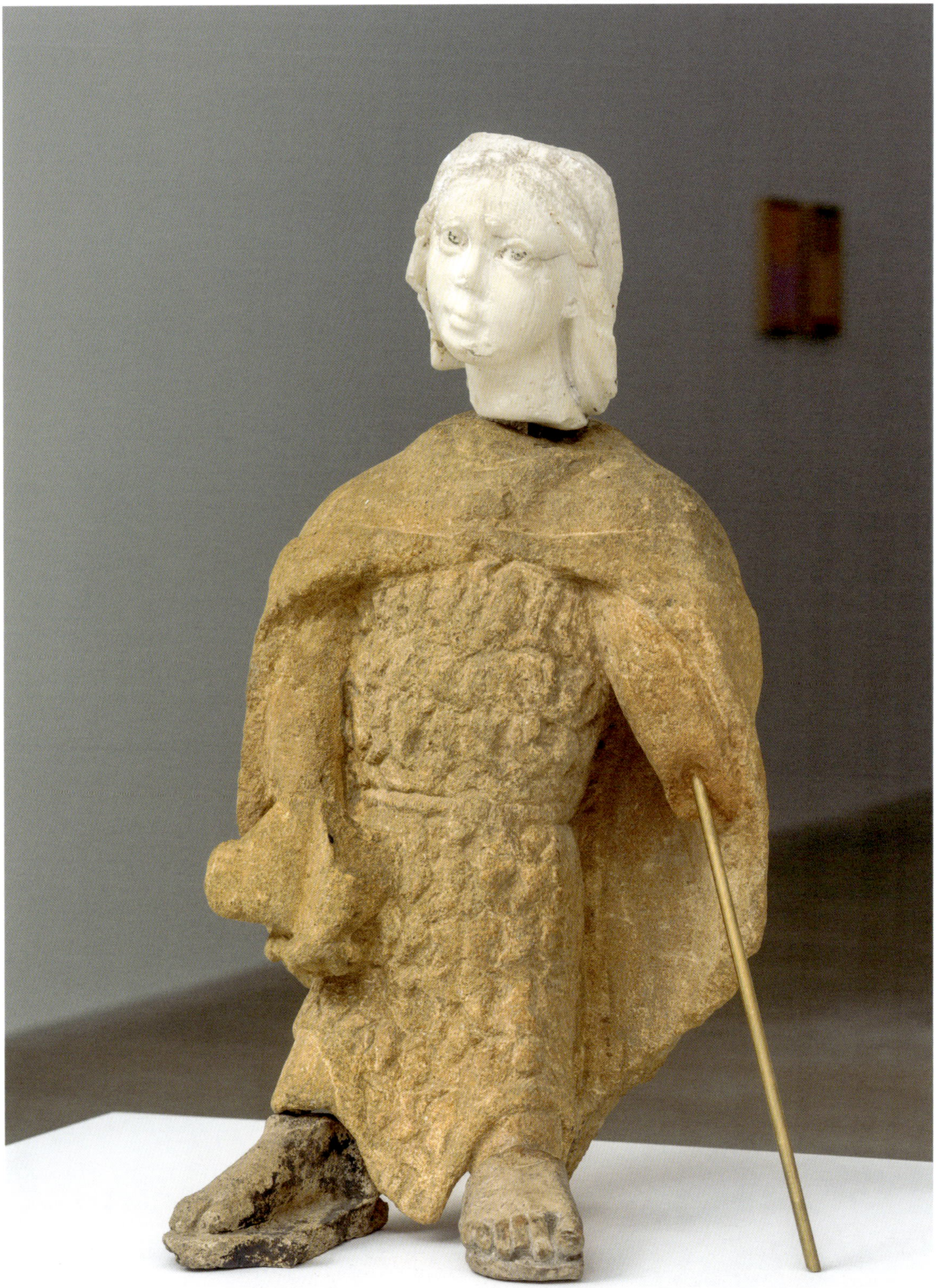

Ali Cherri, *Grafting (Errance)*, 2023 — sandstone headless bust of Saint John the Baptist, France, late eleventh century; alabaster head, France, eighteenth century; terracotta votive feet; metal — 47 × 22 × 32 cm

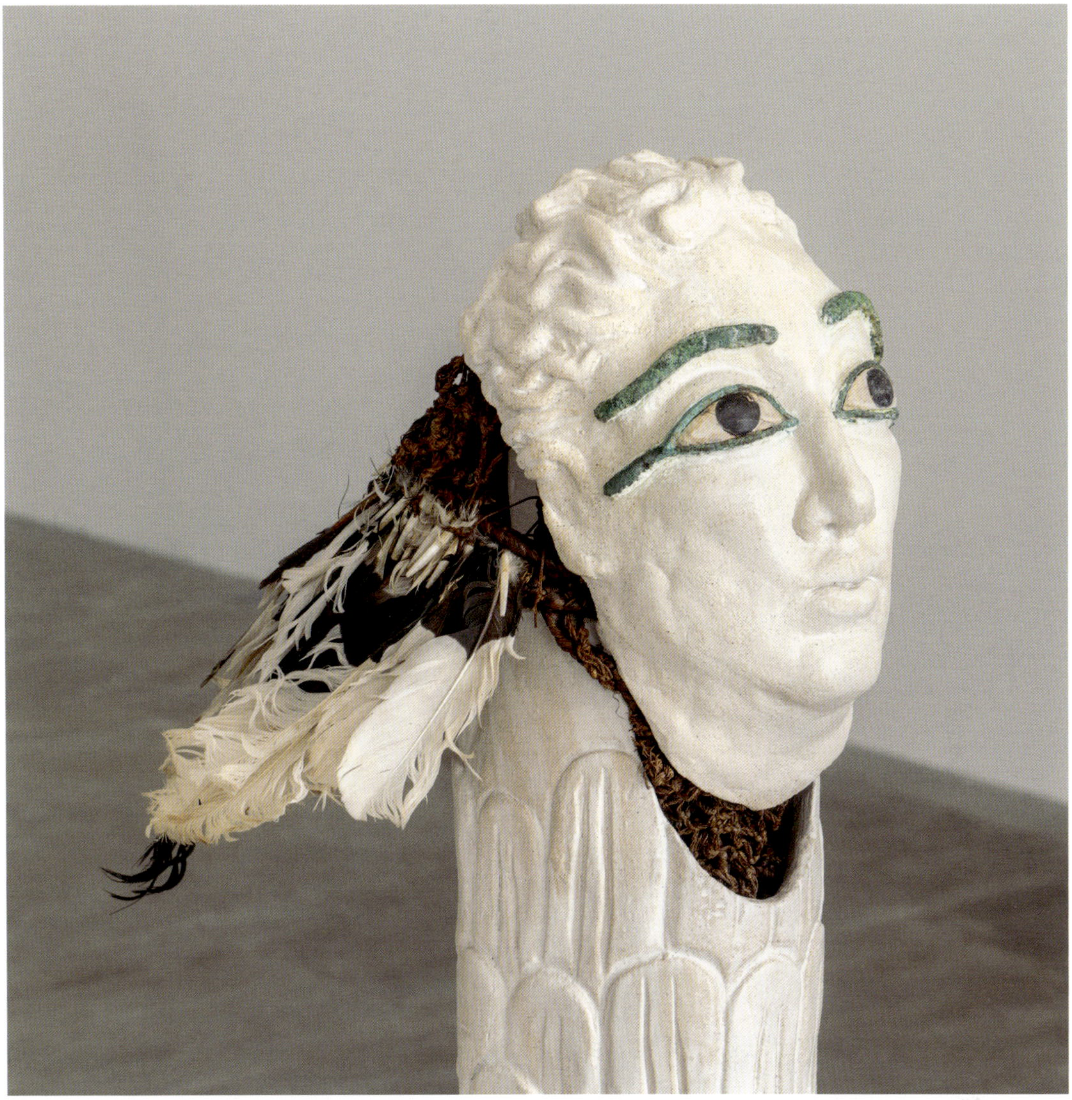

Ali Cherri, *Return of the Beast* (detail), 2021 — fragment of a nineteenth century Roman white marble sculpture with legs and feet (life size); antique Egyptian bronze eyes with matching eyebrows, azurite remains, and inlays; feathered headdress from Angola (Tchokwe culture); glazed stoneware and metal — 130 × 63 × 51 cm

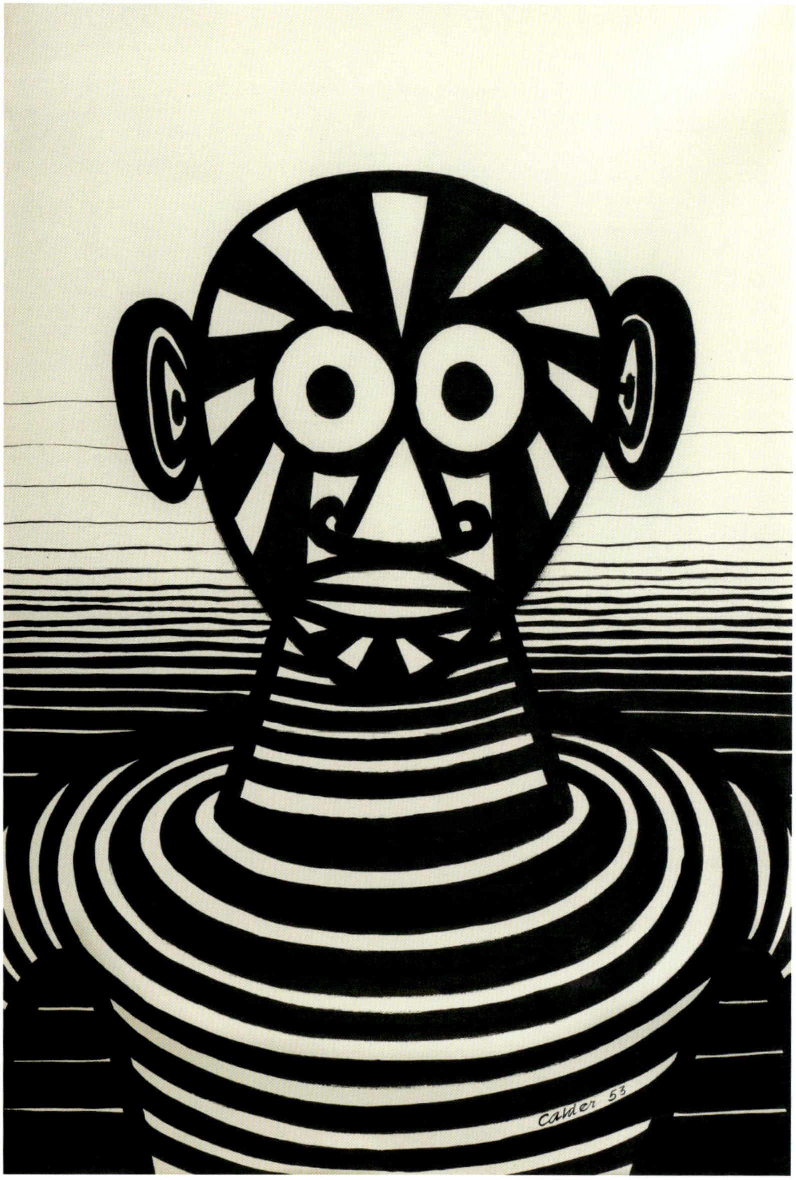

Alexander Calder, *Striped Man, Striped Sweater*, 1953 — gouache on paper — 108 × 73 cm

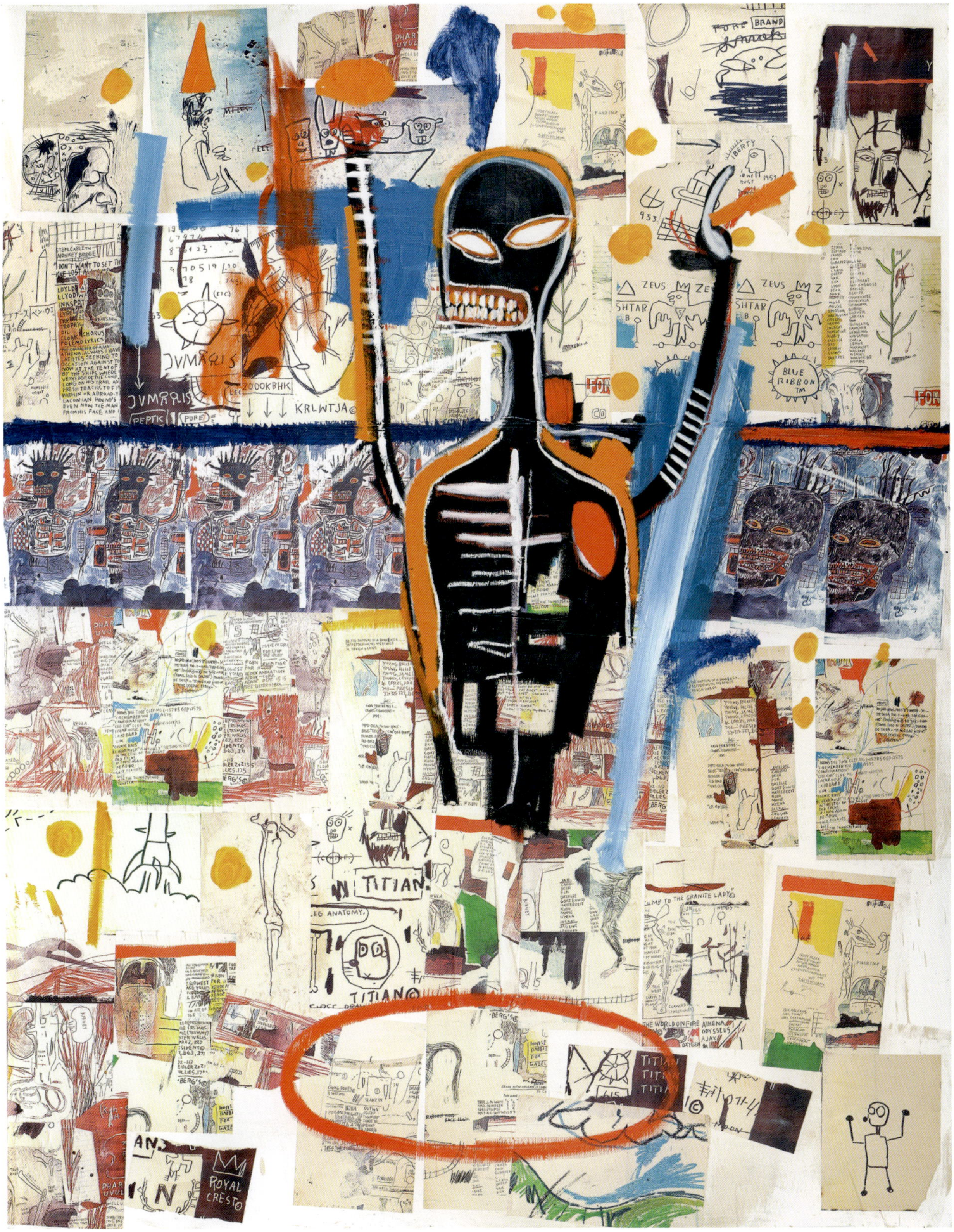

Jean-Michel Basquiat, *Untitled*, 1985 — acrylic paint and printed paper pasted on canvas — 218.3 × 172.7 cm

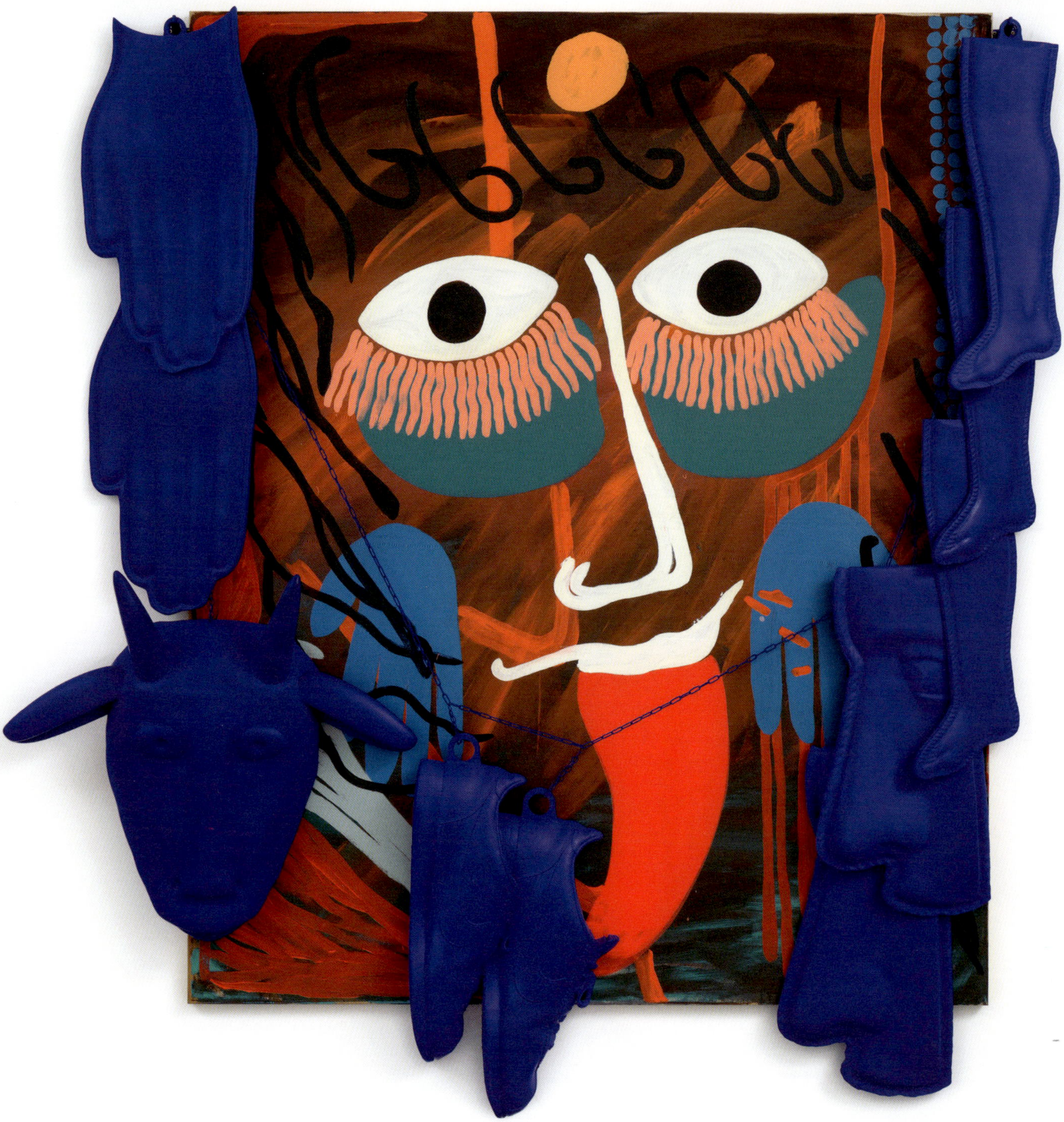

Jeremy Demester, *Kali*, 2022 — oil and acrylic on canvas, resin, and steel — 268 × 255 × 31 cm

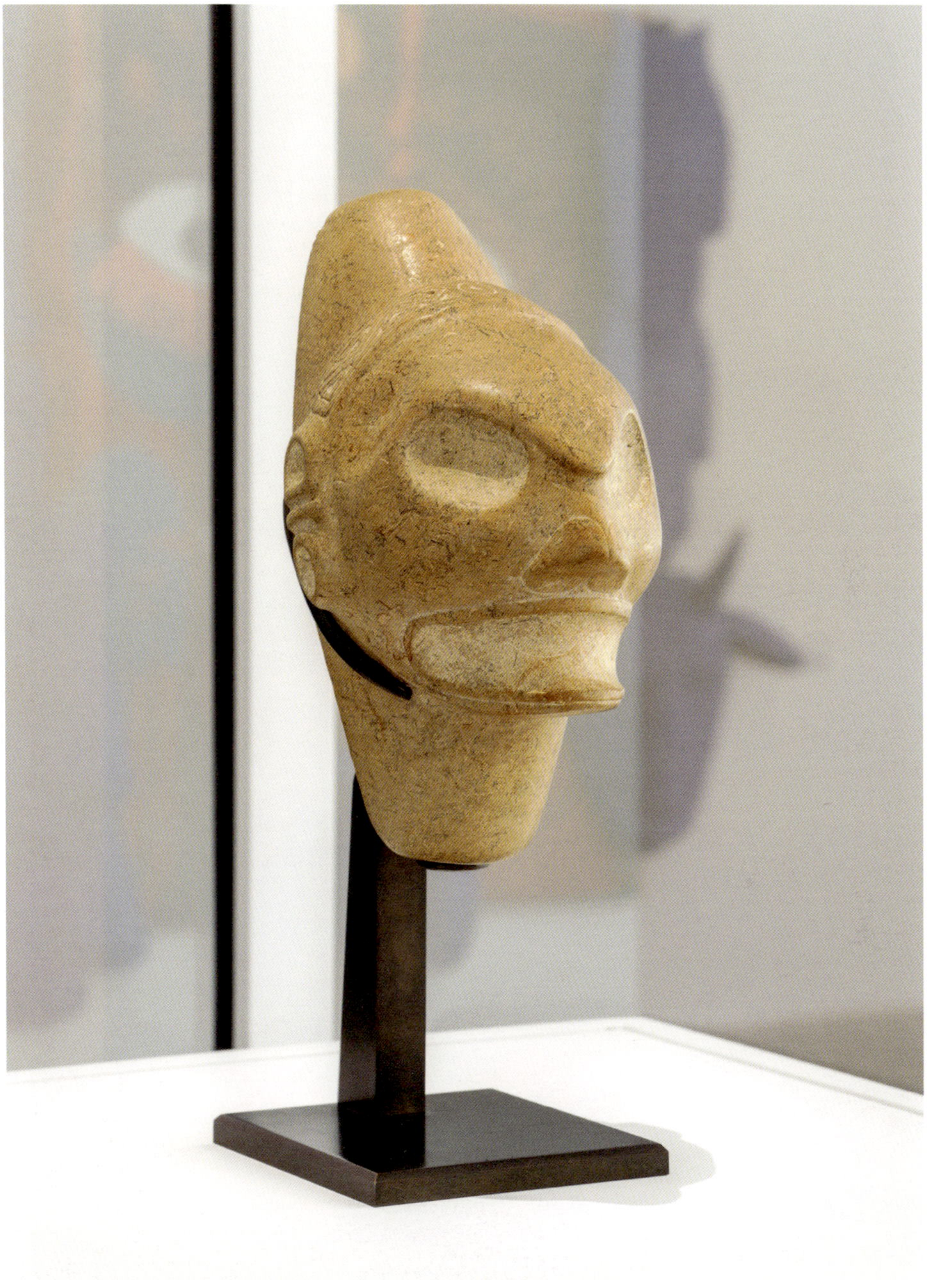

Anthropomorphic sculpture of a skull with schematised features effigy of the deity Zemi,
Dominican Republic, 1200–1450 AD — Beige fossiliferous limestone — 23 × 12 × 12.3 cm

Edgar Sarin, *Variation sur celui du Lararium*, 2023 — solid oak stained with olive oil — 70 × 45 × 14 cm

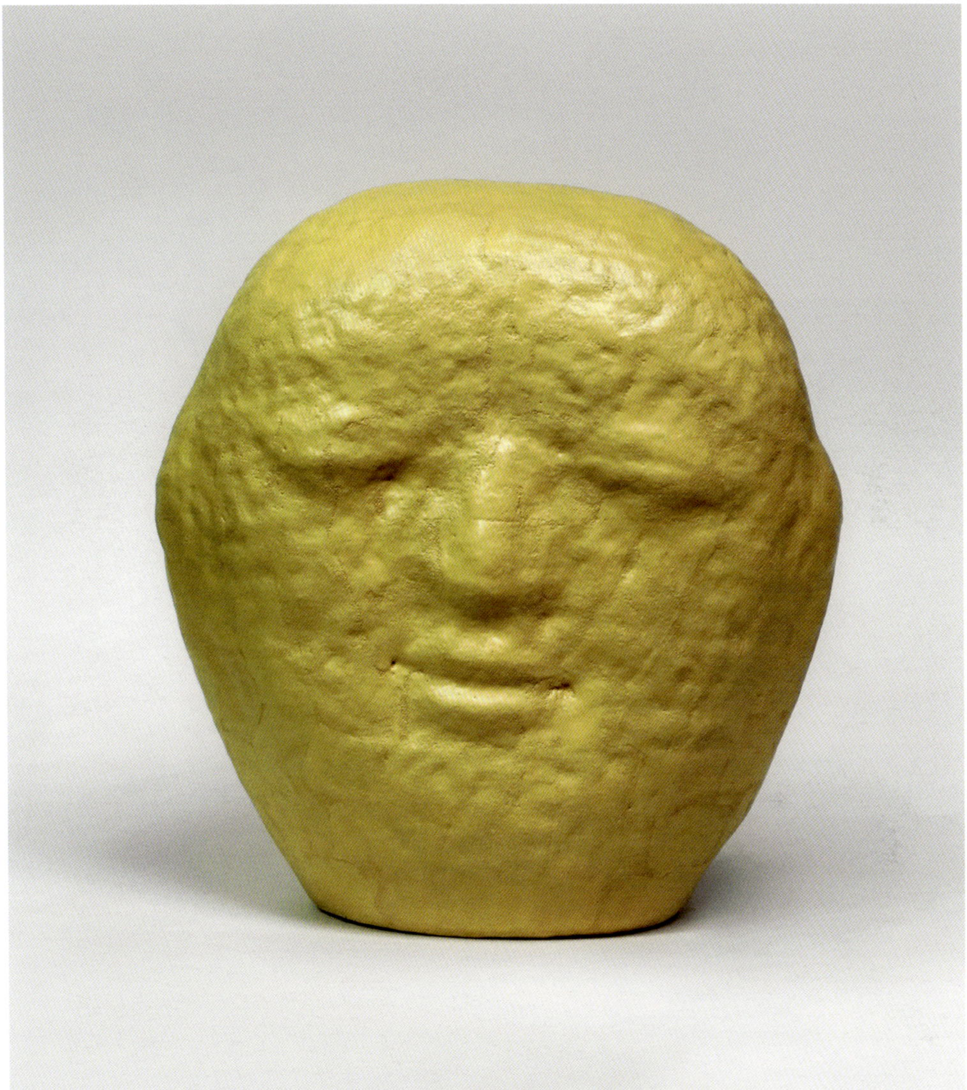

Corentin Grossmann, *Pentagouet jaune*, 2023 — glazed earthenware — 33 × 30 × 16 cm

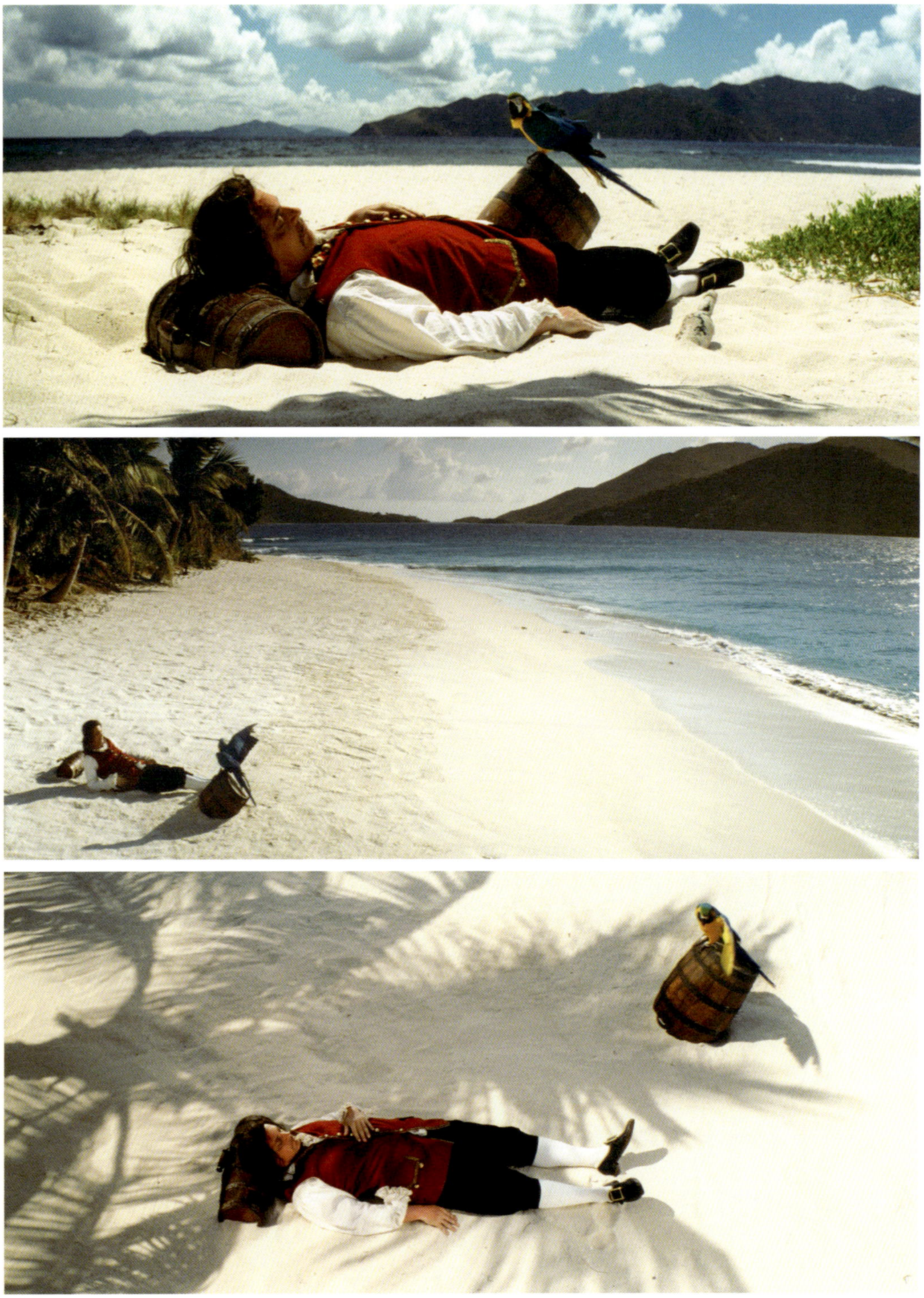

Rodney Graham, *Vexation Island*, 1997 — 35mm film, digitalised — 9' in loop

THE LOOP OF DEEP WATERS

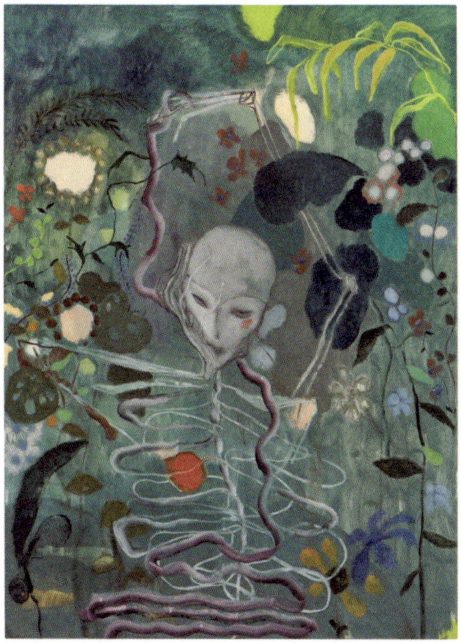

SANYA KANTAROVSKY,
Vagus, 2022, oil on canvas,
190.6 × 139.8 cm

JMG In the beginning, there are landscapes and bodies, landscapes within bodies, a tangled web of situations of the kind that dreams are good at creating. It is hard to understand what constitutes interior or exterior. The eyes are now blinded by a solar light, now plunged into the darkness of the ocean's depths or the heart of the night. One moon, two moons, three moons watch over worlds in which humans are often absent. Sea and mountain merge like the collisions of seasons. From time to time, animals and plants build empires and indulge in rituals. Within this inner island, the eye is invited to roam and lead the rest of the body along for the ride.

YCT What would the ultimate island be? An invisible island, which would not be on any map? Which would emerge then disappear under the water, flickering on the sea's surface? Which would elusively shift? In *Earthsea*, Ursula K. Le Guin's adventure saga, a character in search of the absolute arrives, after traversing several islands and experiencing a series of journeys, within a community living on rafts that form an archipelago of precarious habitats – a floating world set adrift. The character sees freedom in this, a hideout. The absolute horde. But it's not enough for him. So he dives down and goes to look further on. At the bottom of the ocean, he reaches the *ultimate shore*. That might be what we see, inside, when we seek the crystalline island, the absolute elsewhere? A polychrome island-droplet in the form of a cosmic egg like Mark Bradford's *The Loop of Deep Waters*? Or a swarm of fish becoming-water, becoming-machine, becoming-constellation, becoming-island, as in Bruce Nauman's artwork?

JMG *The Loop of Deep Waters* is also a way of returning to the surface, of drawing closer to the mysterious hook that holds this deformed globe through an alternative gravity, an overly heavy weight. Do artists really have a power over the world? Their effect on the real is a kind of slow infusion. They are like scientists ahead of their time, insular mountaineers seeing what we don't yet see. The sleepers in the exhibition are none other than these bodies awaiting revelation, in deep waters. The rooms of the foundation dug under the earth offer a space sheltered from the blinding light of day, they enable the confrontation with these works without place or time, with these characters withdrawn from the world, and these wise or enraged figures. Conversations are sparked. Have we ever seen an iceberg in the Mediterranean Sea, one hundred fish spitting water from their bodies, gulls writing in the sky, and a sleeper blending in with their couch? The melancholy of these visions form enigmatic contemporary vanitas at the heart of Porquerolles. But as soon as we cross the threshold, the eye adjusts to the perception of the material with Pia Krajewski and Janaina Mello Landini's rope, which dissolved itself into a multitude of rhizomes, becoming a solid ramp once again in its ascent to return to the surface, take another breath, rediscover sea spray and fragrant eucalyptus. Then the exploration of the gardens can begin, where you will notably discover a mysterious and musical fruit by Antoine Espinasseau, the fantastic creatures of Corentin Grossmann, a shipwrecked pirate coveting a coconut, famous olives, and a few other well-hidden secrets. Then it is the entire island that you must discover or come back to see, and that each one of you will – consciously or subconsciously – transform into your own inner island.

The night's regular beat
brings news not too different
from those of Caesar's times.
Down the coastline
there's always the sea.

ETEL ADNAN
Night, 2016

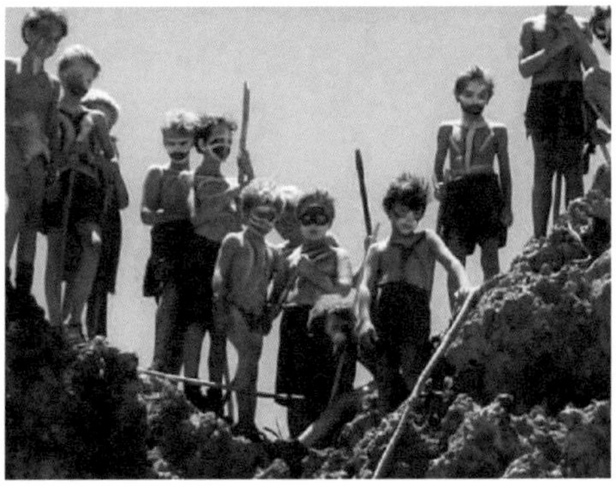

PETER BROOK (director), *Lord of the Flies* (1963)

Antoine Espinasseau, *Fruit*, 2023 — bronze, stainless steel, flowers — variable dimensions

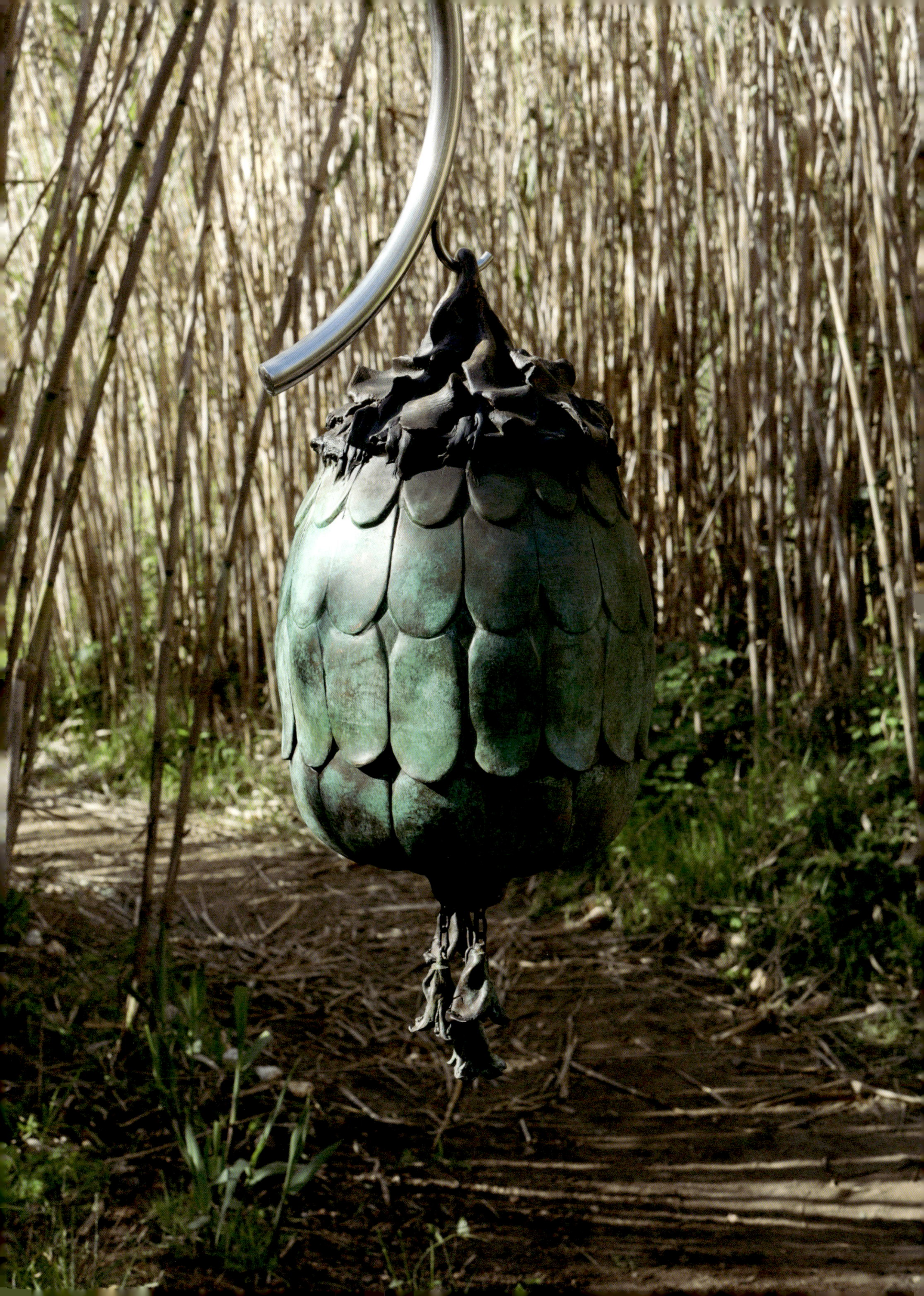

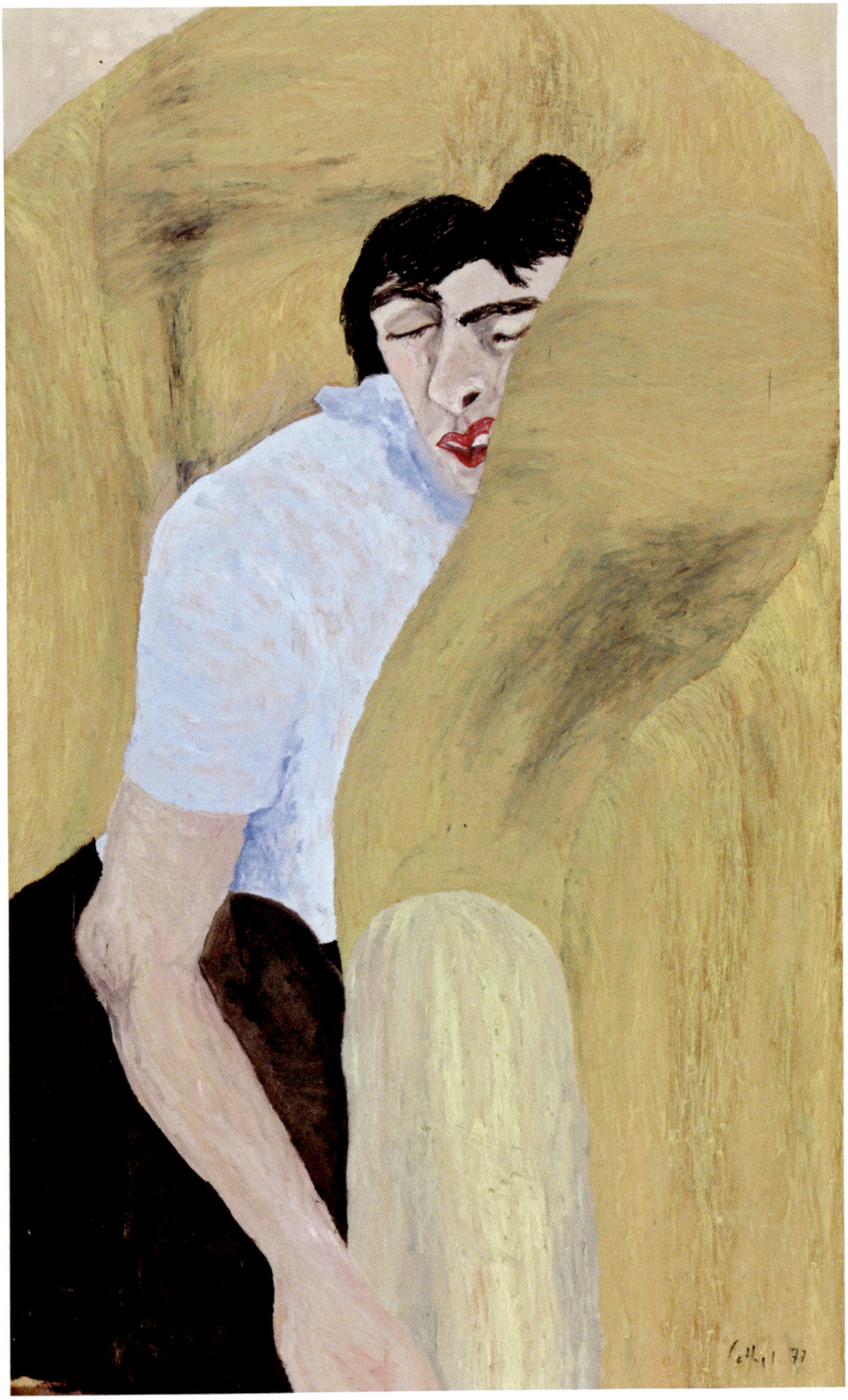

Cathy Josefowitz, *Portrait de Romain*, 1977 — charcoal, pastel, and gouache on paper mounted on board — 158 × 98 cm

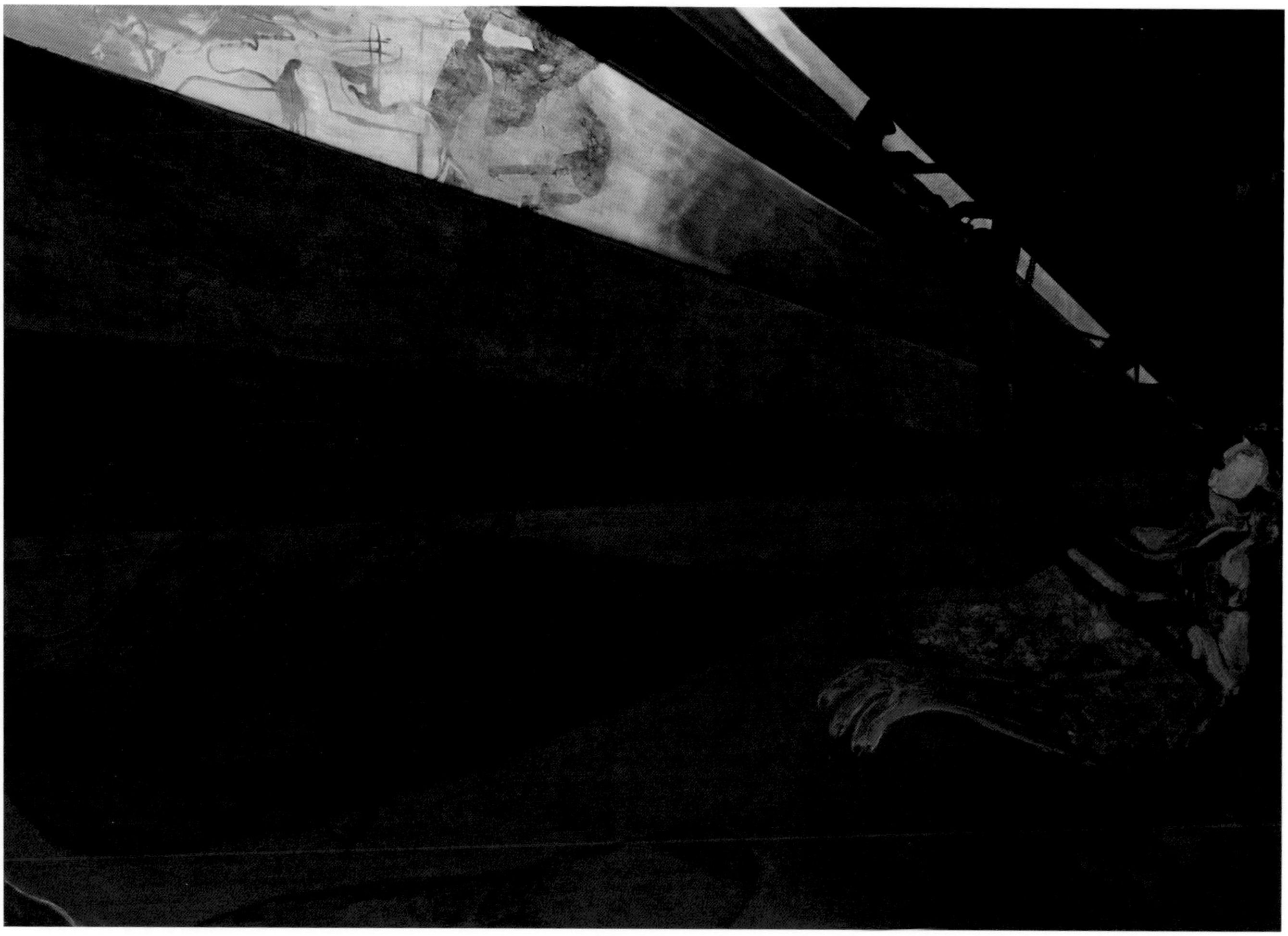

Tim Breuer, *Before Departure*, 2021 — oil on canvas on aluminium — 175 × 246 cm

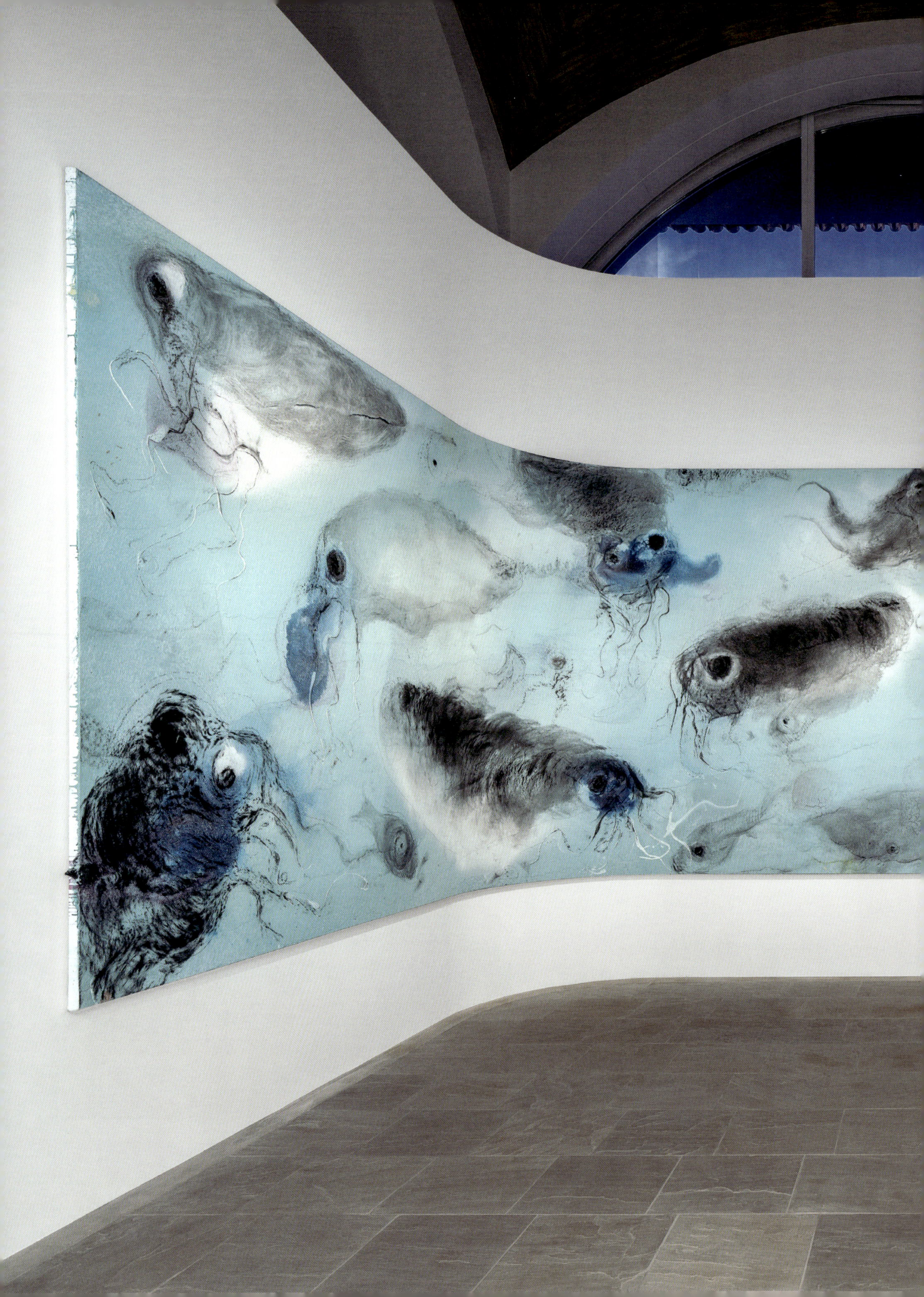

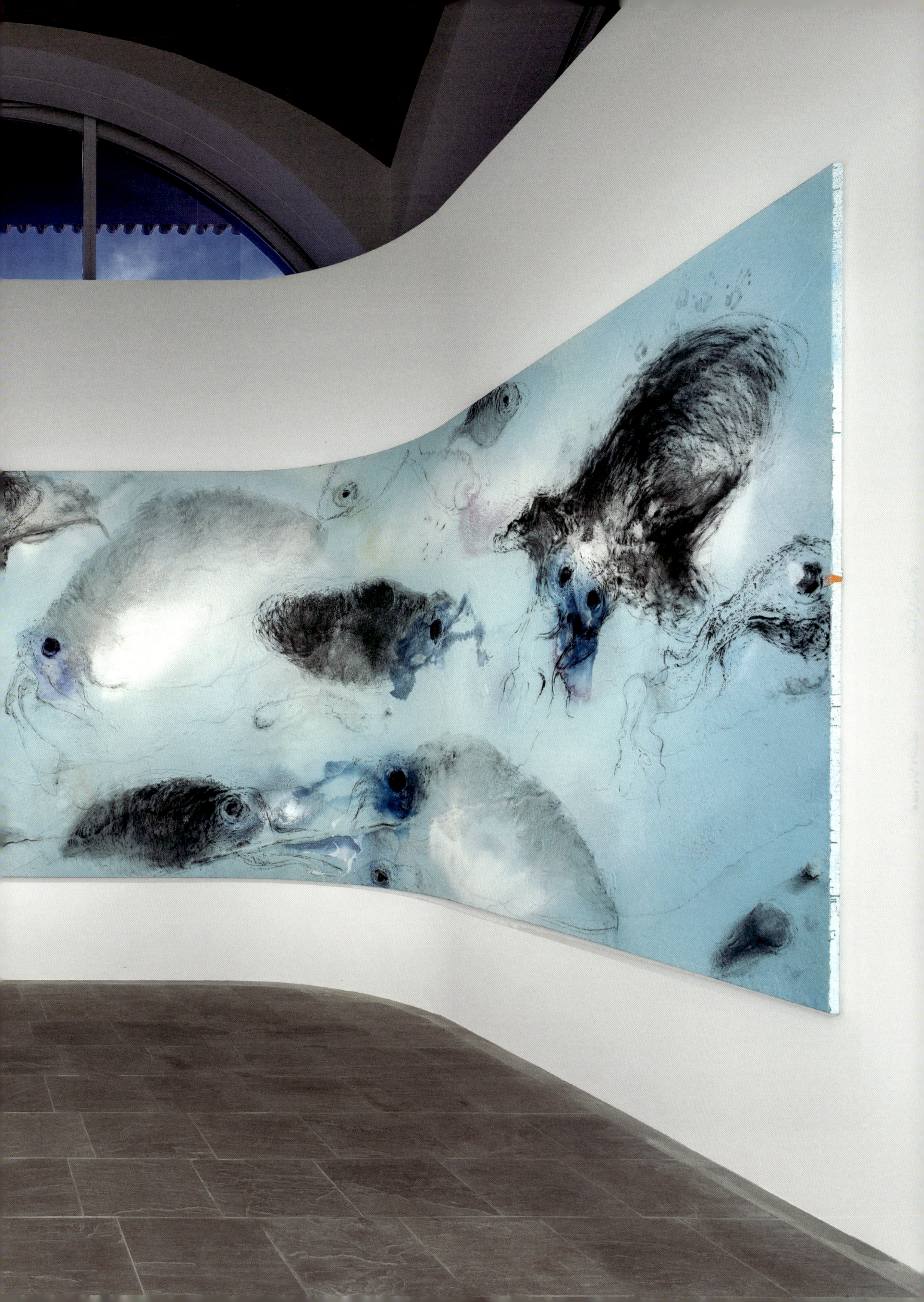

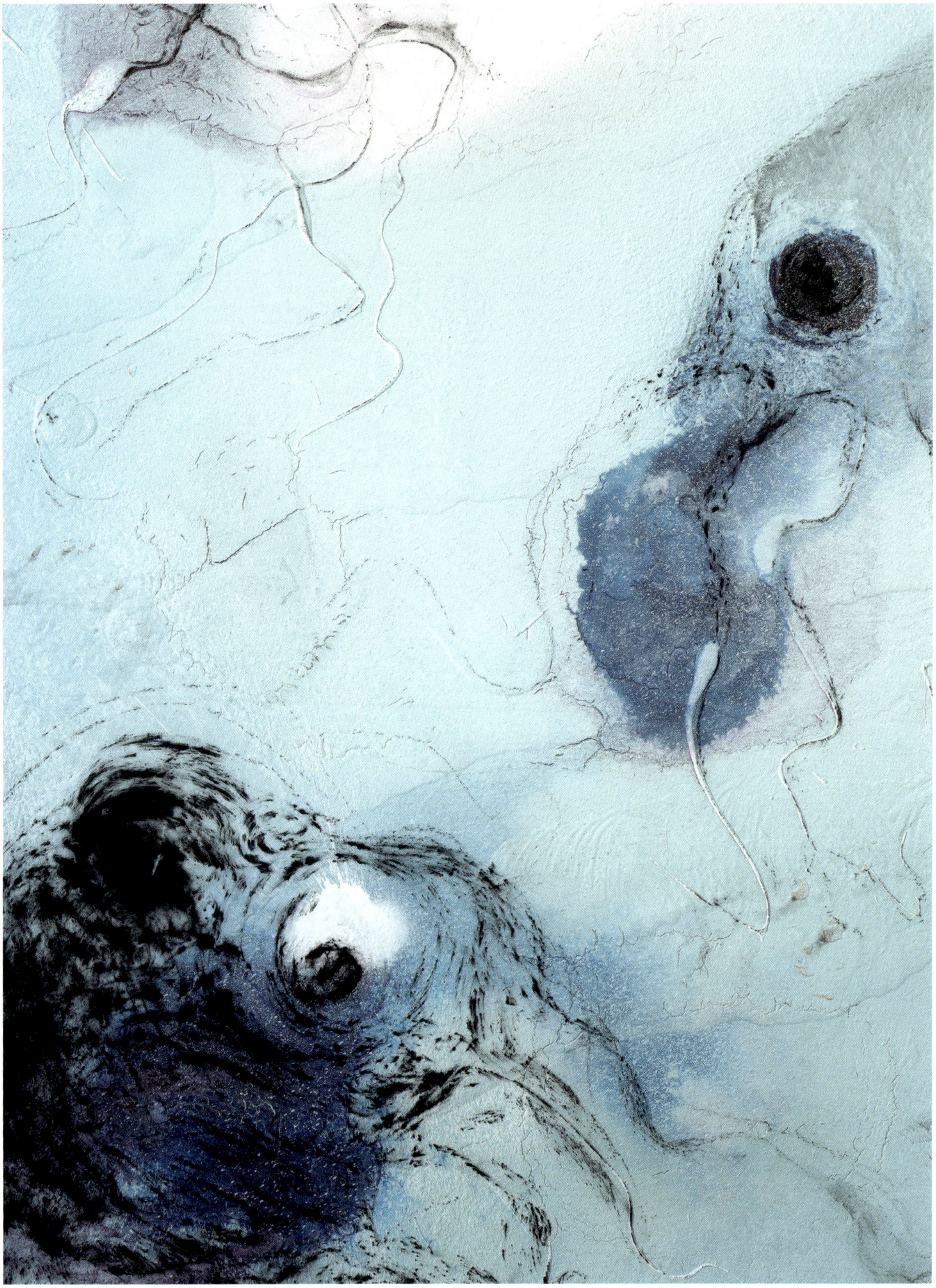

Miquel Barceló, *Not Yet Titled*, 2018 — polyester canvas stretched over a frame, acrylic plaster, gelatine bonding, pigments, and oil — 350 × 1500 cm

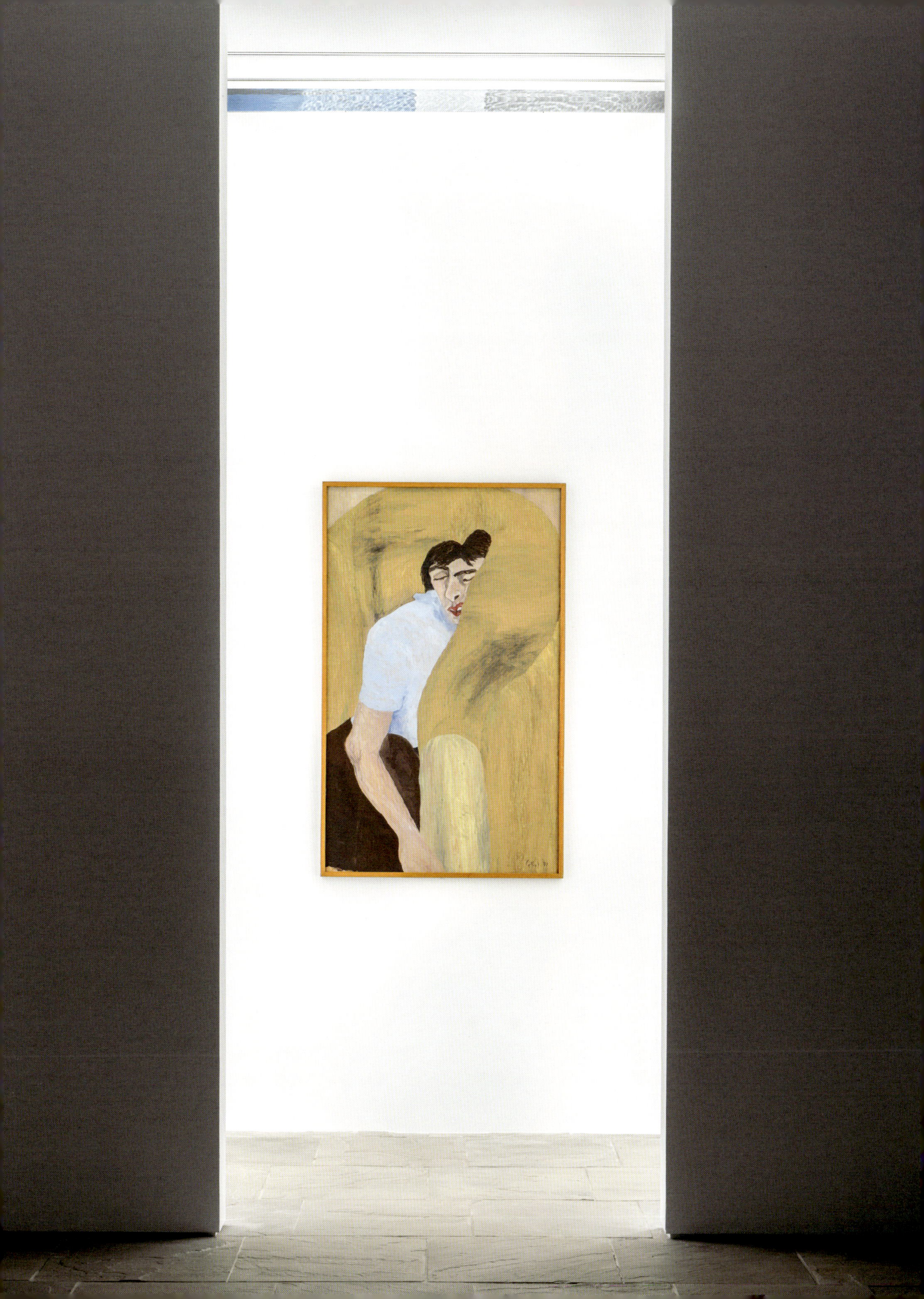

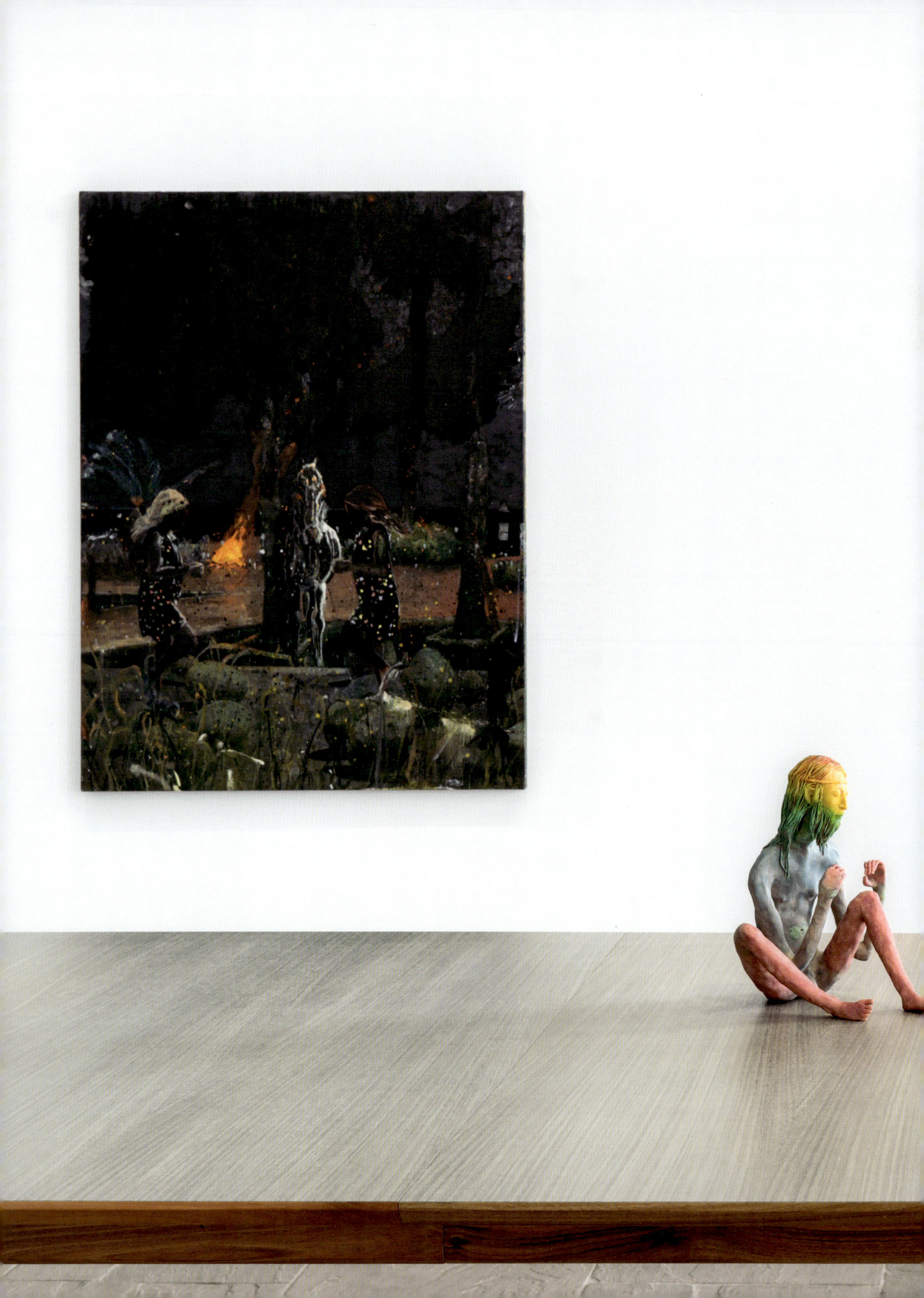

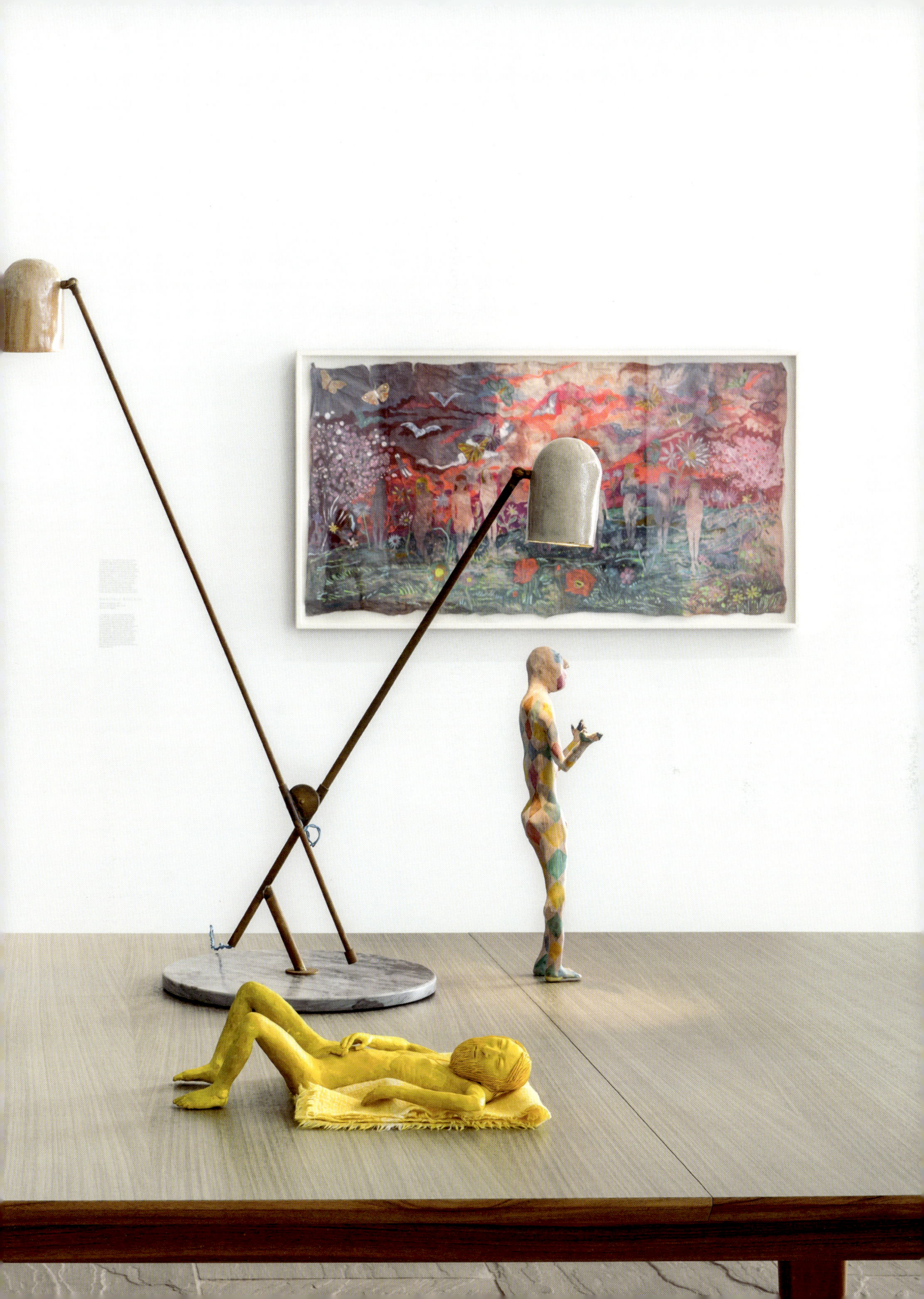

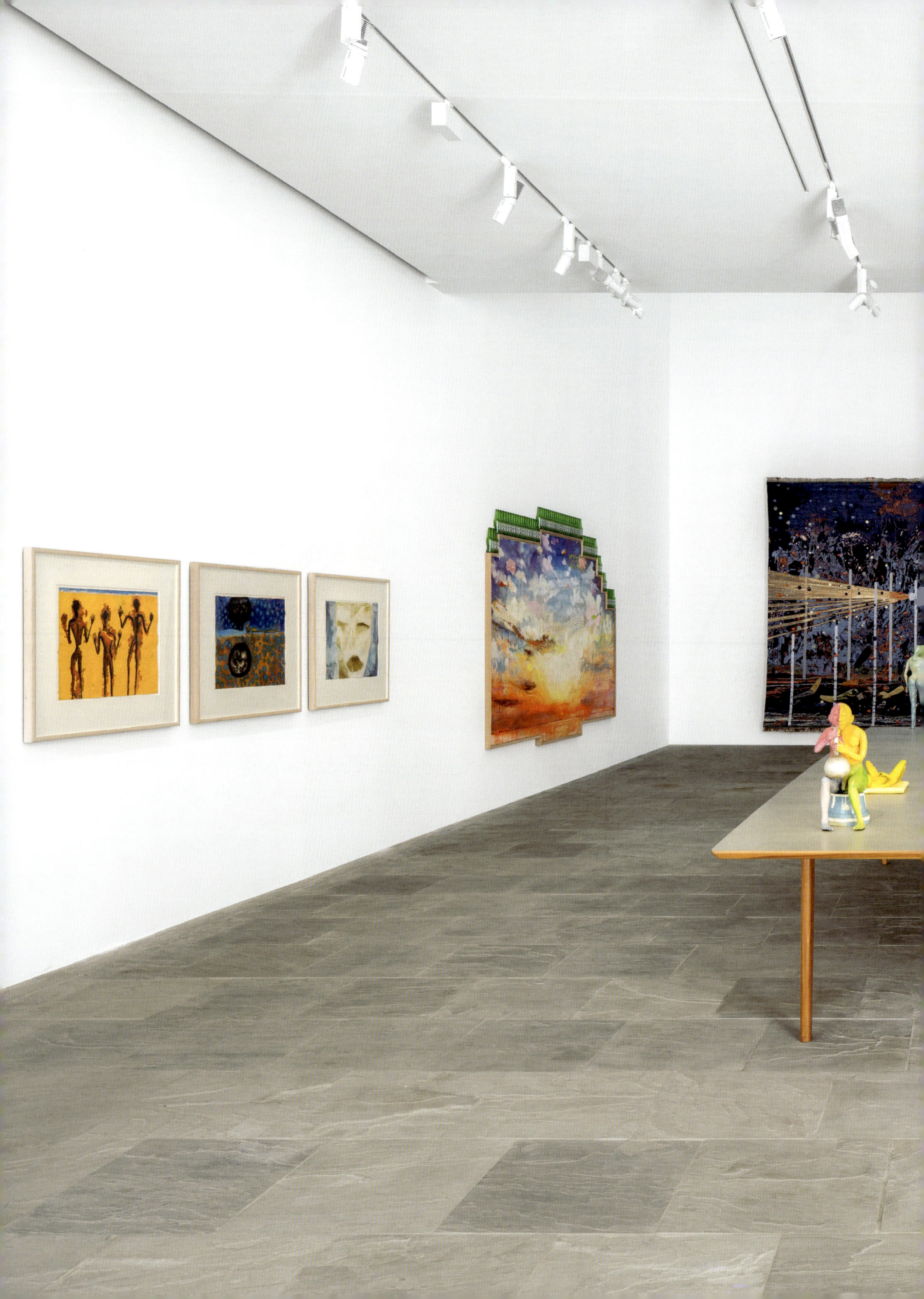

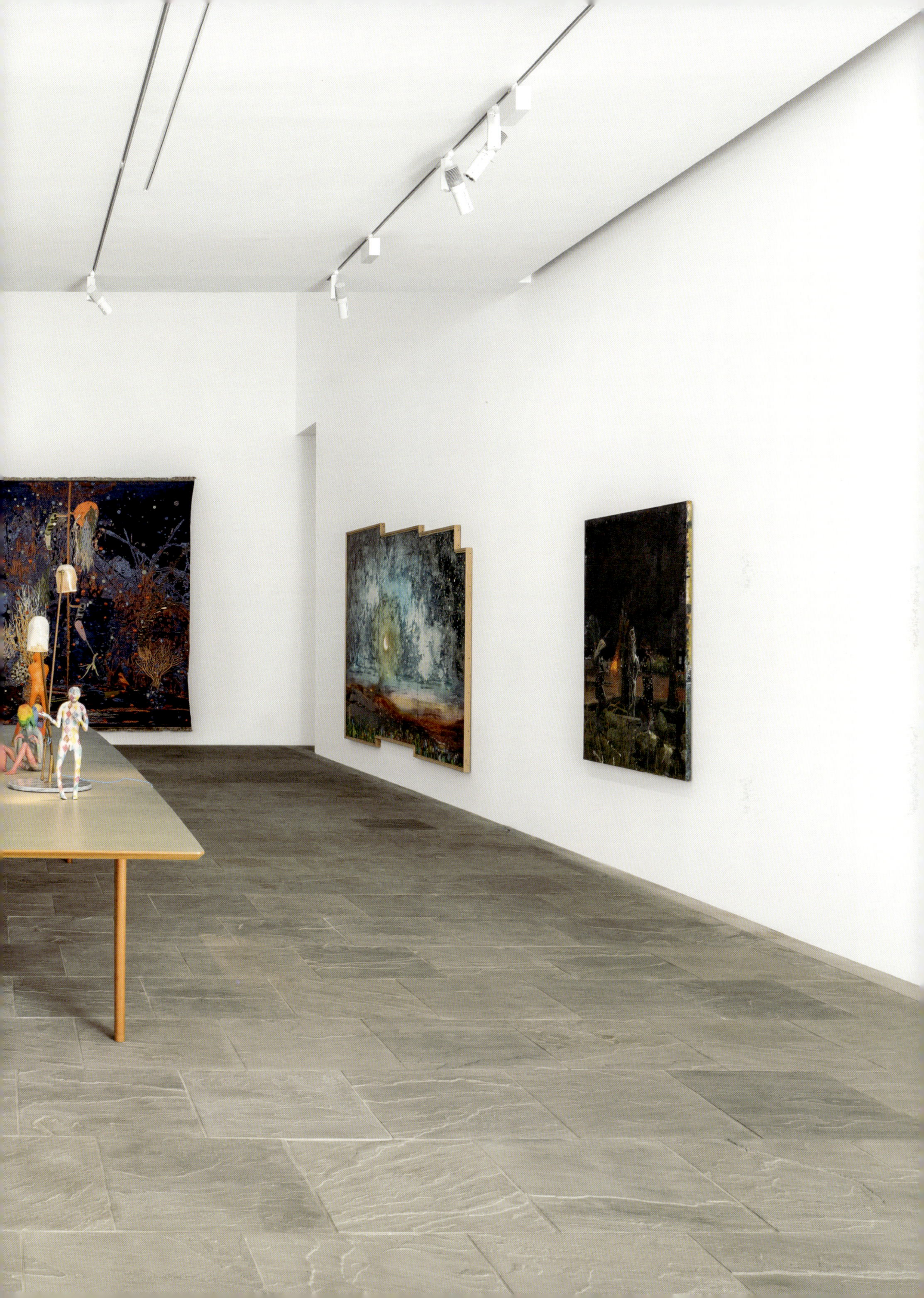

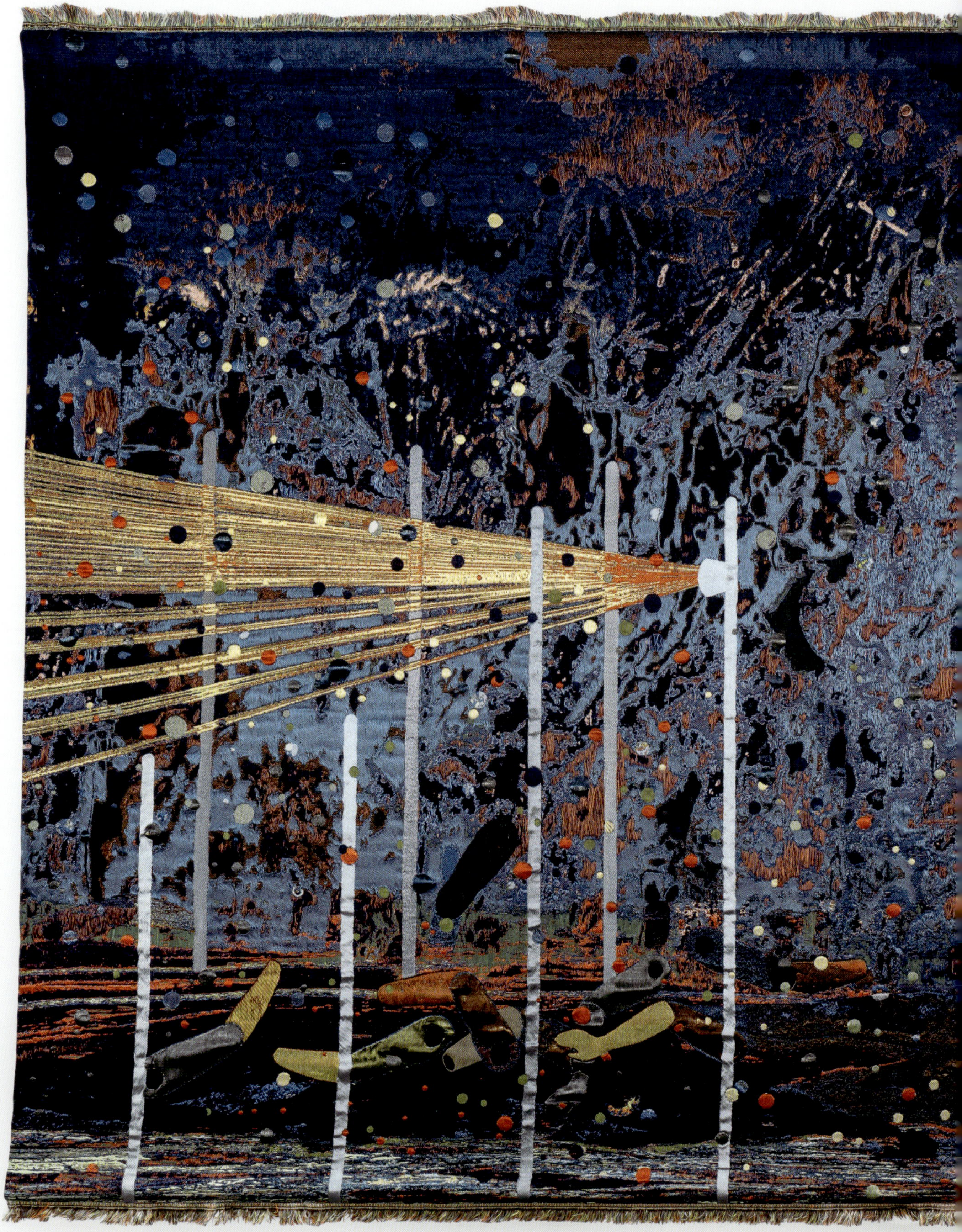

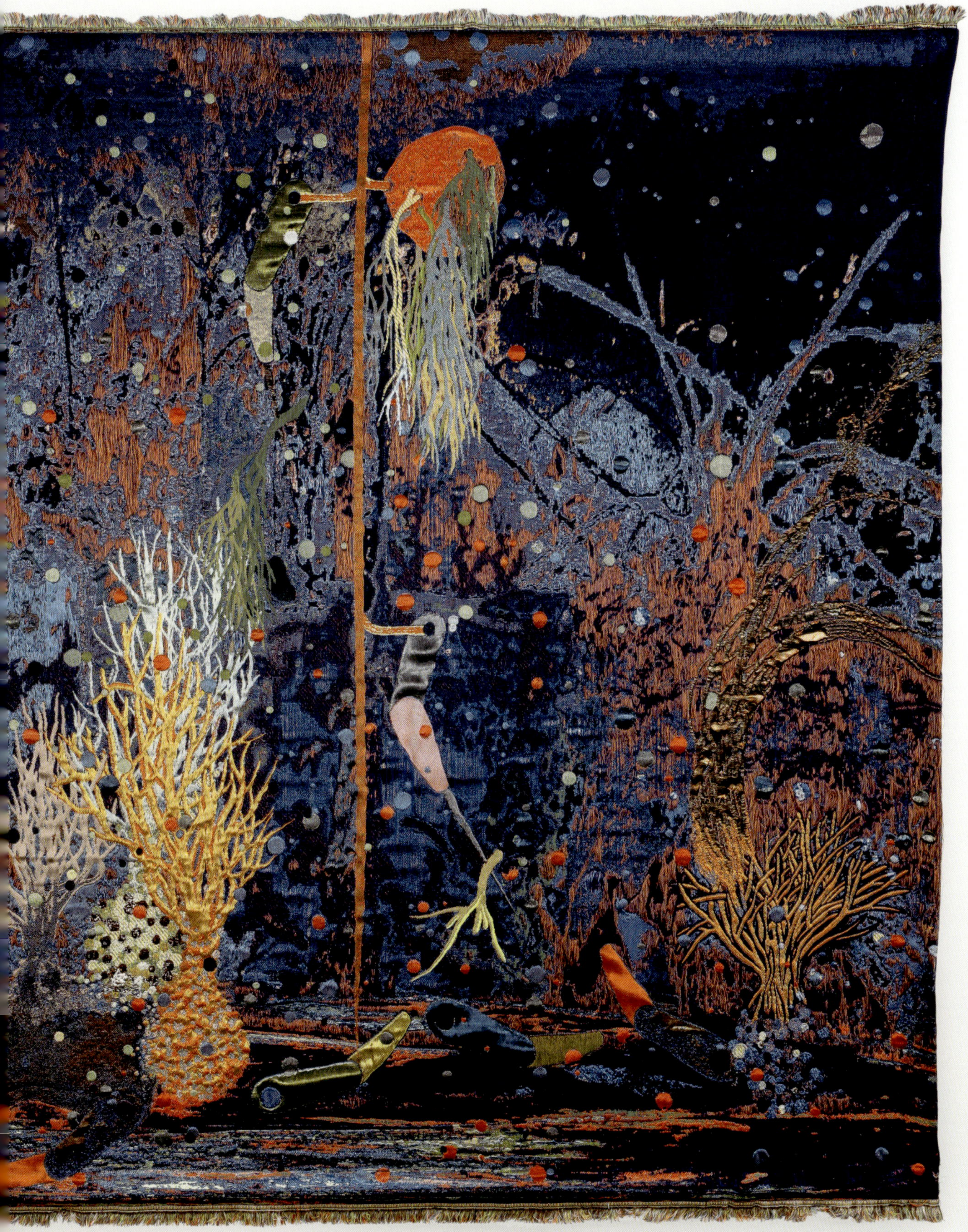

Otobong Nkanga, *Tied to the Other Side*, 2022 — woven tapestry — 350 × 600 cm

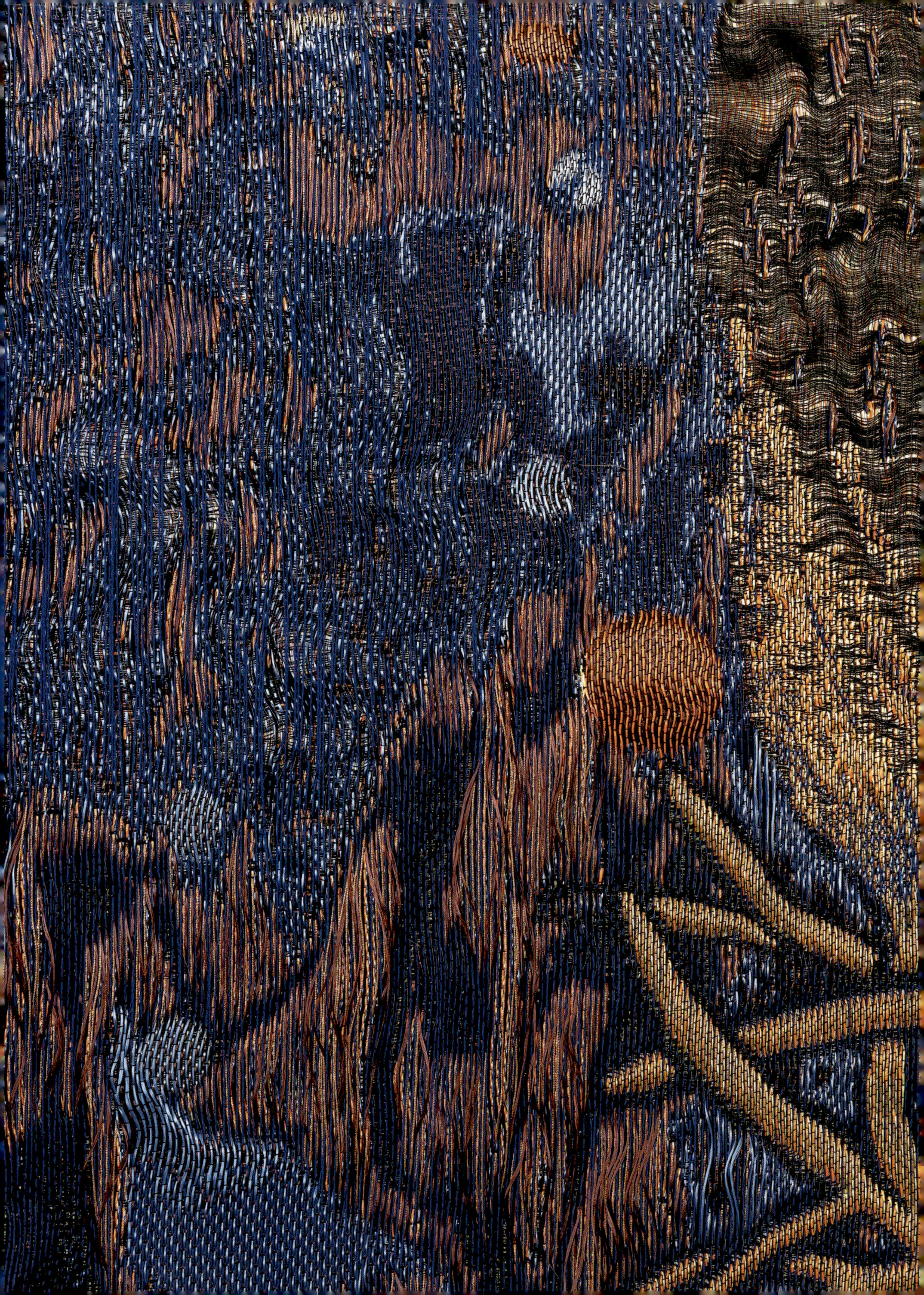

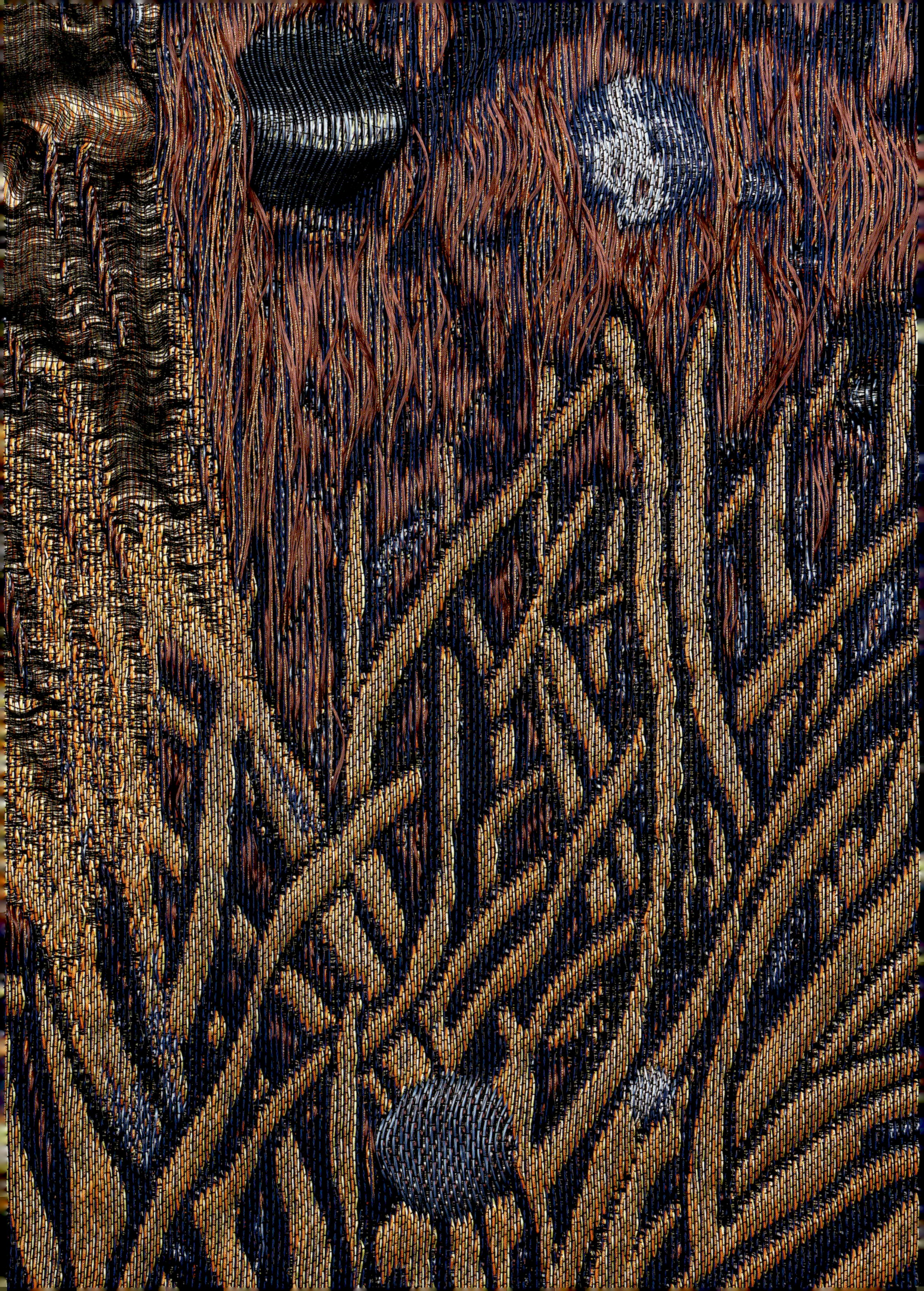

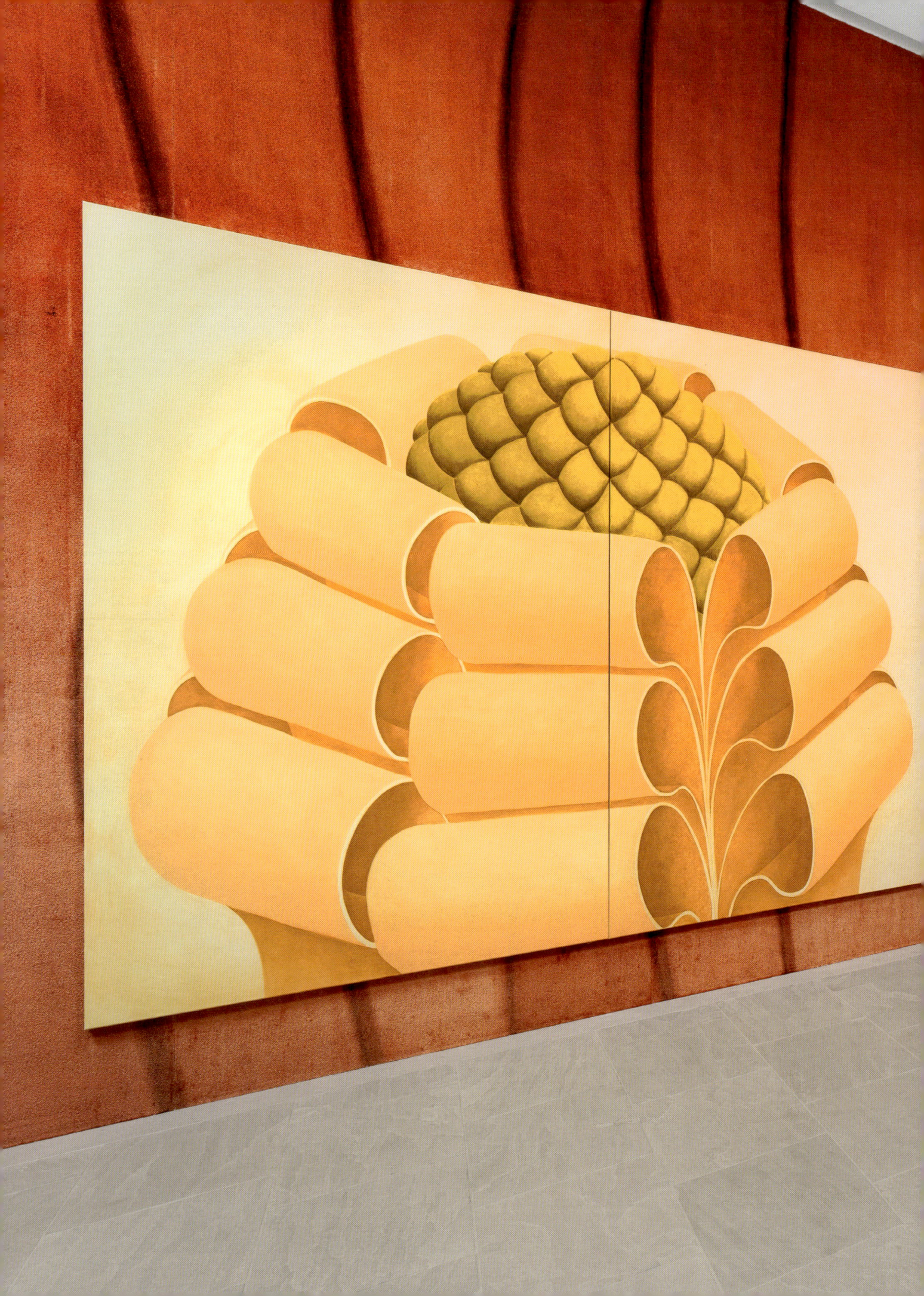

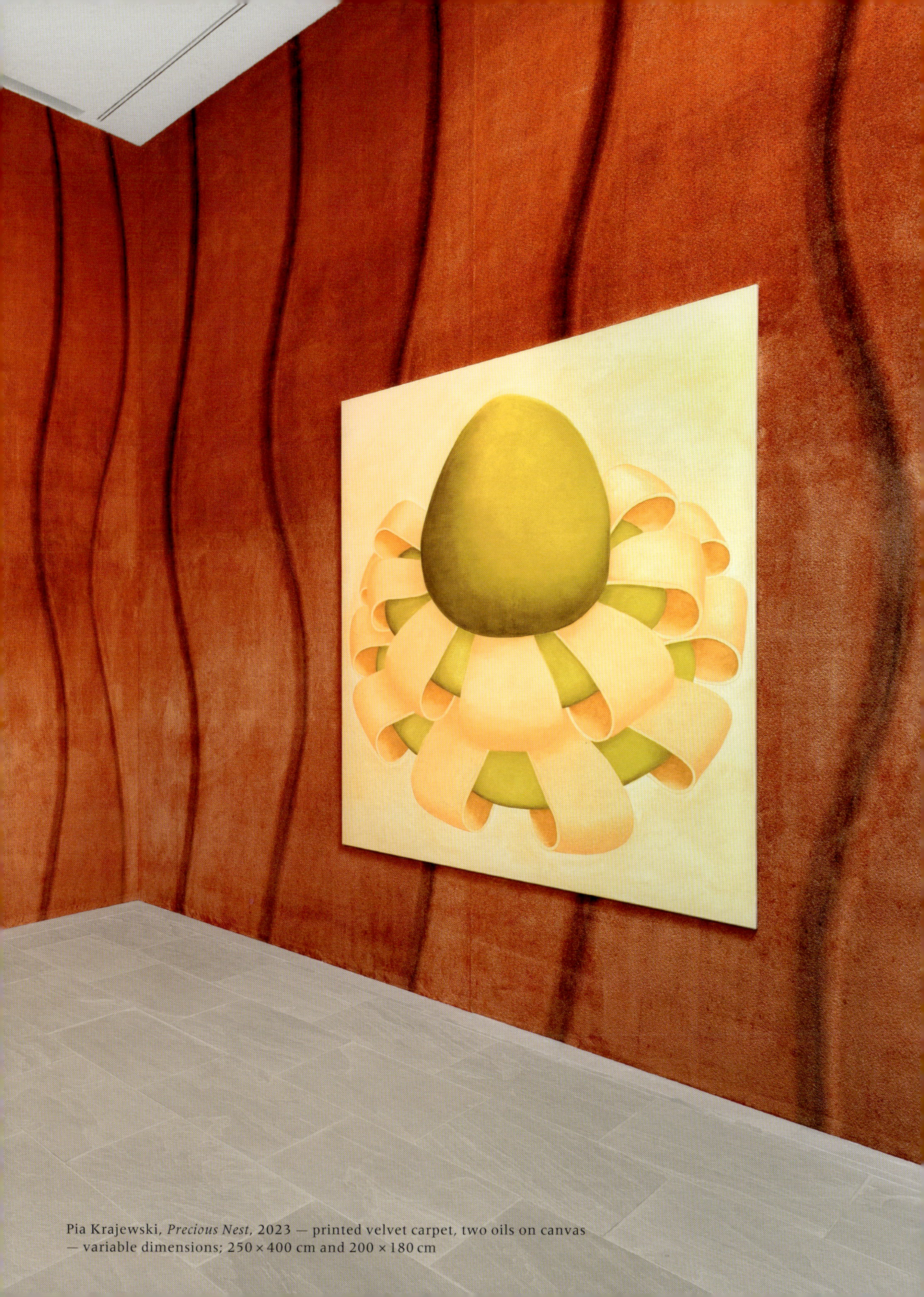

Pia Krajewski, *Precious Nest*, 2023 — printed velvet carpet, two oils on canvas — variable dimensions; 250 × 400 cm and 200 × 180 cm

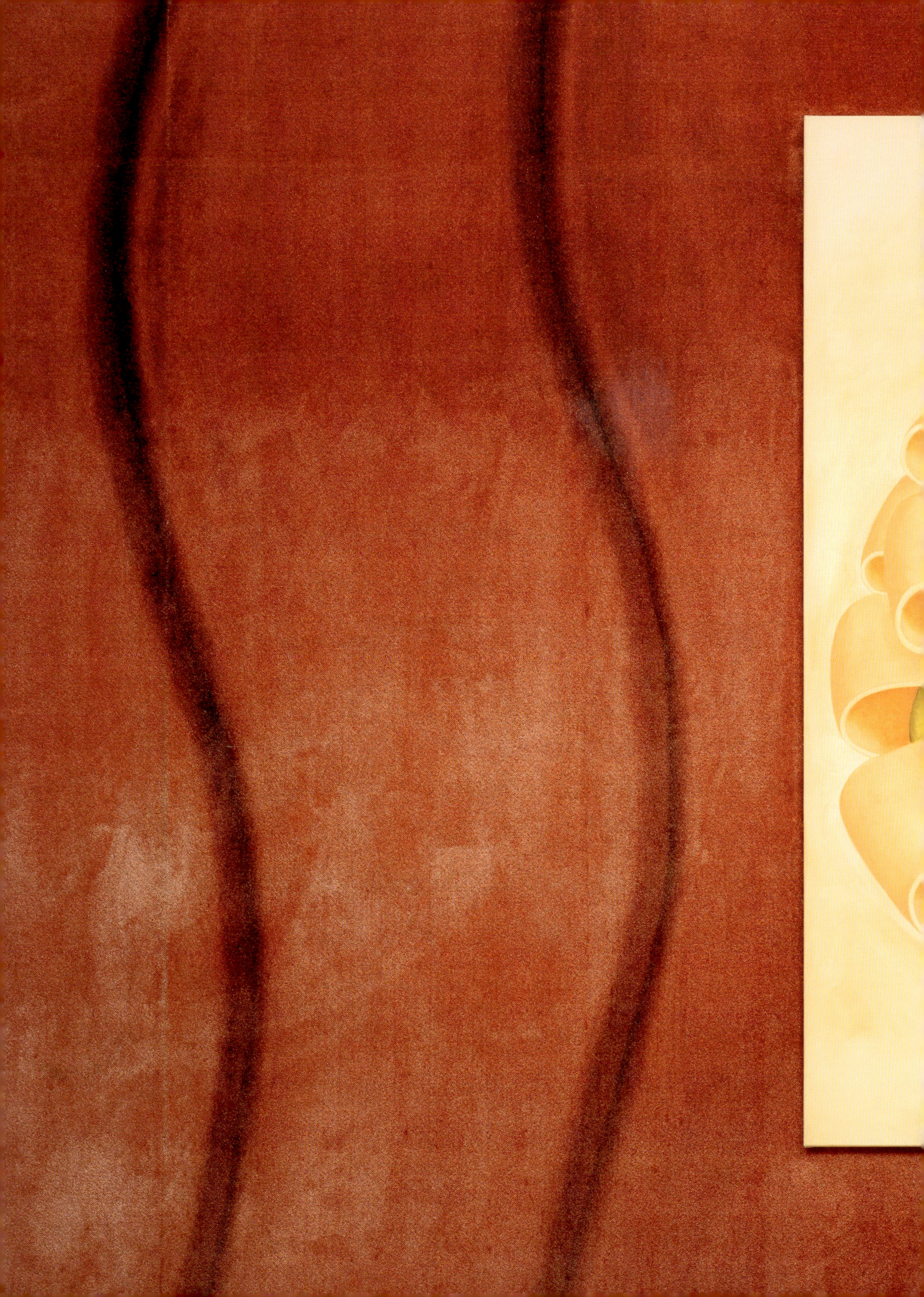

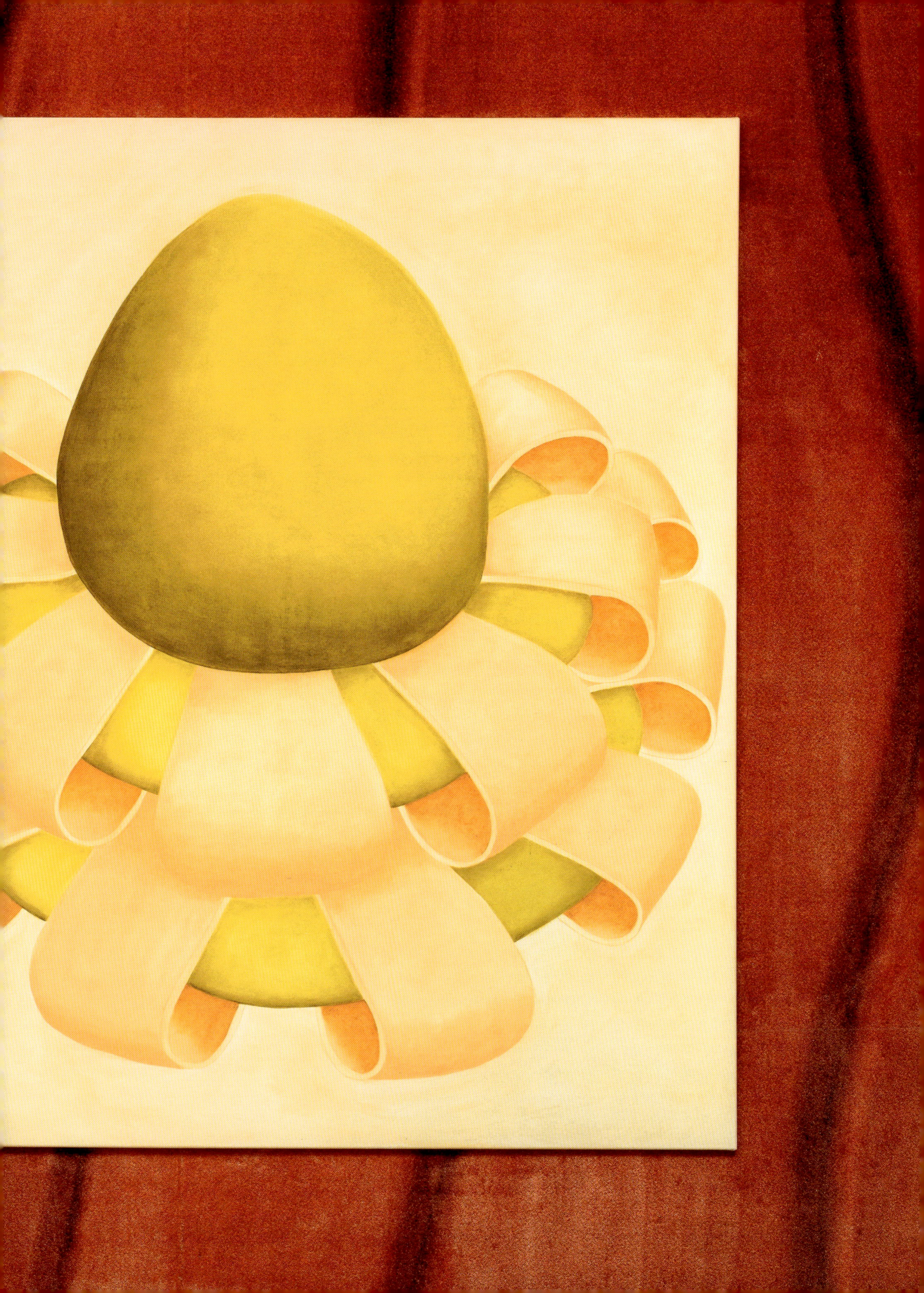

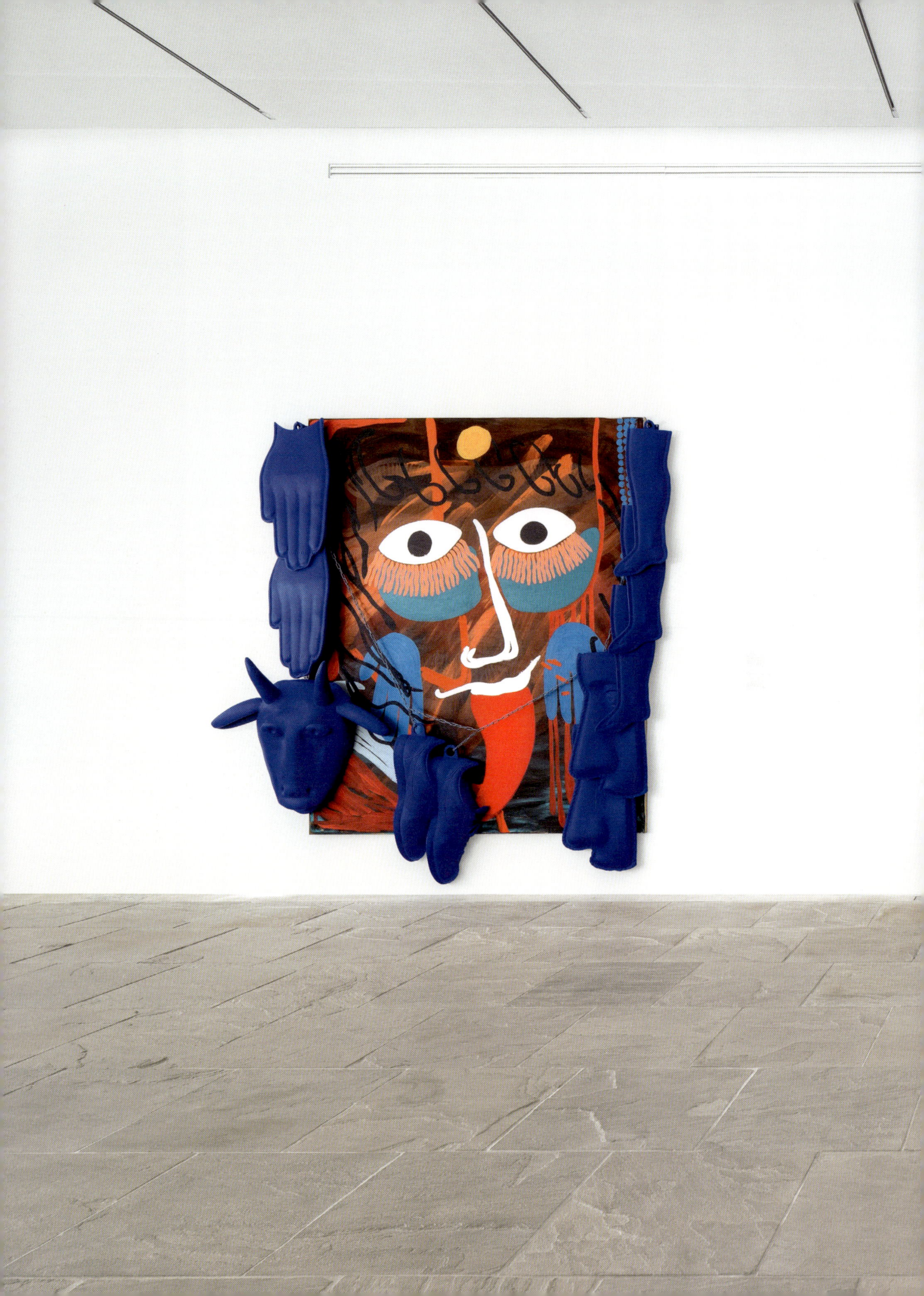

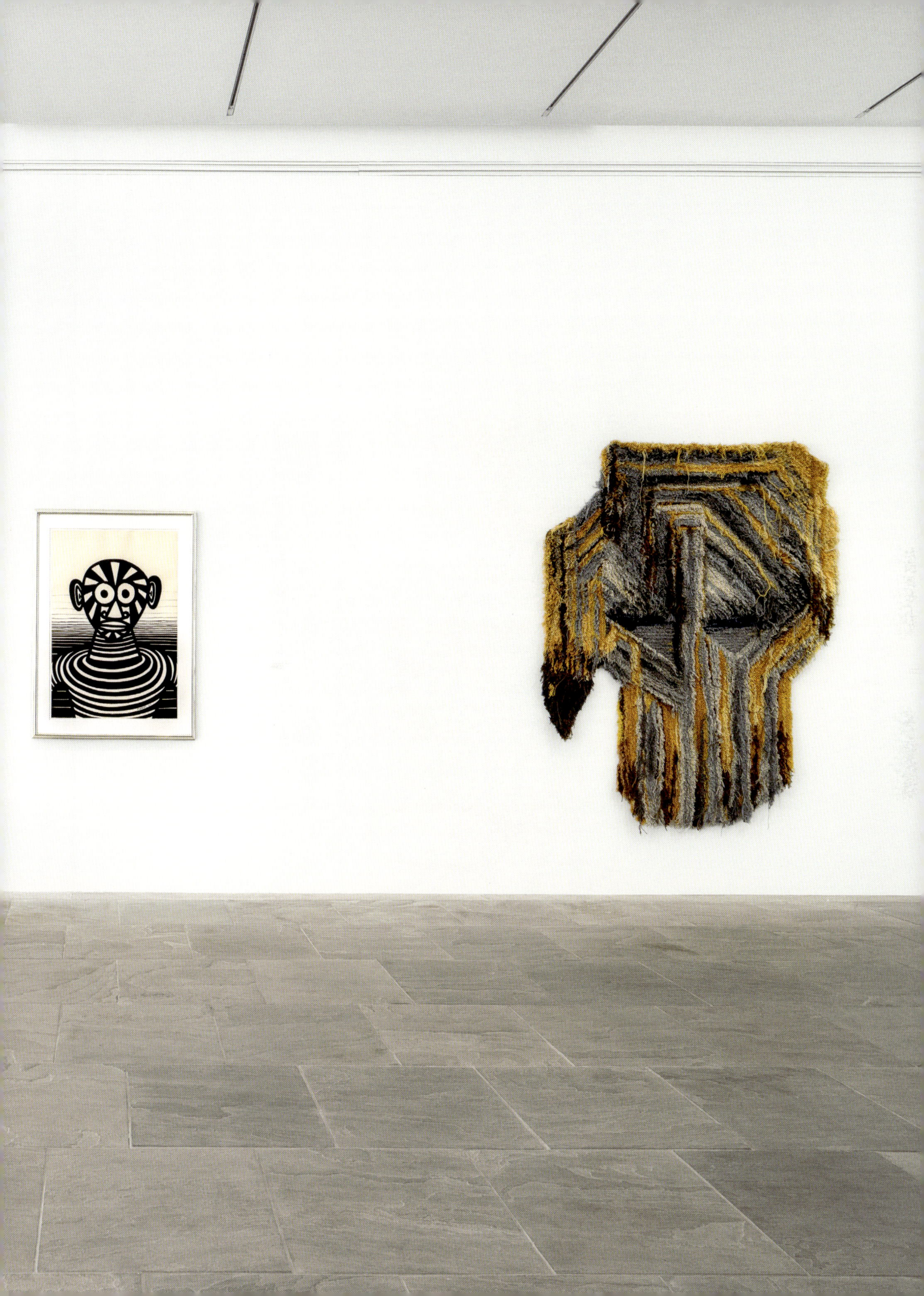

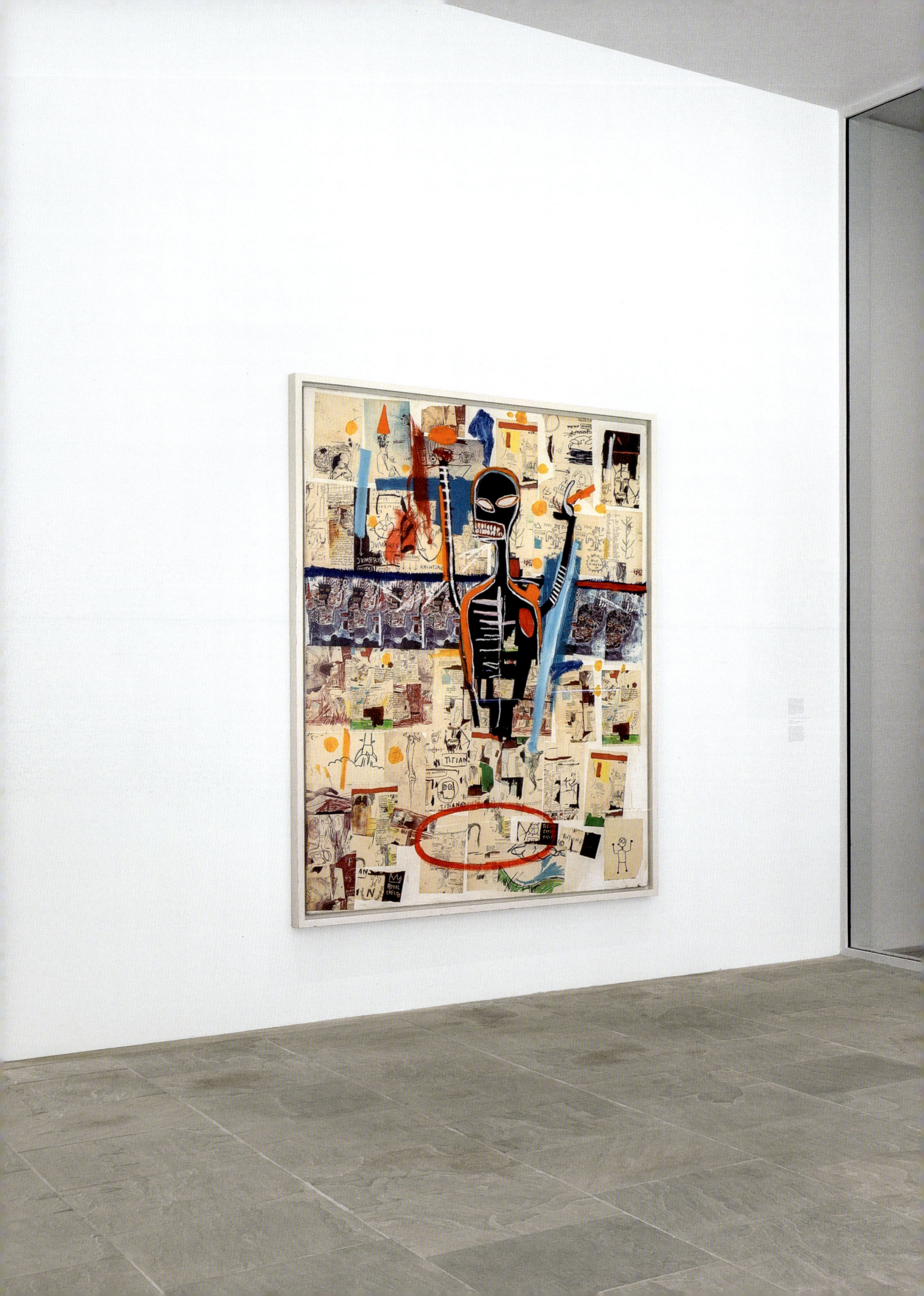
TITIAN

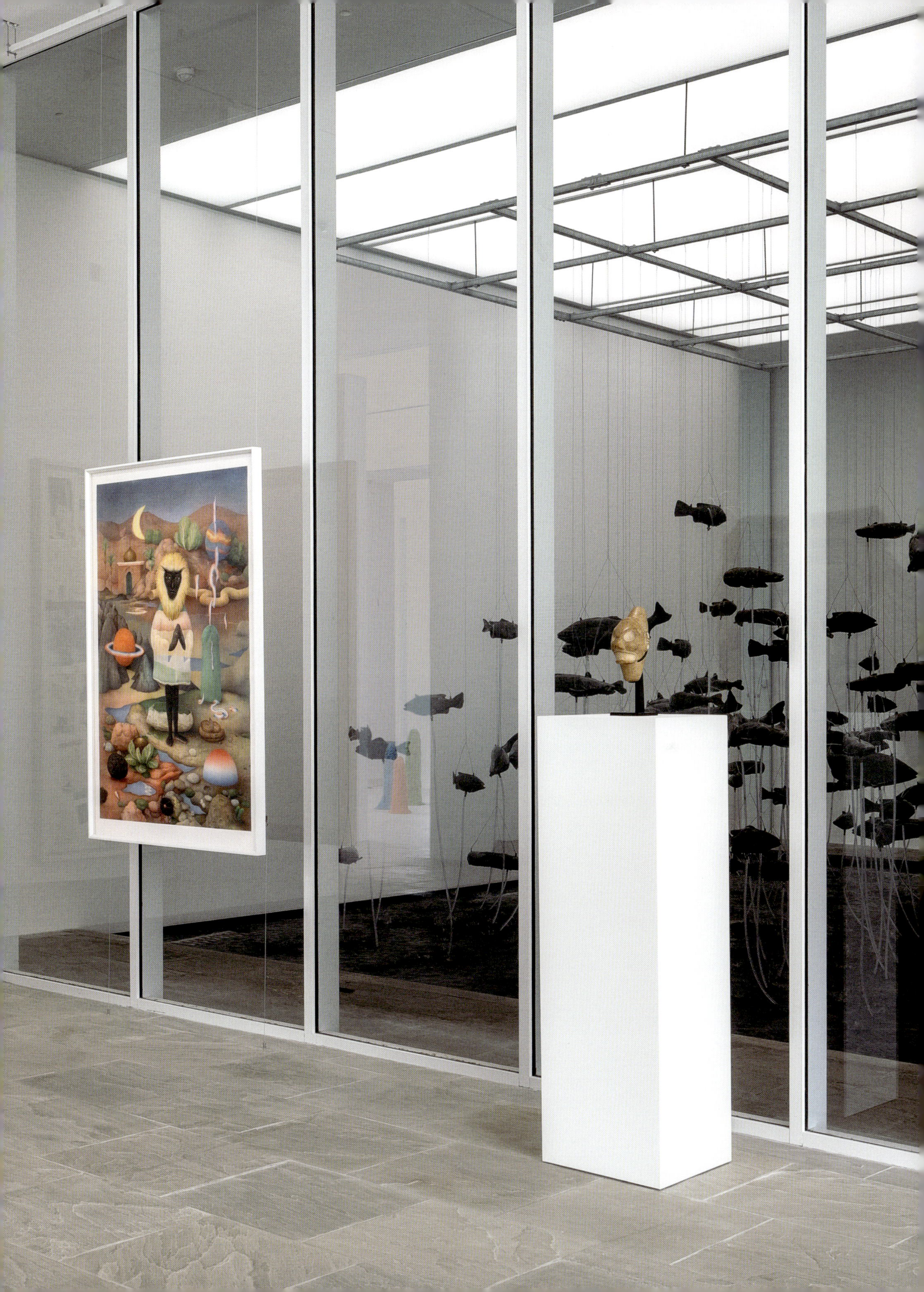

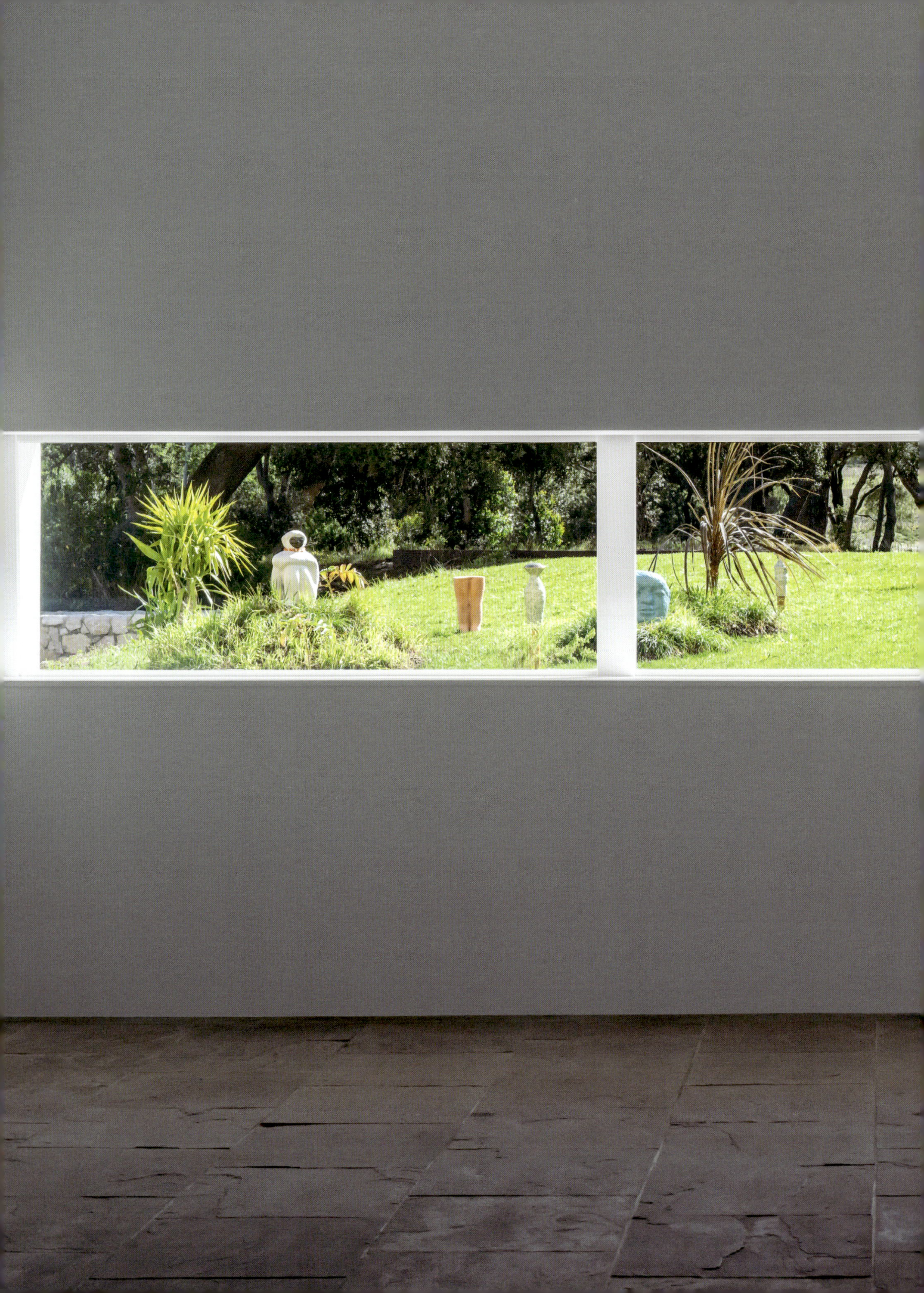

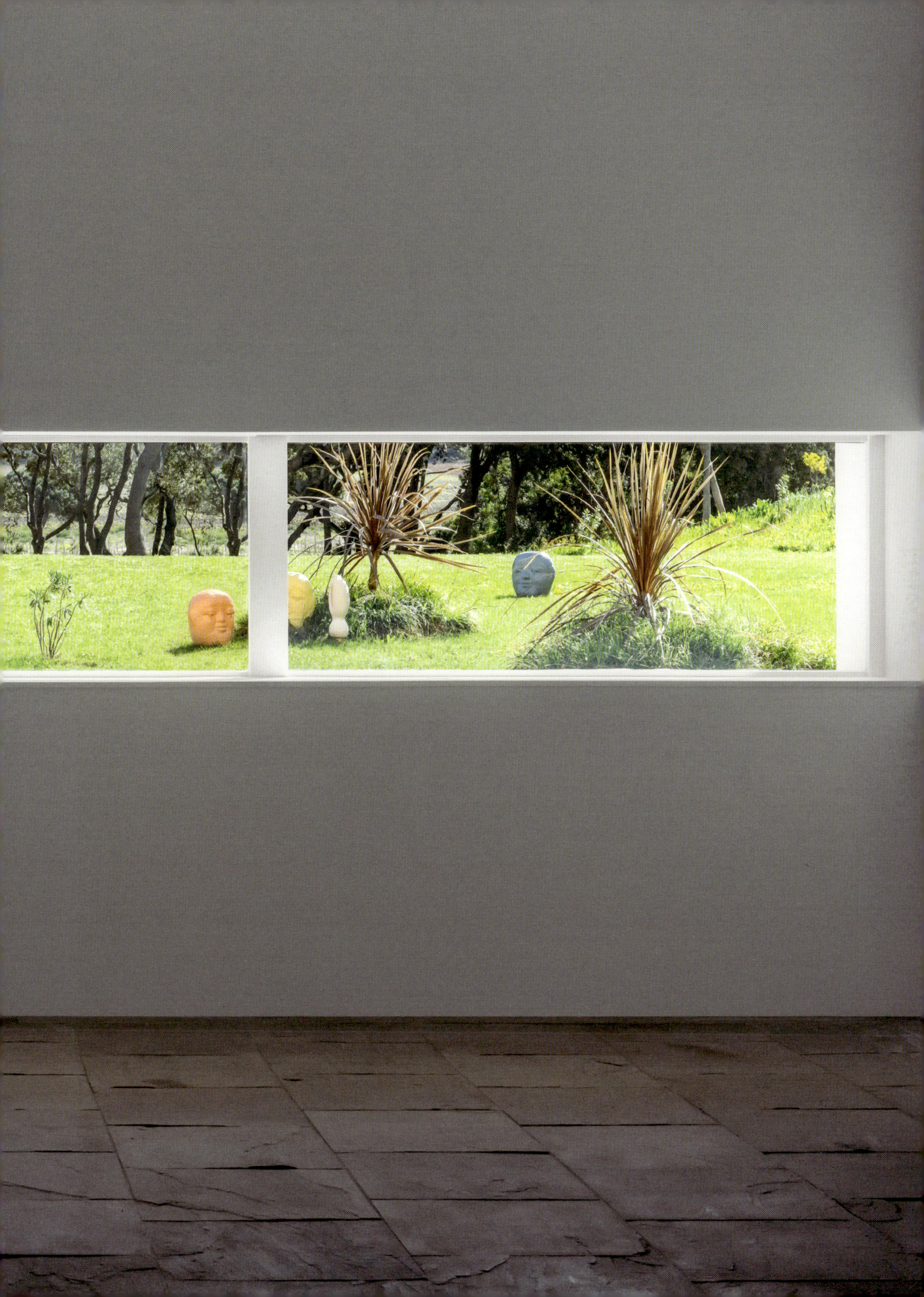

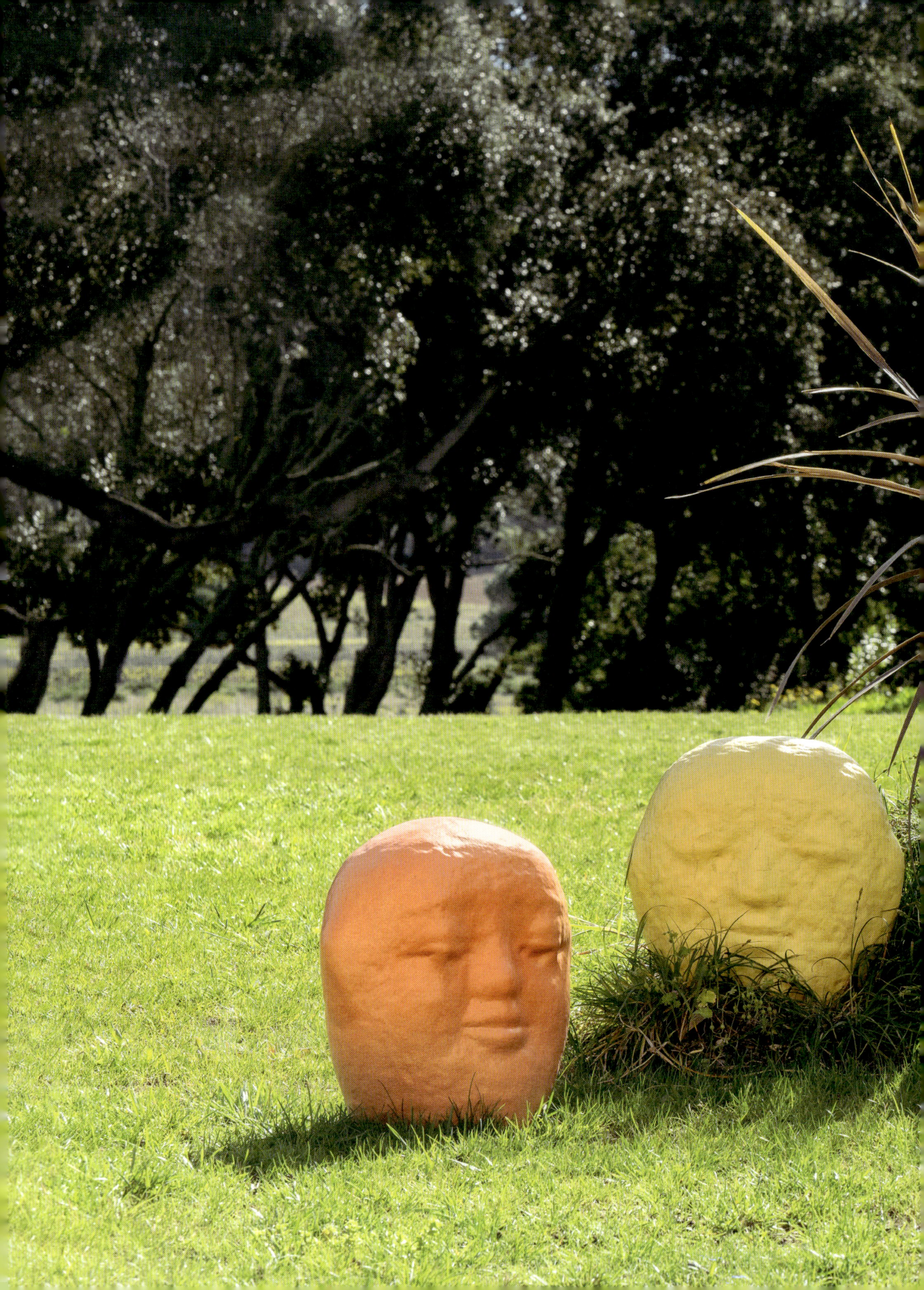

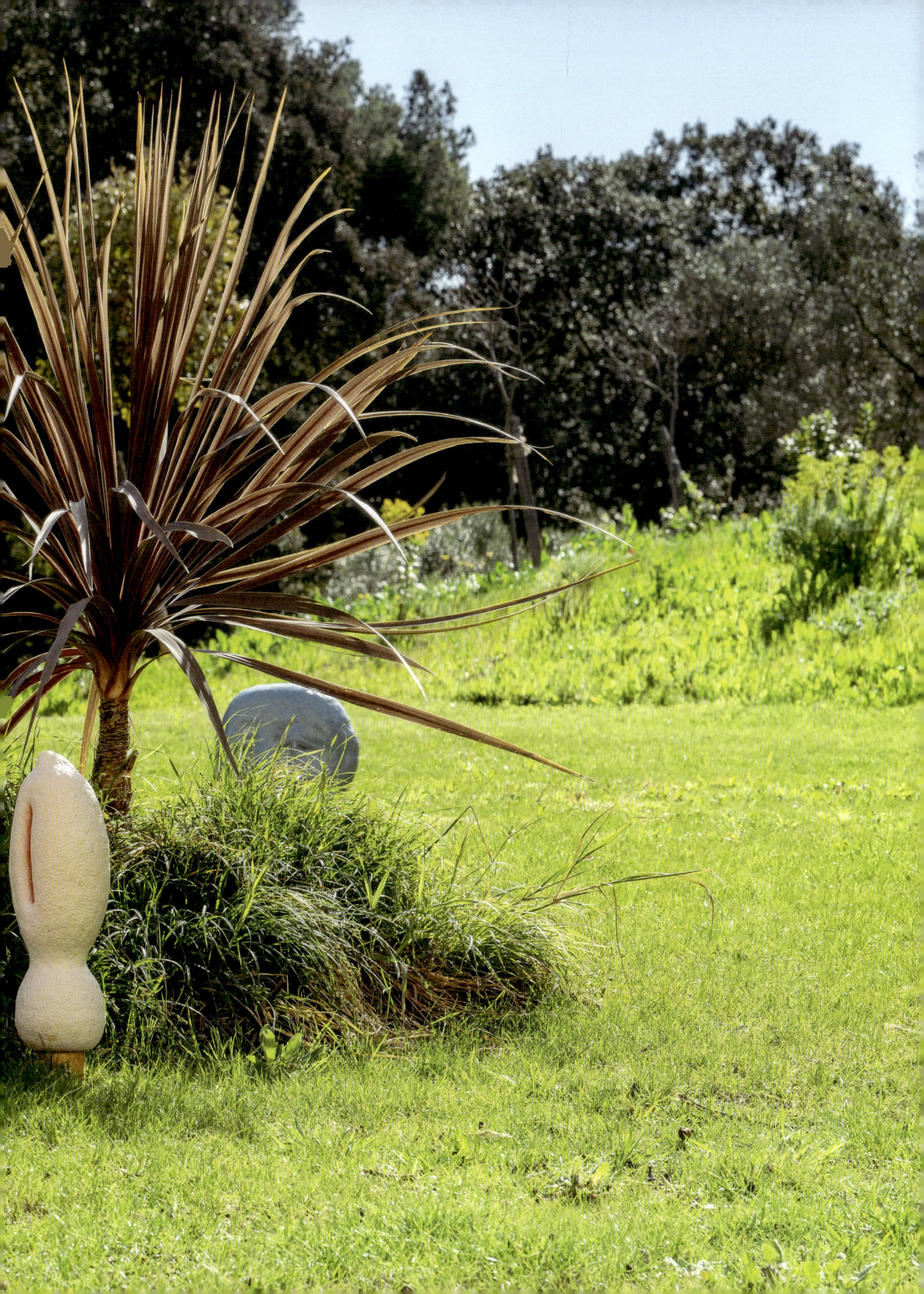

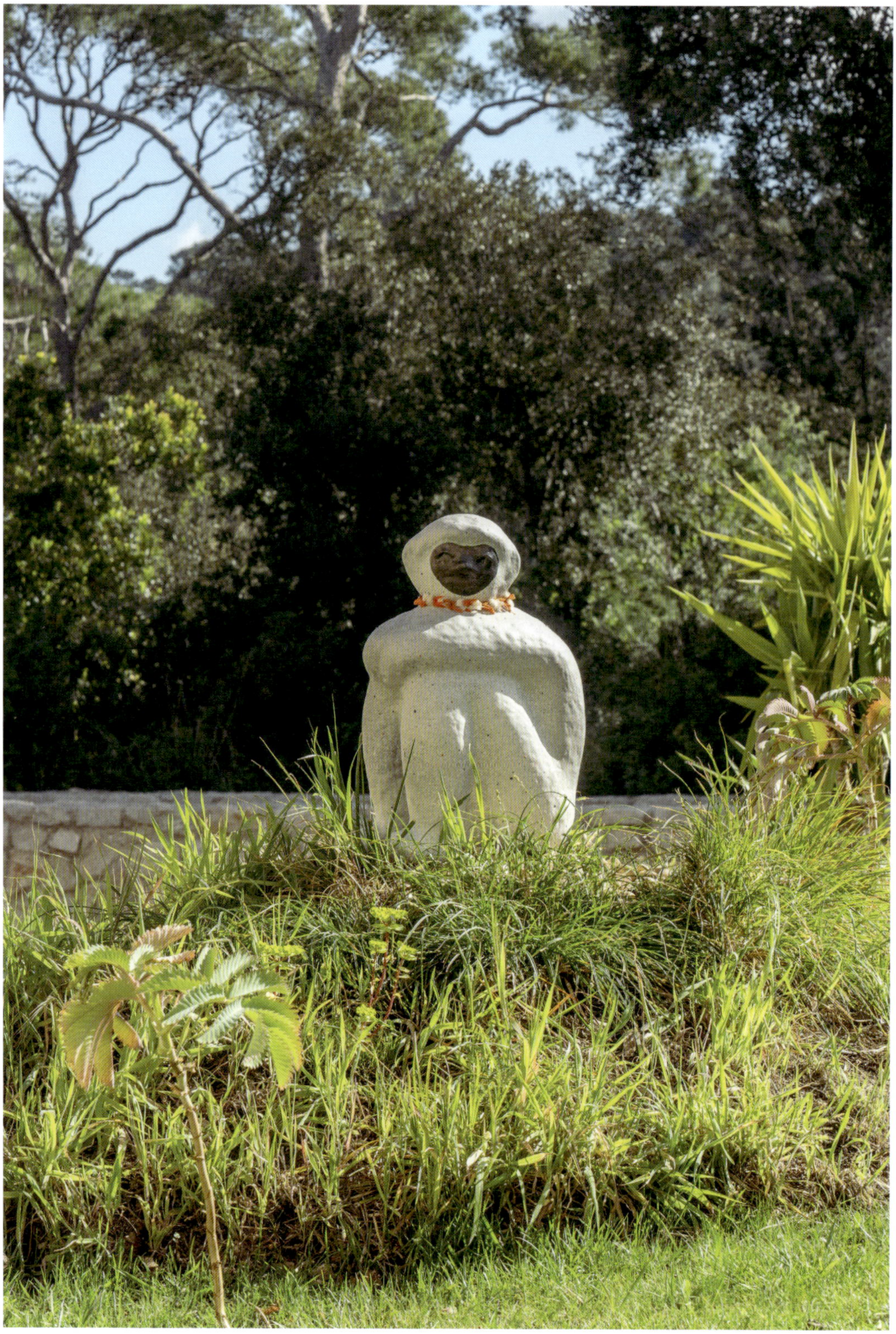

Corentin Grossmann, *M I C M A C*, 2023 — set of glazed earthenware pieces — variable dimensions
Antoine Espinasseau, *Fruit*, 2023 — bronze, metal and flowers — variable dimensions

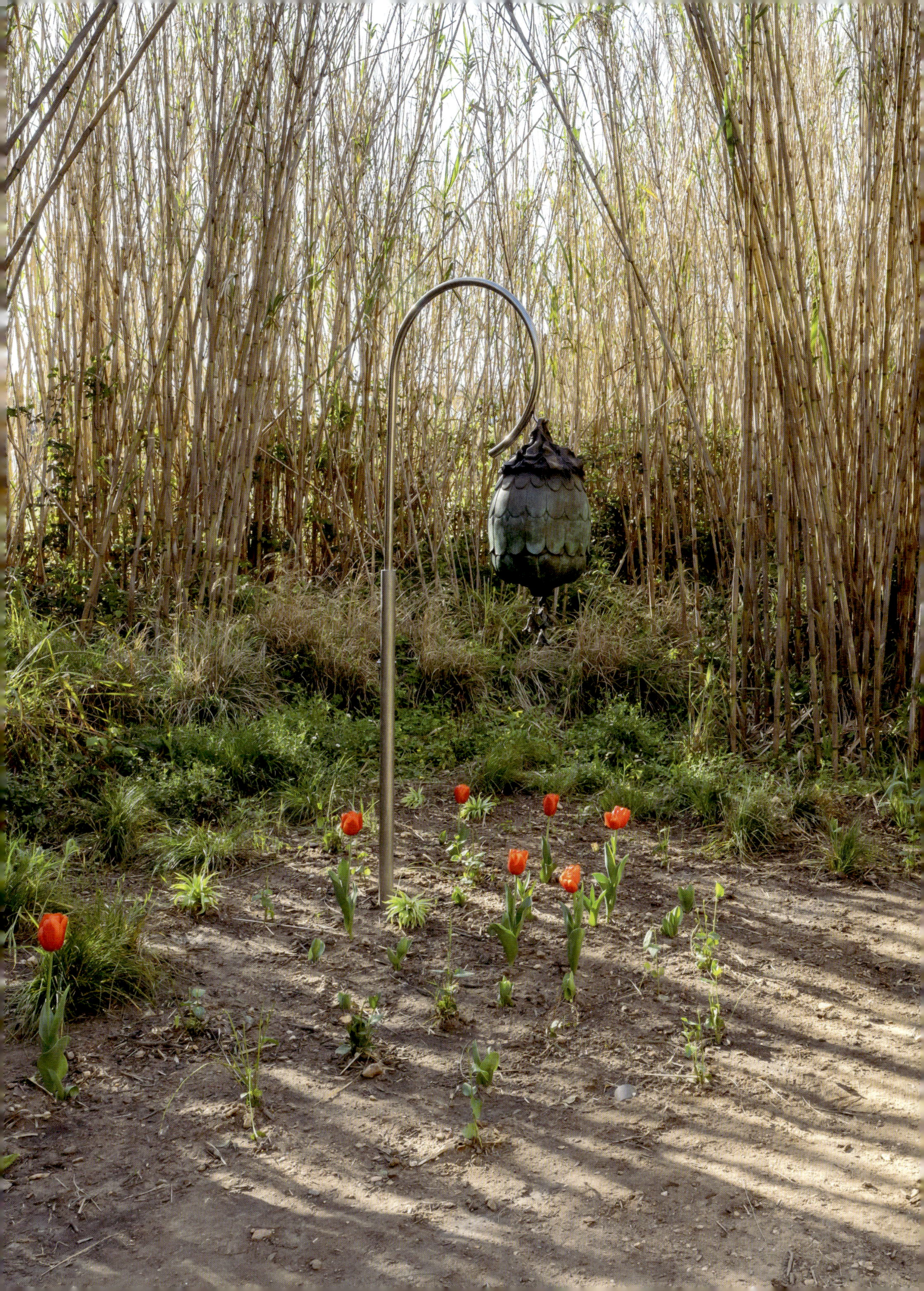

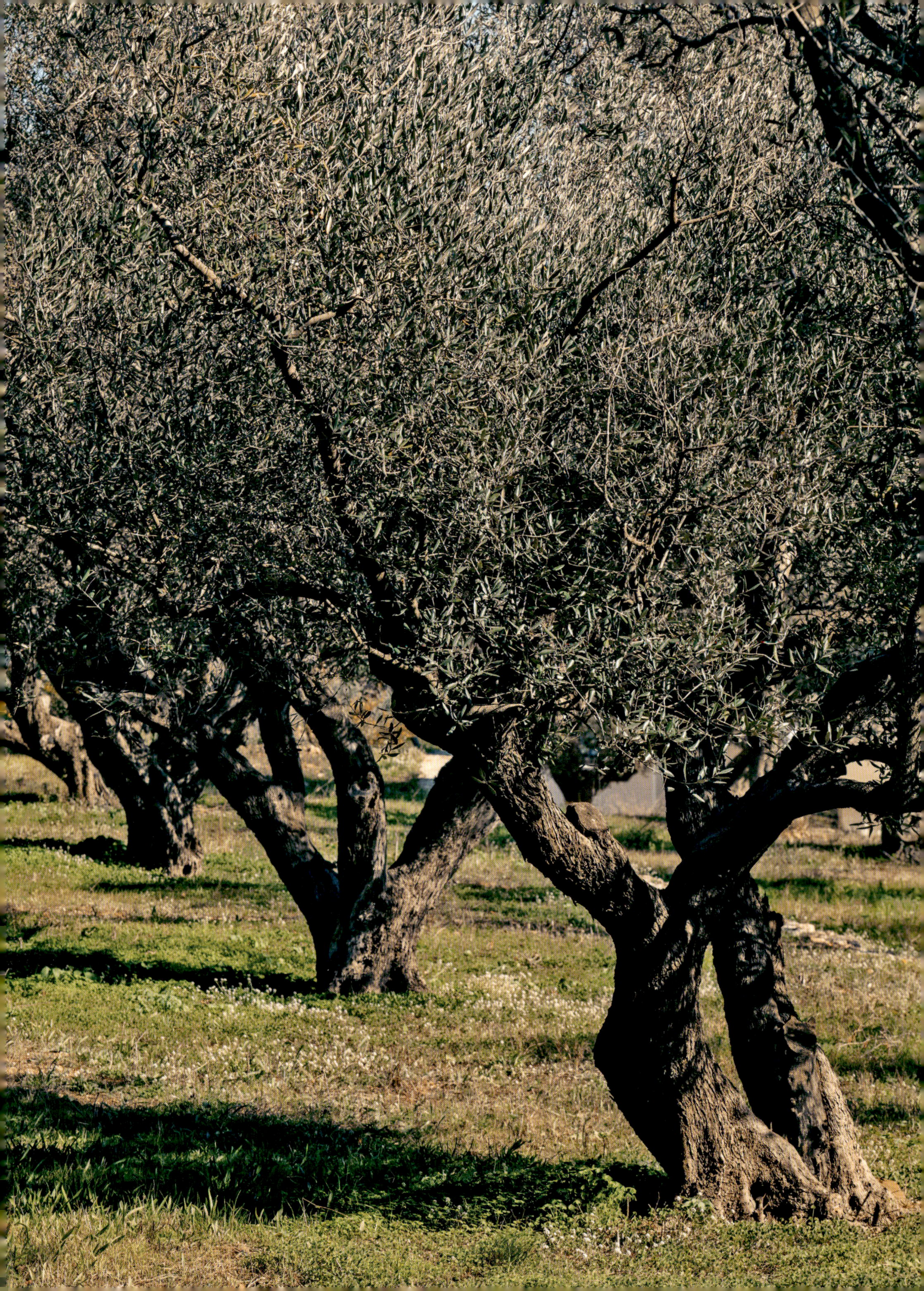

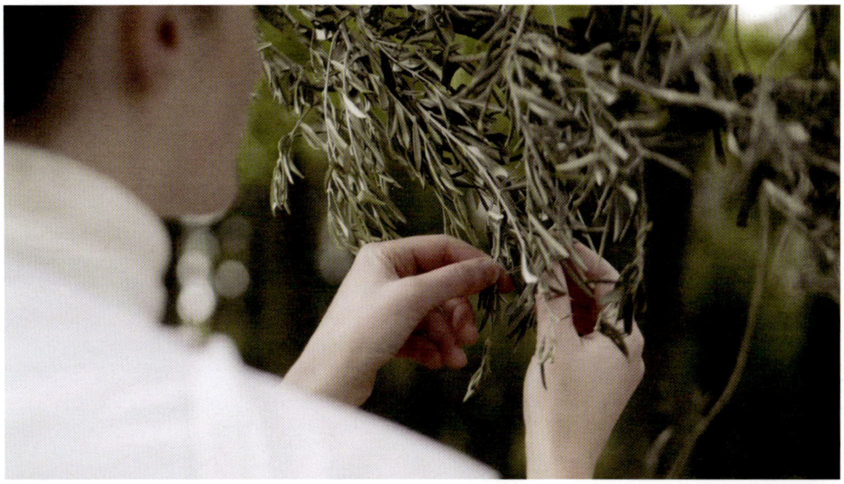

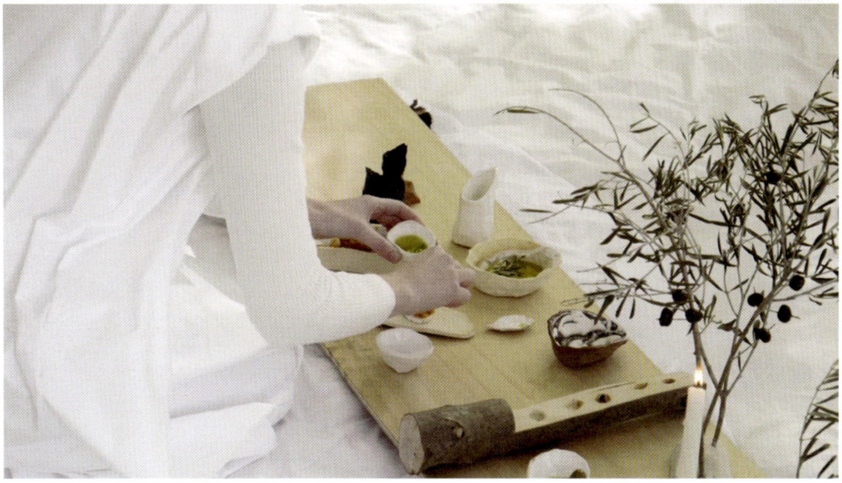

Luz Moreno Pinart & Anaïs Silvestro, *Cérémonie de l'olivier*, 2022–2023 — performance

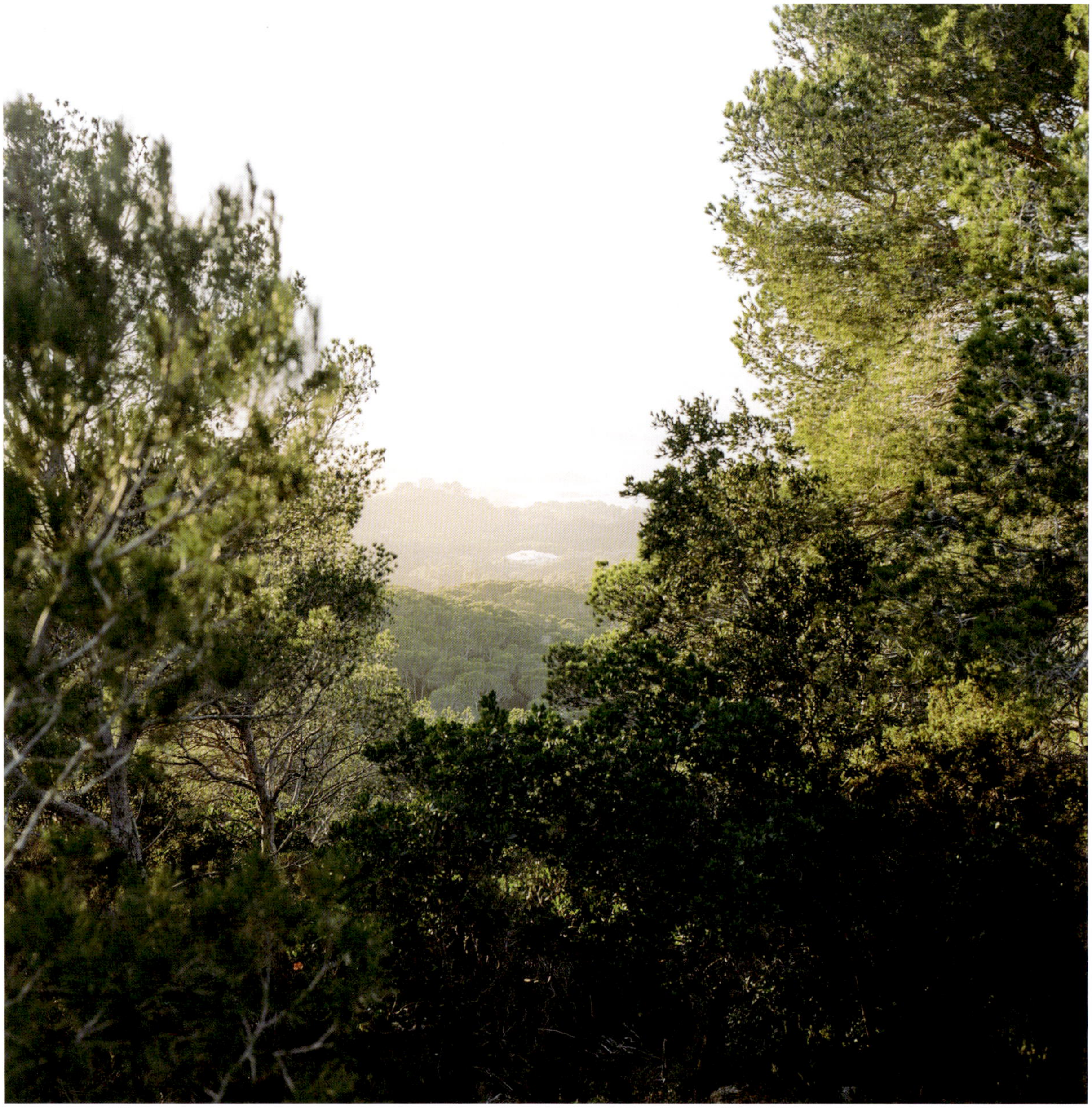

(p. 135) Anthropomorphic sculpture of a skull with schematised features effigy of the deity Zemi, Dominican Republic, 1200–1450 AD, Beige fossiliferous limestone, Carmignac Collection. Photo Nicolas Brasseur

CAROLINE ACHAINTRE

Brutus, 2016
hand-tufted wool, 223 × 180 cm, Villa Datris Collection © Caroline Achaintre, courtesy This Is Arcade, London, and Art:Concept, Paris. Photo Claire Dorn

ETEL ADNAN

Planète 7, 2019
oil on canvas, 33 × 22 cm, Amélie Blanchy Collection © The estate of Etel Adnan / ADAGP, Paris, 2023, courtesy Lelong & Co Gallery

Planète 14, 2020
oil on canvas, 33 × 24 cm, private collection © The estate of Etel Adnan / ADAGP, Paris, 2023, courtesy Lelong & Co Gallery

Planète 20, 2020
oil on canvas, 33 × 22 cm, private collection © The estate of Etel Adnan / Adagp, Paris, 2023, courtesy Lelong & Co Gallery

DARREN ALMOND

Fullmoon@Grand-Cale, 2022
C-print, 121.2 × 121.2 cm, commissioned by Fondation Carmignac © Darren Almond

Fullmoon@Plage Noire, 2022
C-print, 121.2 × 121.2 cm, commissioned by Fondation Carmignac © Darren Almond

Fullmoon@Porquerolles, 2022
C-print, 180 × 180 cm, commissioned by Fondation Carmignac © Darren Almond

Fullmoon@Calanque, 2022
C-print, 121.2 × 263.7 cm, commissioned by Fondation Carmignac © Darren Almond

Fullmoon@Sarranier, 2022
C-print, 121.2 × 263.7 cm, commissioned by Fondation Carmignac © Darren Almond

HAROLD ANCART

Untitled, 2022
oil stick and pencil on canvas, 122 × 152 cm, © Harold Ancart / ADAGP, Paris, 2023, courtesy Gagosian. Photo JSP Art Photography

GIULIA ANDREANI

Roi Requin, 2015
watercolour on paper, 26 × 18 cm, artist's collection © Giulia Andreani, courtesy Max Hetzler Gallery, Berlin, Paris, London. Photo Nicolas Brasseur

Momie de Palerme XXII, 2013
watercolour on paper, 10 × 15 cm, artist's collection © Giulia Andreani, courtesy Max Hetzler Gallery, Berlin, Paris, London. Photo Nicolas Brasseur

Le géologue, 2014
watercolour on paper, 17 × 12 cm, artist's collection © Giulia Andreani, courtesy Max Hetzler Gallery, Berlin, Paris, London. Photo Nicolas Brasseur

La cripta dei cappuccini, 2011
watercolour on paper, 18 × 12 cm, artist's collection © Giulia Andreani, courtesy Max Hetzler Gallery Berlin, Paris, London. Photo Nicolas Brasseur

Crépuscule, 2013
watercolour on paper, 12.5 × 18 cm, artist's collection © Giulia Andreani, courtesy Max Hetzler Gallery Berlin, Paris, London. Photo Nicolas Brasseur

XV (ape), 2011
watercolour on paper, 12.5 × 18 cm, artist's collection © Giulia Andreani, courtesy Max Hetzler Gallery, Berlin, Paris, London. Photo Nicolas Brasseur

Faoucado, 2023
watercolour on paper, 36 × 51 cm, artist's collection © Giulia Andreani, courtesy Max Hetzler Gallery, Berlin, Paris, London. Photo Nicolas Brasseur

Le Rempart, 2015
watercolour on paper, 18 × 12 cm, collection Nina and Jean-Claude Mosconi © Giulia Andreani, courtesy Max Hetzler Gallery, Berlin, Paris, London. Photo Nicolas Brasseur

LUCAS ARRUDA

Untitled (from the Deserto-Modelo series), 2021
huile sur toile, 18 × 22 cm, Lucas Arruda, courtesy David Zwirner

Untitled (from the Deserto-Modelo series), 2021
huile sur toile, 18 × 22 cm, Lucas Arruda, courtesy David Zwirner

JEAN-FRANCIS AUBURTIN

Le Matin (Calanque de Porquerolles), 1894
oil on canvas, 113 × 162 cm, private collection. Photo Nicolas Brasseur

La Grand-Cale à Porquerolles, 1902
gouache on large grey paper, 55.5 × 73 cm, private collection. Photo Nicolas Brasseur

MARCELLA BARCELÓ

Pollination Syndrome, 2021
ink and watercolour on washi paper, 73 × 149 cm, Carmignac Collection © Marcella Barceló, courtesy Anne de Villepoix Gallery. Photo Aurélien Mole

MIQUEL BARCELÓ

Not Yet Titled, 2018
polyester canvas stretched over frame, acrylic plaster, gelatine paste, pigments and oil, 350 × 1500 cm, Carmignac Collection © Marcella Barceló / ADAGP, Paris, 2023. Photo Nicolas Brasseur

JEAN-MICHEL BASQUIAT

Untitled, 1985
acrylic and printed papers on canvas, 218.3 × 172.7 cm, Carmignac Gestion Collection, Management © The estate of Jean-Michel Basquiat / ADAGP, Paris, 2023. Photo Thomas Hennocque

ANNA-EVA BERGMAN

N°11-1955 Lune d'argent, 1955
oil and metal sheet on canvas, 130 × 97 cm, Fondation Hartung-Bergman © Anna-Eva Bergman / ADAGP, Paris, 2023

RAGNA BLEY

La Belle Epoque, 2022
acrylic paint on canvas, 215 × 375 © Ragna Bley, courtesy Pilar Corrias, London

MARK BRADFORD

The Loop of Deep Waters 1, 2014
various techniques,
144.8 × 109.2 cm, Carmignac Collection © Mark Bradford, courtesy and photo Hauser & Wirth

TIM BREUER

Before Departure, 2021
oil on canvas on aluminium,
175 × 246 cm © Tim Breuer, courtesy Champ Lacombe, Biarritz

ALEXANDER CALDER

Striped Man, Striped Sweater, 1953
gouache on paper, 108 × 73.7 cm, Carmignac Gestion Collection © Calder Foundation, New York / ADAG, Paris, 2023. Photo Thomas Hennocque

ALI CHERRI

Grafting (I), 2019
woman's head, Apollo; statue in sculpted stone representing a priest, Normandy; polyurethane foam, metal nails, 110 × 50 × 30 cm © Ali Cherri, courtesy Galerie Imane Farès, Paris. Photo Nicolas Brasseur

Grafting (Errance), 2023
sandstone headless bust of Saint John the Baptist, France, late eleventh century; alabaster head, France, eighteenth century; terracotta votive base; metal, 47 × 22 × 32 cm © Ali Cherri, courtesy Galerie Imane Farès, Paris. Photo Nicolas Brasseur

Return of the Beast, 2021
fragment of a white marble Roman sculpture with legs and feet from the nineteenth century (actual size); eyes in ancient Egyptian bronze with matching eyebrows, remains of azurite and incrustations; feather headdress from Angola (Tchokwe culture); enamelled sandstone and metal, 130 × 63 × 51 cm © Ali Cherri, courtesy Galerie Imane Farès, Paris. Photo Nicolas Brasseur

FRANCESCO CLEMENTE

Fifty One Days on Mount Abu: Hi Full Moon, 1995
watercolour on paper,
53.7 × 70.8 cm, Carmignac Collection © Francesco Clemente

Fifty One Days on Mount Abu XLIV Silence, 1995
watercolour on paper,
53.7 × 70.8 cm, Carmignac Collection © Francesco Clemente

Fifty One Days on Mount Abu XXXVI Sky, 1995
watercolour on paper,
53.7 × 70.8 cm, Carmignac Collection © Francesco Clemente

MARCUS COPE

Reflector, 2021
oil on jute, 170 × 130 cm,
Re Rebaudengo Collection © Marcus Cope, courtesy ARTUNER. Photo BJDeakin_Photography

ANDREW CRANSTON

I Am More Comfortable, 2017
oil and varnish on cardboard book cover, 13 × 22 cm, private collection © Andrew Cranston, courtesy Karma, New York

Starry Night with Donkey (August 1974), 2020
oil on canvas, 225.1 × 160 cm, private collection © Andrew Cranston, courtesy Karma, New York

Island Years, 2022
pigment and gum arabic on cardboard book cover, 22 × 32 cm © Andrew Cranston, courtesy Y.D.C. Photo Modern Art, London

HENRI-EDMOND CROSS

Les îles d'or, 1891–1892
oil on canvas, 59.5 × 54 cm, Paris, musée d'Orsay, © RMN-Grand Palais (Musée d'Orsay) / Hervé Lewandowski

VERNE DAWSON

Macedonia Road, 2013
oil on linen canvas, 182.9 × 213.4 cm © Verne Dawson, courtesy Victoria Miro, London

JEREMY DEMESTER

Kali, 2022
oil and acrylic on canvas, resin and steel, 268 × 255 × 31 cm © Jeremy Demester, courtesy Max Hetzler Gallery, Berlin, Paris, London. Photo def image

PETER DOIG

100 Years Ago (Carrera), 2001
oil on canvas, 229 × 359 cm, Centre Pompidou, MNAM-CCI, Dist, RMN-Grand Palais / Audrey Laurans © Peter Doig, all rights reserved, DACS/ ADAGP, Paris, 2023.

JENNIFER DOUZENEL

Poids du Soleil, 2023
video installation, 8'38" in loop, commissioned by Fondation Carmignac © Jennifer Douzenel

ANTOINE ESPINASSEAU

Anguille, 2022
collage, colour ink-jet print,
60 × 69 cm © Antoine Espinasseau

Candy, 2022
collage, colour ink-jet print,
60 × 69 cm © Antoine Espinasseau

Vendredi, 2022
collage, colour ink-jet print,
60 × 69 cm © Antoine Espinasseau

Fruit, 2023
bronze, stainless steel, flowers, variable dimensions, commissioned by Fondation Carmignac © Antoine Espinasseau. Photo Antoine Espinasseau and Nicolas Brasseur

HELEN FRANKENTHALER

Overture, 1992
acrylic on canvas, 177.8 × 238.8 cm © 2023 Helen Frankenthaler Foundation, Inc. / Artists Rights Society (ARS), New York. Photo Robert McKeever

RODNEY GRAHAM

Vexation Island, 1997
digitized 35mm film, 9' in loop © Rodney Graham Studio. Film still

CORENTIN GROSSMANN

Un doute intersidéral, 2019
graphite, dry pastel, colour pencils, 155 × 113 cm, private collection, France © Corentin Grossmann, courtesy Art:Concept, Paris. Photo Corentin Grossmann

MIMAC, 2023
set of glazed earthenware pieces composed of: *Dazzling Overcup, Blinding Shield of the Kansai Prefecture, Cobalt, Tethys and Venus (nymps), Big Baby, Whispering Conch of Evidences, Yellow Pentagouet, Double Level Folded Eyes, Betty (legs), Kalláïnos, Hanuman*, and *Grinch*, variable dimensions, commissioned by Fondation Carmignac © Corentin Grossmann. Photo Nicolas Brasseur

SIMON HANTAÏ

Sans titre, 1954
oil on canvas, 155 × 220 cm, Frac Bretagne Collection © Simon Hantaï Archives / ADAGP, Paris, 2023. Photo Guy Jaumotte

CAMILLE HENROT

"L'heure de s'enivrer. L'univers a-t-il un sens ?" Hubert Reeves, 2012
ikebana: tinted ornamental garlic (*Allium schubertii*), four-season lemons (*Citrus limon eureka*), and Holly Oak (*Quercus ilex*), H: 181 cm, Frac Île-de-France Collection © Camille Henrot / ADAGP, Paris, 2023. Photo Nicolas Brasseur

DAVID HORVITZ

See the sea being (Audio), 2021
Audio version edited by Yann Chateigné Tytelman. Produced by KANAL - Centre Pompidou, Brussels. Based on an original work by the artist commissioned in 2021 by the Carmignac Foundation. With the voices of: Sena Basöz, Julien Bismuth, Yann Chateigné Tytelman, Javier Cruz, Krysten Cunningham, Sébastien Delire, Kasia Fudakowski, Daniel Gustav Cramer, Stefanie Hessler, Vlatka Horvat, David Horvitz, Jesi Khadivi, Margarida Mendes, Adrien Missika, Ed Steck, Marianna Vecchiellio, and Chiara Vecchiarelli © David Horvitz, courtesy ChertLüdde, Berlin

CATHY JOSEFOWITZ

Portrait de Romain, 1977
charcoal, pastel, and gouache on paper mounted on board, 158 × 98 cm © The estate of Cathy Josefowitz

PIA KRAJEWSKI

Precious Nest, 2023
mural installation: printed velvet carpet, variable dimensions; two oils on canvas, 250 × 400 cm and 200 × 180 cm, commissioned by Fondation Carmignac © Pia Krajewski. Photo Nicolas Brasseur

AGNIESZKA KURANT

Adjacent Possible, 2021–2023
photochromic pigments on the wall, variable dimensions, commissioned by Fondation Carmignac © Agnieszka Kurant. Photo Nicolas Brasseur

A.A.I. 14, 2017
termite mound made of coloured sand, gold, glitter, and crystals, 64.8 × 61 × 61 cm © Agnieszka Kurant, courtesy Tanya Bonakdar Gallery, New York / Los Angeles

A.A.I. 15, 2017
termite mound made of coloured sand, gold, glitter, and crystals, 68.6 × 61 × 61 cm © Agnieszka Kurant, courtesy Tanya Bonakdar Gallery, New York / Los Angeles

A.A.I. 16, 2017
termite mound made of coloured sand, gold, glitter, and crystals, 76.2 × 61 × 61 cm © Agnieszka Kurant, courtesy Tanya Bonakdar Gallery, New York / Los Angeles

A.A.I. 17, 2017
termite mound made of coloured sand, gold, glitter, and crystals, 83.8 × 61 × 61 cm ©Agnieszka Kurant, courtesy Tanya Bonakdar Gallery, New York / Los Angeles. Photo Nicolas Brasseur

A.A.I. 18, 2017
termite mound made of coloured sand, gold, glitter, and crystals, 91.4 × 61 × 61 cm ©Agnieszka Kurant, courtesy Tanya Bonakdar Gallery, New York / Los Angeles. Photo Nicolas Brasseur

A.A.I 19, 2017
termite mound made of coloured sand, gold, glitter, and crystals, 91.4 × 61 × 61 cm © Agnieszka Kurant, courtesy Tanya Bonakdar Gallery, New York / Los Angeles

ROY LICHTENSTEIN

Landscape, 1977
oil and Magna on canvas, 101.6 × 152.4 cm, Carmignac Patrimoine Collection © The estate of Roy Lichtenstein New York / ADAGP, Paris, 2023

TONY MATELLI

Weeds #389, 2017
bronze, 63.5 × 27.9 × 22.9 cm, Carmignac Collection © Courtesy of the artist. Photo Camille Moirenc

JANAINA MELLO LANDINI

Ciclotrama 50 (Wind), 2018
nylon cord, brass, and marble nails, 550 × 1200 × 140 cm, Carmignac Collection © Janaina Mello Landini

LUZ MORENO PINART & ANAÏS SILVESTRO

Cérémonie de l'olivier, 2022–2023, performance © Luz Moreno Pinart & Anaïs Silvestro. Photo Léa Troulard

Sous (le) bois d'olivier, 2023
scent, commissioned by Fondation Carmignac © Luz Moreno Pinart & Anaïs Silvestro

JILL MULLEADY

Badlands, 2010
oil on linen canvas, 46 × 55 cm © Jill Mulleady, courtesy Gladstone Gallery

BRUCE NAUMAN

One Hundred Fish Fountain, 2005
ninety-seven bronze fish of different sizes hung from a metal fence, Carmignac Collection © ADAGP, Paris, 2023. Photo Nicolas Brasseur

OTOBONG NKANGA

Tied to the Other Side, 2022
tapestry woven on Dornier machine, TextielLab, TextielMuseum, Tilburg, The Netherlands; yarns: trevira, elirex, polypropylene exterior, multifilament, mohair, monofilament, fulgaren, sidero, cotton, acrylic, viscose, 350 × 600 cm, private collection Ouissem Barbouchi, Paris © Otobong Nkanga, courtesy Galerie In Situ-fabienne leclerc, Grand Paris. Photo Nicolas Brasseur

ALBERT OEHLEN

Symbol, 1997
oil on canvas, 200 × 200 cm, Carmignac Collection © Albert Oehlen, ADAGP, Paris, 2023. Photo Thomas Hennocque

Hill and Gully Rider, 2018
lacquer and oil on aluminium plates, 260 × 260 cm, Carmignac Patrimoine Collection © Albert Oehlen / ADAGP, Paris, 2023. Photo Nicolas Brasseur

BERNARD PESCE

Les Mèdes, 1980
modern silver print on baryta paper, 60 × 40 cm © Bernard Pesce

BERNARD PLOSSU

Île de Porquerolles, 1976
modern silver print on baryta paper, 9 × 13.8 cm, La Banque, musée des Cultures et du Paysage, Hyères © Bernard Plossu

Île de Porquerolles, 1976
modern silver print on baryta paper, 9 × 13.8 cm, collection of the artist © Bernard Plossu

Île de Porquerolles, 1976
modern silver print on baryta paper, 9 × 13.8 cm, collection of the artist © Bernard Plossu

Île de Porquerolles, 1976
modern silver print on baryta paper, 13.8 × 9 cm, La Banque, musée des Cultures et du Paysage, Hyères © Bernard Plossu. Photo F. Joncour

Île de Porquerolles, 1976
modern silver print on baryta paper, 13.8 × 9 cm, La Banque, musée des Cultures et du Paysage, Hyères © Bernard Plossu. Photo F. Joncour

Île de Porquerolles, 1976
modern silver print on baryta paper, 13.8 × 9 cm, La Banque, musée des Cultures et du Paysage, Hyères © Bernard Plossu. Photo F. Joncour

SIGMAR POLKE

Untitled (Lapis-Lazuli), 1998
pure lapis lazuli pigment and resin on canvas, 240 × 200 cm, Carmignac Patrimoine Collection © The estate of Sigmar Polke, Cologne / ADAGP, Paris, 2023

MICHEL REDOLFI

Beyond, 2023
sensory sound sculpture, Carmignac Collection © Michel Redolfi

AUGUSTE RODIN

La Voix intérieure ou *Méditation sans bras* [*The Inner Voice*, or *Meditation without arms*], 1896
bronze, 146 × 75.5 × 55 cm, Musée Rodin, Paris. Photo Nicolas Brasseur

CHRISTINE SAFA

La mer, par-delà ton épaule III, 2023
oil on linen canvas, 146 × 135 cm © Christine Safa, courtesy Lelong & Co Gallery, Paris. Photo Nicolas Brasseur

EDGAR SARIN

Variation sur celui du Lararium, 2023
solid oak stained with olive oil, 70 × 45 × 14 cm © Edgar Sarin, courtesy Michel Rein, Paris/Brussels. Photo Nicolas Brasseur

NORBERT SCHWONTKOWSKI

Sopot, 2010
oil on canvas, 200 × 180 cm © Norbert Schwontkowski, courtesy of Contemporary Fine Arts, Berlin. Photo Jochen Littkemann

Ohne Titel (AHAB), 2002
oil and pigment on canvas, 132 × 160 cm © Norbert Schwontkowski, courtesy of Contemporary Fine Arts, Berlin. Photo Jochen Littkemann

KIKI SMITH

Woman with Wolf, 2003
porcelain, 37 × 12 × 20 cm © Kiki Smith, courtesy Lelong & Co Gallery, Paris

Tahitian Girls with Feathers, 2005
set of two porcelain pieces, 22 × 20 × 20 cm each © Kiki Smith, courtesy Lelong & Co Gallery, Paris

LÉON SPILLIAERT

Faune au clair de lune, 1900
Indian ink wash, paintbrush, black chalk, coloured pencil on paper, 48.9 × 63.6 cm, private collection. Photo Daniel de Kievith

TURSIC & MILLE

The Blue Landscape, 2019
oil on board in an oak frame, in three parts, 246.3 × 373.7 cm © Tursic & Mille, courtesy Max Hetzler Gallery, Berlin, Paris, London. Photo def image

Melancholic Sunset, 2018
oil on boards, sixty-four Heineken bottles, 214 × 372 cm © Tursic & Mille. Photo def image

Sisyphe (Time Mass), 2016–2023
oil on board, oak base, 97 × 120 × 80 cm © Tursic & Mille, courtesy Max Hetzler Gallery, Berlin, Paris, London. Photo Nicolas Brasseur

FRANCIS UPRITCHARD

Long, 2009
table: lino, figurines: modelling clay, iron wire, paint, 88.4 × 169.2 × 540 cm © Francis Upritchard, courtesy Kate MacGarry, London

Moon Monkey and Dancing Monkey Urn, 2016
ceramic, 39 × 42.5 × 42.5 © Francis Upritchard, courtesy Kate MacGarry, London

FRANK WALTER

Untitled (Grey Bird on Black Cliff), c. 1970
oil on Polaroid film cartridge box, 10 × 8.1 cm, courtesy Walter Family Collection. Photo Kenneth M. Milton Fine Arts Conservator

Untitled (Black Bird, Black Headlands), c. 1970
oil on Polaroid film cartridge box, 10 × 8.1 cm, courtesy Walter Family Collection. Photo Kenneth M. Milton Fine Arts Conservator

Untitled (Abstract Red-Roofed Village), c. 1970
oil on Polaroid film cartridge box, 10 × 8.2 cm, courtesy Walter Family Collection. Photo Kenneth M. Milton Fine Arts Conservator

Untitled (Solo Black Bird Flying Low), c. 1970
oil on Polaroid film cartridge box, 10 × 8.1 cm, courtesy Walter Family Collection. Photo Kenneth M. Milton Fine Arts Conservator

Untitled (White-Edged Harbor, Green Hills), c. 1970
oil on Polaroid film cartridge box, 10.1 × 8.1 cm, courtesy Walter Family Collection. Photo Kenneth M. Milton Fine Arts Conservator

Untitled (Hurricane Headlands), c. 1970
oil on Polaroid film cartridge box, 10.1 × 8.2 cm, courtesy Walter Family Collection. Photo Kenneth M. Milton Fine Arts Conservator

Untitled (Hurricane Sky and Sea), c. 1970
oil on Polaroid film cartridge box, 10.1 × 8.2 cm, courtesy Walter Family Collection. Photo Kenneth M. Milton Fine Arts Conservator

Untitled (Green Path, Black Mountains, Pink Sky), c. 1970
oil on Polaroid film cartridge box, 10 × 8.3 cm, courtesy Walter Family Collection. Photo Kenneth M. Milton Fine Arts Conservator

Untitled (Green Hills, Blue Evening Sky), c. 1970
oil on Polaroid film cartridge box, 9.9 × 8.2 cm, courtesy Walter Family Collection. Photo Kenneth M. Milton Fine Arts Conservator

Untitled (Yellow Sky, Black Bute, White Sun), c. 1970
oil on Polaroid film cartridge box, 9.8 × 8 cm, courtesy Walter Family Collection. Photo Kenneth M. Milton Fine Arts Conservator

Untitled (Yellow Sky, Black Headlands), c. 1970
oil on Polaroid film cartridge box, 9.8 × 8 cm, courtesy Walter Family Collection. Photo Kenneth M. Milton Fine Arts Conservator

Untitled (Black Hills, Yellow Sky), c. 1970
oil on Polaroid film cartridge box, 9.8 × 8 cm, courtesy Walter Family Collection. Photo Kenneth M. Milton Fine Arts Conservator

Untitled (Pink Sky, Greenland), c. 1970
oil on Polaroid film cartridge box, 10 × 8.2 cm, courtesy Walter Family Collection. Photo Kenneth M. Milton Fine Arts Conservator

Untitled (Waterfall and Hurricane Sky), c. 1970
oil on Polaroid film cartridge box, 9.8 × 8 cm, courtesy Walter Family Collection. Photo Kenneth M. Milton Fine Arts Conservator

Untitled (Steep Cliffs, Red Sky, White Sea), c. 1970
oil on Polaroid film cartridge box, 9.8 × 8 cm, courtesy Walter Family Collection. Photo Kenneth M. Milton Fine Arts Conservator

Untitled (Self-Portrait in a Tree), c. 1970
oil on Polaroid film cartridge box, 9.8 × 8 cm, courtesy Walter Family Collection. Photo Kenneth M. Milton Fine Arts Conservator

Untitled (Purple Night, Green Headlands), c. 1970
oil on Polaroid film cartridge box, 10 × 8.2 cm, courtesy Walter Family Collection. Photo Kenneth M. Milton Fine Arts Conservator

Untitled (Purple Night Sky), c. 1970
oil on Polaroid film cartridge box, 10.2 × 8.2 cm, courtesy Walter Family Collection. Photo Kenneth M. Milton Fine Arts Conservator

Untitled (Black Bird, Black Mountain), c. 1970
oil on Polaroid film cartridge box, 10 × 8.3 cm, courtesy Walter Family Collection. Photo Kenneth M. Milton Fine Arts Conservator

CHRISTOPHER WOOL

Untitled, 2007
enamel on linen canvas, 304.4 × 243.84 cm, Carmignac Collection © Christopher Wool

Unless otherwise noted, all photographs of Porquerolles Island and the Villa Carmignac are © Nicolas Brasseur. p. 35, Michael J. Robertson Collection and Christopher A. Slapak; p. 36, Galleria d'Arte Moderna Torino, GAM - Galleria Civica d'Arte Moderna e Contemporanea. Su concessione della Fondazione Torino Musei. Photo Saroldi, 2009; p. 46, courtesy the artist and Ingleby, Edinburgh, private collection, photo John McKenzie; p. 49, Spencer Finch Studio and James Cohan Gallery; p. 50, courtesy Jennifer Douzenel; p. 86, ADAGP, Paris, 2023; p. 101, ADAGP, Paris, 2023; p. 121, collection George Ortiz; p. 122, © British Lion Films/Studio-canal Films Ltd., 1973; p. 139, Aishti Foundation Collection, Bayreuth, Laban, courtesy the artist and Capitain Petzel, Berlin; p.140, Carlotta Films, all rights reserved; p. 170, courtesy Romain Laprade; p. 172, courtesy Antoine Espinasseau.

ADNAN, Etel. *Night.* New York: Nightboat Books, 2016.

AL-MALA'IKA, Nazik. *Revolt Against the Sun: The Selected Poetry of Nazik al-Mala'ika; A Bilingual Reader*. Edited and translated by Emily Drumsta. London: Saqi Books, 2020.

BALLARD, J. G. *Concrete Island.* London: J. Cape, 1974.

BENJAMIN, Walter. *The Storyteller Essays.* New York: New York Review of Books, 2019. [Translator's note: includes stories written in Ibiza in 1932–1933.]

BIOY CASARES, Adolfo. *The Invention of Morel* (1940). Translated from the Spanish (Argentina) by Ruth Simms, preface by Jorge Luis Borgès. New York: New York Review of Books, 2003.

BLANQUI, Auguste. *Eternity by the Stars* (1872). Translated from the French by Frank Chouraqui. New York: Contra Mundum Press, 2013.

BUTLER, Samuel. *Erewhon; or, Over the Range*. London: Trubner, 1872.

CAVENDISH, Margaret. *The Description of a New World, Called The Blazing-World*. London: A. Maxwell, 1668.

DAUMAL, René. *Mount Analogue: An Authentic Narrative* (1952). Translation and introduction by Roger Shattuck with a post-face by Véra Daumal. London: Vincent Stuart, 1959.

DELEUZE, Gilles. *Desert Islands and Other Texts: 1953–1974.* Edited by David Lapoujade. Los Angeles: Semiotext(e), 2004.

DESCOLA, Philippe. *Les Formes du visible. Une anthropologie de la figuration*. Paris: Éditions du Seuil, 2021.

DESPRET, Vinciane. *Our Emotional Makeup: Ethnopsychology and Selfhood*. New York: Other Press, 2004.

GLISSANT, Édouard. *Caribbean Discourse: Selected Essays* (1981). Translated by Michael Dash. Charlottesville: University Press of Virginia, 1989.
—. *The Collected Poems of Edouard Glissant*. Translated by Jeff Humpreys. Chicago: University of Minnesota Press, 2005.
—. *Poetics of Relation* (1990). Translated by Betsy Wing. Ann Arbor: University of Michigan Press, 1997.

GOLDING, William. *Lord of the Flies*. London: Faber and Faber, 1954.

GRAFF, Laurent. *Au nom de Sa Majesté*. Paris: Le Dilettante, 2015.

HOFMANN, Werner. *Das entzweite Jahrhundert, 1750–1830*. Munich: Beck, 1995.

HOPTMAN, Laura, ed. *The Forever Now: Contemporary Painting in an Atemporal World*. New York: Museum of Modern Art, 2014.

LAWRENCE, D. H., *The Man Who Loved Islands: Sixteen Stories by D. H. Lawrence* (1927). London: Riverrun Editions, 2021.

HUXLEY, Aldous. *Island*. London: Chatto & Windus, 1962.

INGOLD, Tim. *Lines: A Brief History*. Oxon: Routledge, 2007.

JAMESON, Fredric. *Archaeologies of the Future: The Desire Called Utopia and Other Science Fictions*. London: Verso Books, 2007.

LATOUR, Bruno. *Politics of Nature: How to Bring the Sciences into Democracy* (1999). Translated by Catherine Port. Cambridge: Harvard University Press, 2004.

LE CLÉZIO, J. M. G. *Le flot de la poésie continuera de couler* [Poetry Is a Stream That Continually Flows]. With Dong Qiang. Paris: Philippe Rey, 2020.

LE GUIN, Ursula K. *The Language of the Night: Essays on Fantasy and Science Fiction*. Edited by Susan Wood. New York: Putnam Adult, 1979.

MELVILLE, Herman. "The Encantadas, or Enchanted Isles" (1854). In *The Piazza Tales*. New York: Dix and Edwards, 1856.

MEUNIER, Jacques. *On dirait des îles*. Paris: Flammarion, 1999.

PESSOA, Fernando. *The Book of Disquiet* (1982). Translated and edited by Zenith Richard. London: Penguin Classics, 2002.

PIC, Muriel. *Élégies documentaires*. Paris: Éditions Macula, 2016.

SAHLINS, Marshall. *Islands of History*. Chicago: Chicago University Press, 1987.

SCHALANSKY, Judith. *Atlas of Remote Islands: Fifty Islands I Have Never Set Foot On and Never Will*. Translated from the German by Christine Lo. London: Penguin Books, 2010.

SCHLESSER, Thomas. *L'Univers sans l'homme*. Vanves: Hazan, 2016.

SEGALEN, Victor. *Les Immémoriaux*. In *Œuvres I*. Edited by Christian Doumet. Paris: Gallimard, 2020.

SEKIGUCHI, Ryōko. *Nagori. La nostalgie de la saison qui vient de nous quitter*. Paris: POL, 2018.

STEYERL, Hito. *I Will Survive*. Edited by Florian Ebner et al. Leipzig: Spector Books, 2021.

THIELLEMENT, Pacôme. *Les Mêmes Yeux que "Lost"*. Paris: Léo Scheer, 2011.

TUYMANS, Luc. *Die Erschütterung der Sinne*. Edited by Ulrich Bischoff. Dresden: Sandstein Kommunikation, 2013.

VERNE, Jules. *The Mysterious Island* (1875). Translated by Jordan Stump. New York: Random House Modern Library, 2001.

VIGARELLO, Georges. *Une histoire des lointains. Entre réel et imaginaire*. Paris: Éditions du Seuil, 2022.

WELLS, Herbert George. *The Island of Doctor Moreau*. London: Heinnemann, 1896.

ZHONG MENGUAL, Estelle. *Apprendre à voir. Le point de vue du vivant*. Arles: Actes Sud, 2021.

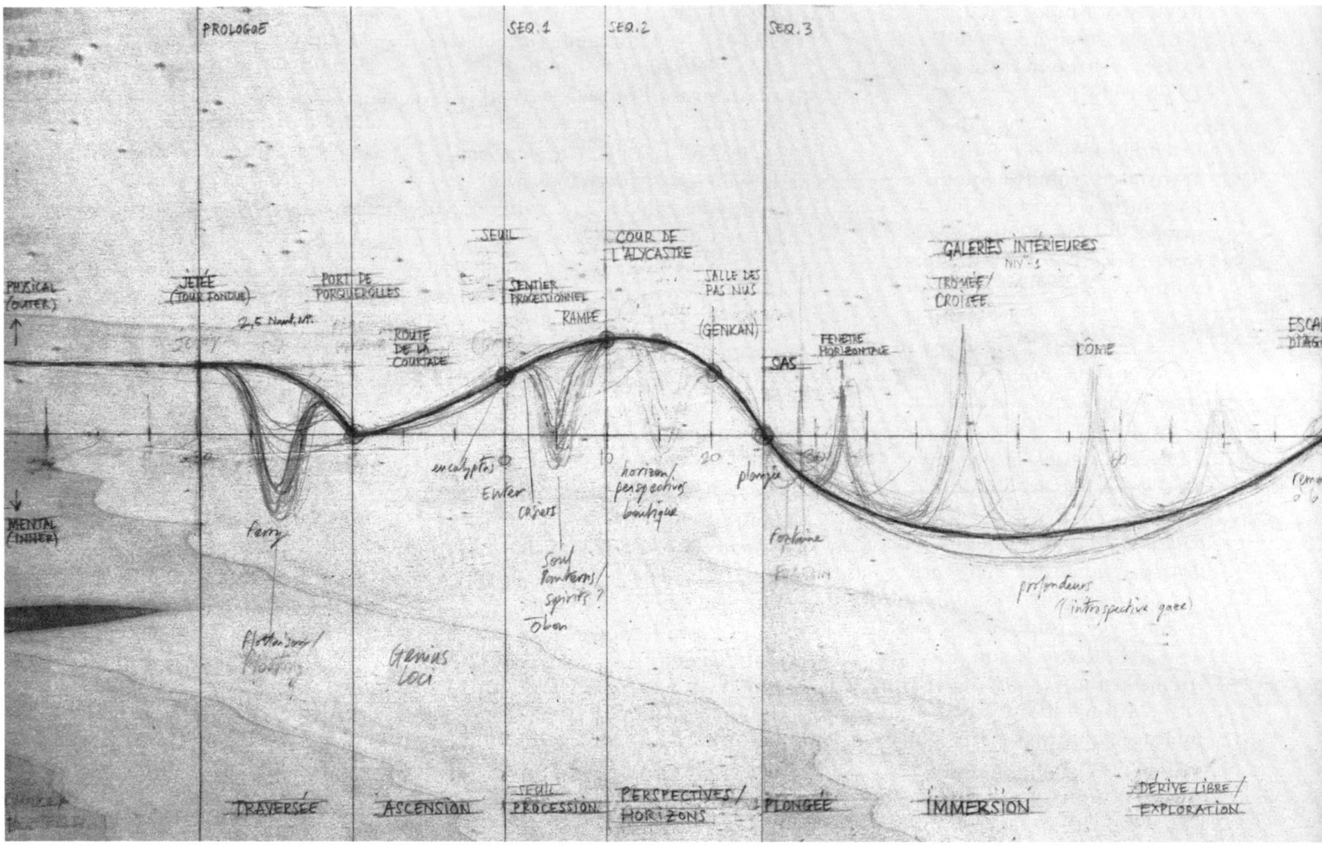
PROLOGUE
SEQ.1
SEQ.2
SEQ.3
PHYSICAL
(OUTER)
MENTAL
(INNER)
JETÉE
(TOUR FONDUE)
PORT DE
PORQUEROLLES
ROUTE
DE LA
COURTADE
SEUIL
SENTIER
PROCESSIONNEL
RAMPE
COUR DE
L'ALYCASTRE
SALLE DES
PAS NUS
(GENKAN)
SAS
FENETRE
HORIZONTALE
GALERIES INTÉRIEURES
NIV -1
CROISÉE
DÔME
ferry
eucalyptus
Enter
casiers
horizon/
perspectives
boutique
plongée
fontaine
10
20
profondeurs
(introspective gaze)
Genius
Loci
TRAVERSÉE
ASCENSION
SEUIL
PROCESSION
PERSPECTIVES/
HORIZONS
PLONGÉE
IMMERSION
DÉRIVE LIBRE/
EXPLORATION

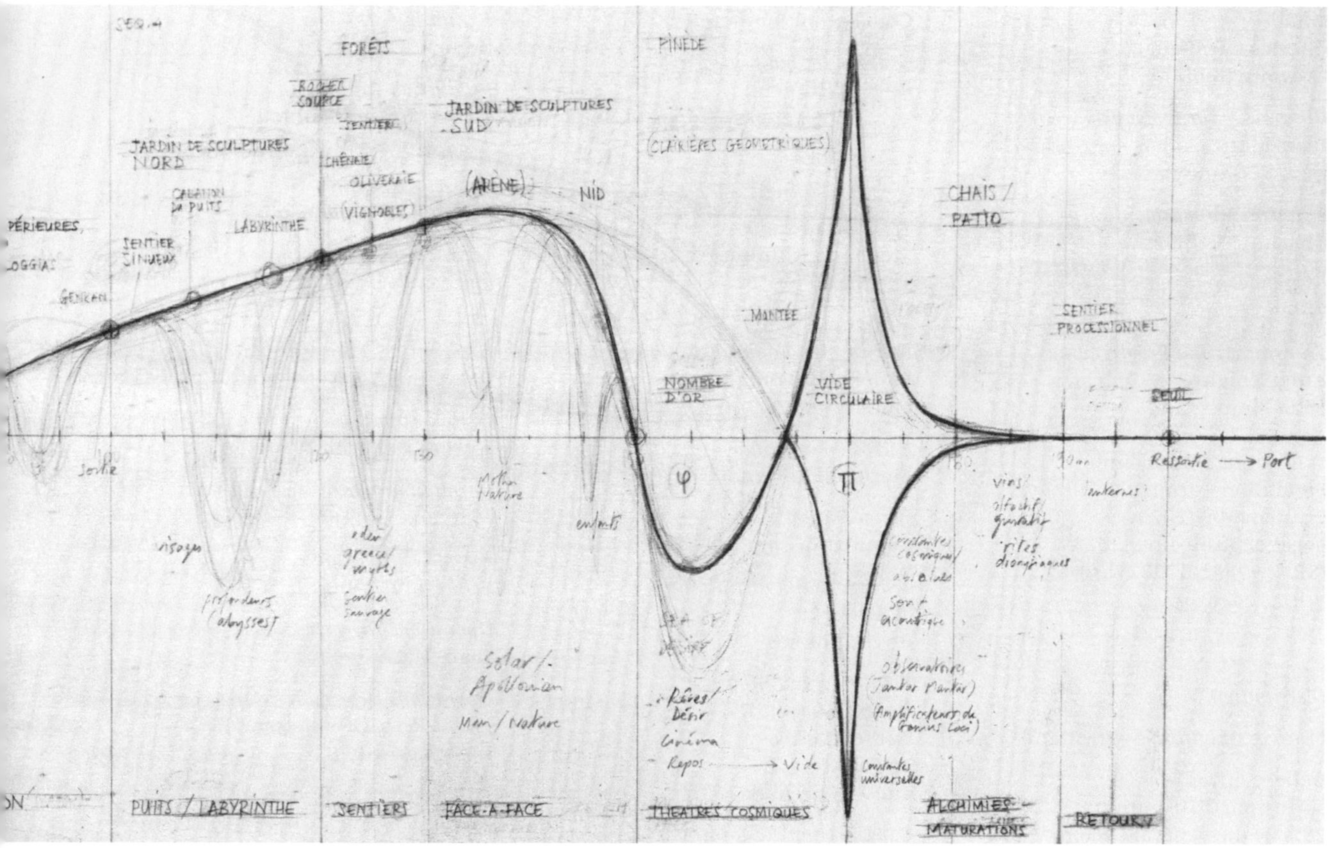

The title *The Inner Island* is shared with a drawing by Stephan Zimmerli – Charles Carmignac's partner in the band Moriarty – which shows the visitor circuit in the manner of a voyage of the mind, oscillating around a surface line. This curve also serves as a score for the soundtrack of the exhibition, played live at the occasion of the opening, devised by singer Barbara Carlotti.

The Inner Island
From 29 April to 15 November 2023

Guest Curator
Jean-Marie Gallais

Fondation and Villa Carmignac would like to thank the artists, art lenders, and institutions who contributed to this exhibition.

Editors
Charles Carmignac
Grégoire Robinne

Directors of the Publication
Jean-Marie Gallais
Kévin Le Squer

Editorial Management
Charlotte Othman

Graphic Design
Roland Brauchli

Translation and Proofreading
Anna Knight
Julia Monks

Printed: May 2023
Legal deposit: June 2023
ISBN: 978-2-37372-170-6
Price: 39 euros

Distribution

France, Belgium, Switzerland

Belles Lettres
Diffusion-Distribution
25, rue du Général Leclerc
94270 Le Kremlin-Bicêtre
T +33 1 45 15 19 70
www.bldd.fr

North America (USA and Canada), Latin America, UK, Asia, Australia, Middle East

ARTBOOK D.A.P.
75 Broad St, Suite 630
New York, NY 10004
www.artbook.com

Exhibition

Set Design
Jasmin Oezcebi, assisted by Judith Quirot

Construction
EMA Création, Alice de Bortoli, and Produzioni Milano

Lighting
ACL – Atelier de Conception Lumière

Graphic Design
Roland Brauchli

Signage
Coll'o Doc and Œil de Lynx

Translation and Proofreading
Stéphanie Quillon and Sarah Moroz

Mediation
Fræme, Lorena Puerta, Yola Rey Büchler, and Carlotta Sanna

Reception and Shop
Marianne International

Poster Design
Camille Gasser

Transport and Installation of Artworks
Bovis, Fræme

Printing and Framing
Benoît Soardi, Cadre Exquis, La Palette, and Studio AZA

Conservation-Restoration
La Réserve

Insurance
Morel & Cie

Media Partners
AD, Beaux-Arts, France Bleu, Le Monde, M Le Monde, L'Obs, Télérama

With the support of
Le Bonbon, Fnac, Gares & Connexion, JC Decaux, Lumens Box, Métropole, MK2

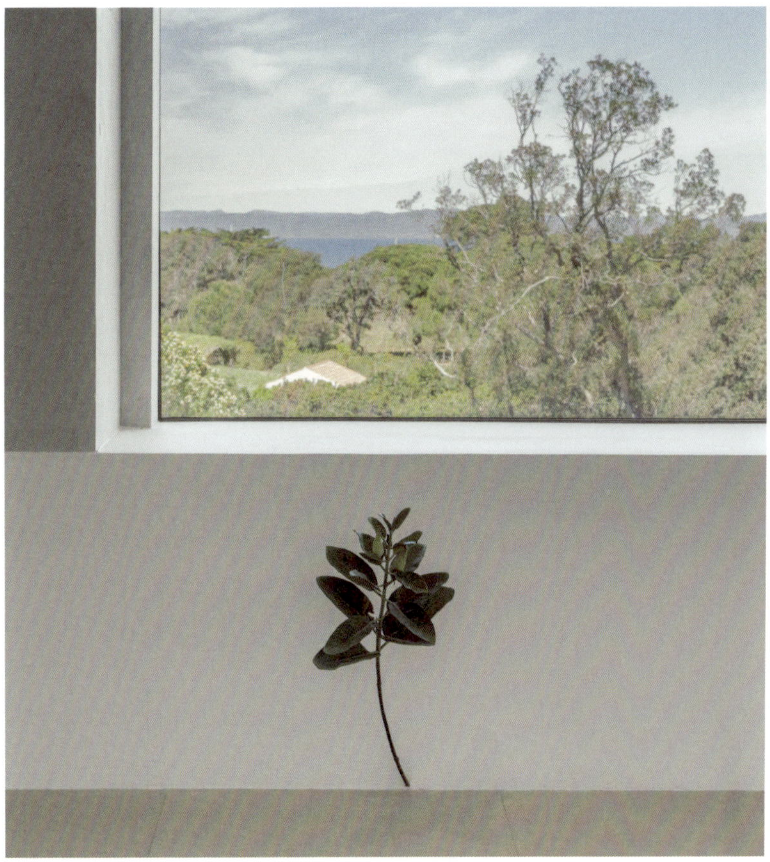

Tony Matelli, *Weeds #389*, 2017 — Bronze — 63.5 × 27.9 × 22.9 cm